A Survivor's Guide Series:
Surviving Ireland:
An Auld Yank's Adventures in County Cork

(...and You Can Too)

Tom Richards

How an 'Auld Yank Learned to Survive in Southwest County Cork, Ireland

Come for a week and stay for a lifetime.
That's the beauty and magic of Ireland!

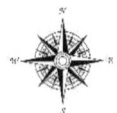

About How an 'Auld Yank Learned to Survive in Southwest County Cork Ireland:

This 'Aulder Yank, now sixty-eight years old, has now survived Ireland for over Forty-Three Years. When I moved here permanently in June, 1982, and lived in Navan, County Meath, the country was very, very different than it is now.

The first series, A *Survivor's Guide Living in Ireland*, talks about how I came to live here and what happened to me, my family and the job that I managed to land. That series, which was launched in 2005 and finished in 2021, continues to be relevant.

This Brand-New memoir and travel guide picks up in March, 2024. After I write about this astounding journey of living in Eyeries Village, County Cork, I'll also include most, but not all, of *A Survivor's Guide to Living in Ireland*. Call it a bonus for those who purchase this first book in a new series of *A Survivor's Guide* by Tom Richards.

In this new Memoir and Travel Guide, I have the most recent information on the price of homes and how to get a Visa. Too, this memoir, which is also something of a journal, tells you about the places I've visited and which I recommend. Visiting this country might be the best thing you can do to determine if you want to eventually live in Ireland permanently.

Living here has been a wonderful experience but heartbreaking, too. Having left Navan to move here in November, 2010, I met the woman of my dreams, Carmel Murray, who came to live here with me and my kitten Sasha, bringing along with her wonderful dog, Jack. It was here that, having semi-retired from my marketing agency, I started to write novels and screenplays full time. Carm became my Muse: she read everything that I wrote and critiqued the prose. I followed all of her advice, which is why *Dolphin Song*, the novel, went to #1 across the world so quickly. My dear Carmel, with the nickname Pookey, now resides in a nursing home in the town of Trim in County Meath. She's been diagnosed with Early Onset Alzheimer's Disease and she doesn't remember me. This means that today, I live alone as I have done for over two years since she was taken first to the hospital. I've managed to survive, just barely, and now have a new puppy named Bluebell who makes me laugh and smile all the time, helping me to make the best of life without Carm, my almost-wife.

That gives you some basic background. As of now, I've lived in Eyeries for going on fourteen years. So much has happened since Carm had to leave: I've been all over Ireland, to the United States and to London. This has coloured what I'll now write about and I'll start with this:

In this new series, Tom Richards writes about how you, too, can come to the beauty to Southwest Ireland to live a life of Tranquillity and Peace. So many people that I've met, mostly American but not all, want to live in Ireland but find that it can be difficult to get a Visa of any kind. In the Memoir below, I'll do my best to illustrate the steps you need to go through to move here, get a work permit and a job, find an affordable home and enjoy the same sort of life that I do now.

Blessings on all of you on this day, two days after Saint Patrick's Day, 2024

When Tom Richards started this memoir and guide for visitors to Ireland

19 March 2024,
Eyeries Village,
Beara Peninsula,
Southwest County Cork

(I finished this Book on 9 October 2024 with the Memory of my Partner Carmel Murray who, in spite being in a Nursing Home, is still right at my side watching and commenting as I write)

Tom Richards
Eyeries, Beara, Bantry,
County Cork Ireland

How an 'Auld Yank Learned to Survive in Southwest County Cork, Ireland

ISBN:
© Copyright Storylines Entertainment Ltd, 2005 - 2021.
All rights reserved
The moral right of Tom Richards to be identified as the Author of this Work is asserted.
Conditions of Sale
All rights reserved. Except for brief passages quoted in newspaper, magazine, radio or television reviews, no part of
this book may be reproduced in any form or by any means, electronic or mechanical, including scanning, photocopying or recording,
or by any information storage or retrieval system without prior permission from the publisher.
First published in 2024 by
Storylines Entertainment Ltd.
(A Survivor's Guide to Living in Ireland, provided to you for FREE at the end of this memoir, was first published in Dunshaughlin,
County Meath, 2005)
Many of the names in this book have been changed to protect the innocent and ensure that the author is not slugged in the nose.
Cover Design by Touqeer Shahid.

Find him on fiverr.com at Touqeershahid95
To contact the author email tomrichards141@gmail.com

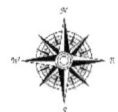

Dedication

To all of those I've lost over the past 3 years:
Liam O'Neill, film producer, writer, director and best friend;
My father, Bill Richards and my Mom, Mary Richards;
To Ron Raben, my teacher, a Good Jew who taught me some Hebrew;
To Carmel Murray who I miss with all my heart;
To Jack our wonderful dog who we really thought was the Canine Version of Prime Minister Winston Churchill
To the many people who welcomed me in Eyeries when I first moved here and saved my life following my Heart Attack:
Also to the Villagers of Eyeries and good friends in Castletownbere, County Cork;
The EMT drivers who rushed me to the Cork University Hospital;
My Surgeon and the many nurses who became my friends, who not only saved my life but helped me to recover;
To Harsha Ganatra, a wonderful woman from India who checks in on me all the time;
To Donal, Jay and the rest of the family in Causkey's Bar;
To Tony, Frank, English Kieran, Kieran the Fisherman, Michael the Talented Owner of our Local Gardening Centre, Ger the Englishman and the many, many people and families that I've learned to count on as amazing friends;
To my great, great friends in the United States, particularly the Rolling Meadows High School Class of 1974, Rolling Meadows Illinois.
And to you, all of you who read this, that your wish for a wonderful life will take place soon.

Table Of Contents

Chapter One: How I Came to Leave Navan, County Meath and Move to Eyeries Village in Stunning Southwest County Cork 1

Chapter Two: How I Came to Buy Our Home in this Beautiful Village and How You Can Too 6

Chapter Three: The Outrageous Prices of Homes - and Just about Everything - in Today's Ireland (and no, it's not a Joke!) 14

Chapter Four: What You Have to Do to Visit, Work or Live in Ireland (and for many foreigners it's a real Mess) 30

Chapter Five: In Eyeries, County Cork, I 'Made My Stand' for the Rest of My Life 37

Chapter Six: Why I Choose to Stay in Ireland 44

Chapter Seven: A Welcoming, Stunning & Peaceful Location 50

Chapter Eight: Touring this Area and What to Bring with You. Don't Forget about the Irish Weather. 63

Chapter Nine: What Do All Irish People Constantly Talk About? Why, *The Weather*, of Course! 78

Chapter Ten: Taking Ireland Just as It Is. The Lesson I Learned Many Years Ago. And If You Come Here, You Should, Too. 86

   A Survivor's Guide to Living in Ireland 95

Ireland 2021: Thoughts of optimism *100*

Map of Ireland *105*

Preface: Notes from a Long-Gone Yank *106*

Prologue *108*

   Chicago, Illinois   August 15, 1982 108

Guideline One: Don't Believe Anything You Have Read, It Probably Isn't True *115*
Guideline Two: The Economy — a Chink of Light *128*
Guideline Three: How to Get a Job and a Visa, and Also Survive *137*
Guideline Four: Can't Get a Job? Then Do it Yourself *162*
The Coming of Irish Entrepreneurship *163*
Ireland as a Centre for Business *169*
Population *169*
Infrastructure *171*
Opportunities for the Entrepreneur *173*
Home Construction *180*
Additional Construction Related Industries *181*
Computer Support *182*
Health Care *184*
The Food Industry *185*
Franchise Opportunities *186*
Coffee Bars *187*
Call Centre Support *187*
Software Development *188*
International Export Opportunities *189*
Financial Services *189*
On Being an Artist *190*
Other Opportunities *191*
Some Advice on Doing Business in Ireland *192*
Your Right to Remain in this Country *193*
Guideline Five: How I Bought Myself a Little Corner of the Irish Dream *195*

Guideline Six: How to Buy a Piece of Irish Heaven for Yourself 214
Choosing the Right Estate Agent 219
New Construction 221
And A Final Word About Prices 224
Guideline Seven: Ireland is Expensive. Or Is It? 230
What's So Expensive About It? 239
The Cost of Higher Education 249
Do I Bring Everything or Do I Leave It All Behind? 253
Guideline Eight: Come for the Pleasure of it All 255
The Captivation of Ireland 263
Guideline Nine: Deconstructing Your Nationalisms 268
Listen rather than talk. You might learn something. 276
Ireland isn't Disney World 278
Forget your net worth. No one else is going to give a fig about it.
.... 283
If you get homesick, go home for a visit before you drive everyone crazy. 287
Learn to drive on the other side of the road. 290
Be open to the wonders around you. 291
De-construct your Nationalism before you do anything else. 295
Guideline Ten: Despite Everything You'll be Criticised So Get Used to It 297
Guideline Eleven: Come to the Ireland We All Love 306
Guideline Twelve: Holidays. Learning to Love Them Like the Irish 322
Christmas 323
Hallowe'en 329
Saint Patrick's Day 332

And the Summer Holidays 335

Guideline Thirteen: Toward an Understanding of Ireland's
Sporting Mania 339

Guideline Fourteen: Living & Dying the Irish Way 347

Saying Goodbye 349

A Walk with Past Friends 352

Guideline Fifteen: When You Come Here You Might Never Leave
.... 355

Guideline Sixteen: Now What? Plan, That's What! 361

Guideline Seventeen: Learn to Talk Like the Irish, A Dictionary of
Irish Slang and Phrases 365

Afterword 381

References 383

Acknowledgements 390

Chapter One:
How I Came to Leave Navan, County Meath and Move to Eyeries Village in Stunning Southwest County Cork

Due to the personal nature of the many problems that came between me and my ex-wife, I won't go into much detail. Just say that like many couples we went our separate ways. However, that wonderful woman, Bernadette, is still a great mother and grandmother and I know she wishes me well just as I do her.

Following my decision to leave the family home in Navan, County Meath, I moved to Trim, about 8 miles south. An absolutely wonderful town to live in, I became single for the first time in years.

You who read this, know that magic really does happens. Right after I moved to this town made famous by the feature film *Braveheart*, I flew to Florida where I visited my father, Bill Richards, at his apartment in Freedom Plaza, Sun City. Following a wonderful visit with him, I flew back through Boston which was a piece of Serendipity. I could have flown home to Ireland through New York, Chicago or Atlanta but my round-trip ticket was a bit less expensive by flying direct from Tampa to Boston. Now here's where it gets fun.

With a fairly long layover, I went outside of the Arrivals Hall and stretched my legs. Coming back into the Departures Hall, I had a final bottle of local beer at a small bar right near the gate. Only later did I find out that Carmel Murray was also having a quick bottle of beer near me. Later, she told me how she had seen me sitting only a few feet from her. Yet I never set eyes on her. When the flight to Shannon Airport in County Limerick, Ireland, was announced, I was one of the first to board the flight. I'll never forget what happened next.

I was sitting in Seat 36A reading a novel when a woman with long auburn hair and a sunny smile sat down in the seat right next to me. The flight was crowded and as I turned a page of my novel, I heard the flight attendant ask the woman in the seat next to me for her boarding pass.

"You're miss Carmel Murray?" the flight attendant asked. "I'm afraid you're sitting in the wrong seat."

"No I'm not," Carm replied looking over at me. "I'm right where I should be."

"But see the boarding pass? You should be sitting in seat 37C, not 36C."

Carmel looked up at the female flight attendant and frowned.

"My boarding pass was printed incorrectly. When I made my reservation I selected Seat 36C."

A female passenger came up to the flight attendant and tapped her on the shoulder. "I don't mind sitting in the seat behind the once I selected. No matter where I sit, I'll get to Shannon."

"See?" Carm said, smiling first at the woman passenger and then me. "We're all set."

I put my book down and glanced at her. She looked stunning and I thought that I'd never seen someone so beautiful.

"I'm Tom Richards," I said as I held out my hand.

"I'm Carm," she replied. "But you can call me Pookey."

"Pookey? What's a Pookey?" I asked, mystified. "I've never heard that name and I've lived in Ireland for years!"

"Pookey is my nickname," Carm replied. "So you're a Yank living in Ireland? Where?"

"Right now, in Trim, County Meath."

"Trim! That's where I'm going too. My parents live in Trim as do most of my sisters. I have a great job in Boston but I decided it was time to go home to visit them."

As the Aer Lingus jet was pushed back from the gate I could tell that Carm was growing very, very nervous. "Carmel, are you okay?" I asked her.

"I hate flying. I only fly when I have to. I get so nervous and anxious I want to throw up."

I nodded and smiled. Explaining that I was the son of a pilot and had flown on aircraft since I was a boy, and had taken flying lessons for years, I explained what all the strange noises were as our aircraft taxied out to the runway.

As the airplane began its take-off roll, Carm grabbed my hand and clung to it. For the next ten minutes, she wouldn't let go. In all my life, no female stranger on an aircraft had taken my hand like that. As we took off and climbed to our cruising altitude, I bought Carm a bottle of wine and one for me, too. As we flew out over the Atlantic, I thought I was the luckiest man alive. We talked for a bit and then ate the dinner that the flight attendant had given to us. When the trays were taken away, the woman next to me, no longer such a stranger, fell asleep still holding my hand and I fell asleep, too.

When I woke up, I found Carmel standing over me. Her long auburn hair fell into my face. Looking down at me, she said, "Tom, do you mind if I kiss you?"

And that was it. Carm and I landed in Shannon then, following an hour's delay, we reboarded and took off for Dublin. Carm and I kept in touch but we both thought we'd never see each other again. She was with her parents and I was in my apartment near her. I also knew that she had to go back to Boston to go to work.

But strange things do happen. Carm and I kept in touch by email and telephone and, a year later almost exactly to the day, Carm phoned me to tell me that she had come home to Trim, permanently. "I've decided to take care of my parents," Carm said. "They're both getting older and it's time I moved from Boston back here."

"I thought you were married?" I asked her. "We never talked about any relationships we might have."

"I'm divorced. I know that you're single. You weren't wearing a wedding ring."

"I left her," I explained. "Soon, we'll be separated and then divorced."

"It looks like you're going to go through the same thing that I did a few years ago."

Over the coming months, Carm told me all about her life in Boston and how she'd had been diagnosed with a melanoma that almost killed her. "But I survived and, within a few years, following all of those continuing treatments, I hope the doctors will tell me that I'll be cancer-free."

I understood just a bit about cancer. I understand much more now. But isn't it very strange and somewhat odd how meeting a stranger on an airplane can change your entire life? That simple conversation was the beginning of our relationship.

Carm's father, Tommy, died in her arms about ten years ago. I'd met him and her mother, Josie, in Trim and grew very close to Josephine. Visiting their family home all the time, I was treated like a son-in-law. Knowing that I would get a divorce as soon as I could, she knew that I would take care of Carm, her youngest child, like no one else.

Following a discussion with her mother, Carm moved down permanently to Eyeries almost fourteen years ago. We've been together ever since and turned our little cottage (which I'll discuss in the next chapter) into a loving home. But now that Carm is in a nursing home, I look around at the empty house with a great deal of pain and sadness but also much, much, much happiness at the memories that we made. I know that Carm is still here, looking at me as I write this. God bless you, Carm. I love you and know you're right next to me.

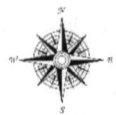

Chapter Two:
How I Came to Buy Our Home in this Beautiful Village and How You Can Too

I started coming to Eyeries in 1997 when I was working on the screenplay version of Dolphin Song. I did some research with my friend and producer of the film and together, we decided that I should go to the Artist Retreat, Anam Cara, which is located about a mile's walk from the Village.

When I first went down to Anam Cara, I met the owner, Sue Forbes-Booth, a woman originally from Salt Lake City, Utah, who had decided to move here after her husband died. I worked on the screenplay and, when I ran into trouble, Sue was great at helping me tease out new ideas and telling me where I'd gone wrong. She acted rather like a 'mother' for all of us who were staying there together then. In fact, I had the pleasure of meeting a distant cousin of mine, Mary Bradford. She was a writer and a poet and an absolutely wonderful person. I also met an artist there and I've stayed in touch with her. Anne Tracey lives in New Mexico and came over to create more art. Her paintings are stunning and she's had any number of exhibitions, for all I know, all over the United States.

At the end of every day, we'd all sit at a large table while Sue served us dinner. She's a very, very good cook and, having helped her clean up, we all had a cup of tea, talked a bit, and then went to bed.

As part of our stay at Anam Cara, Sue offered to take us all around the area in her large comfortable SUV. We all climbed in and I well remember how she drove us first down to Allihies for a drink at a local pub. Next stop Eyeries. We walked into Causkeys Bar and we all sat down while the owners poured us whatever we ordered. I was staggered by the beauty out the large picture window at the back of the pub. Later, when Sue took everyone back to Anam Cara, I decided to stay and talk with Donal Causkey, the owner of the bar with his wife Jay. (For more information on Anam Cara and its artist retreats, visit: https://www.anamcararetreat.com/)

I asked Donal what it was like to live in a small village? He stated that living here was very peaceful. We also discussed the possibility of me purchasing a house near the village centre and he told me that few were available. But if I did buy a place in the Village, I'd be welcome with open arms.

"We have a lot of foreign tourists that come here every year," Donal explained. "We also have many foreigners living just outside the village. Here, you'll never be treated as a 'blow in' even though you're a Yank."

I laughed like hell at his comment. I'd always been a blow in since I came to Ireland in 1982. And now I would be accepted as a part of the village if I moved there? It was hard to believe.

Having finished my pint of Guinness, I walked out the front door and rather than turn right as I planned for my walk back to Anam Cara, I turned left instead. Strolling down the only Main Street, I marvelled at the colourful houses that lined it and then saw a light blue house on the left-hand side of the street with a For Sale sign hanging from it. The Estate Agent handling the sale of the property was JJ O'Sullivan (for more information on this wonderful man's Estate Agent Company - real estate agent for those of you in the United States) - see their website: https://jjbeara.com/. I highly recommend J.J. to anyone thinking of moving over here and looking for a property of any kind in the area. I really did purchase my Main Street home from him. He negotiated well for me. But see below for what he did and how much cash he saved me on this rather complex transaction). The front of the house didn't look like much, to be honest. I didn't try to look through the front windows but no one seemed to be home. I walked down a small narrow road at the right-hand side of the house and it was then that my opinion of that property was changed forever.

"The view are absolutely stunning!" I said to myself. "Look at all the small islands and the whitewater crashing onto the rocks. The sea is only about a half-mile away. I wish that Carm could see it to tell me what decision to make. But she's still in Boston so...well, why the hell wait? It would make a perfect home for the two of us."

Running back to the front of the house, I looked up again at the For Sale sign and saw the phone number to the Estate Agent. Pulling out my mobile phone I dialled and a very pleasant voice answered.

When J.J. learned that I was interested in the house, he told me to wait there. Twenty minutes later he drove up and, walking to the back garden, we sat down at a small outdoor table. As it turned out, or so the Estate Agent said, the house had been on the market for over two years. Owned by Finbar and Rose Quill, the house was their summer home. The Quill's were very wealthy but the crash of the Irish economy in the early 2000's meant that they, as well as many other wealthy people, were selling what they didn't use very often.

J.J. told me that the couple were looking for over ☐300,000 for that property and I told J.J. that they were nuts! No one would pay that much for a home even one that had such fantastic views of the sea.

"J.J. I offer then ninety-thousand euro to get the ball rolling," I said to him. "If they don't accept that initial offer, that's fine by me.

Tell you what. Let's make it ninety-thousand five hundred euro. But that's it."

J.J. coughed into his hand and looked at me. "Tom, they'll never accept that. But here's where I agree. The price that they're asking is far too much. I phone the clients and start to negotiate with them."

"They're you're clients? But how will you negotiate so I can buy this house for a fair price?"

"Tom, you're also my client. Remember, I make commission not only from the seller but also the buyer. It's a much fairer system than in America."

J.J. and I made an appointment to see the interior of the property the very next day. When I met him at the front door, he escorted me throughout the two-storey home that also had a large attic.

"Tom, the present couple who lives here is only renting it. When and if you buy it, they'll be out by the end of that month. But look around. What a lovely cottage, isn't it?"

The cottage was built in 1903. It had been partly demolished then rebuilt by the Quill's. With one large master bedroom, a tiny second bedroom, and an attic that was used by the Quill's grandchildren as a bedroom of sorts, the first floor also had a gigantic family bathroom.

"J.J. the bathroom even has a Jacuzzi in it!" I exclaimed as I looked around. "And what are those controls? Does it also have a radio? And the small fireplace! If my girlfriend comes down here, I'll make her a nice hot bath and light the fire. Then she'll be so snug and warm that she's bound to fall in love with it like I have."

We went downstairs and I looked at the solid oak floors in the living room and the very small kitchen that reminded me of a galley in a boat. The kitchen came with a cooker and a Belfast sink, as well as a small Hoover refrigerator / freezer.

When we walked out of the living room and down three steps, J.J. pointed out the huge glass window on the far side of that room. The view was astonishing. Even better than the one in the back garden because we were slightly higher. When I walked out the back door and onto a pebbled deck, I happened to look up and saw another deck just above us.

I climbed the steps and, when I came to the top, I turned around and beheld an entire vista of white clouds and surging blue seas.

"Tom, that's Coulagh Bay and from here, the next stop is Canada."

"No kidding, J.J.," I said as I came back down the steps. "Look, I have to go back to work tomorrow in Dunshaughlin, County Meath."

"Right near Dublin, right? I'll call the Quill's and start the process. And hopefully, within three months you'll get the key and can move here permanently."

Readers, I'm afraid that it took far longer than three months. Finbar Quill and I called each other almost every day. As J.J. continued with the negotiations, we came closer and closer to an agreed sales figure. Finally, we were only one-thousand euro away from a firm agreement.

"Finbar, we're only a few quid away from an agreement," I said to Mister Quill on the phone as I sat in my office at work. "As you know, I live in County Meath. Why don't I come down tomorrow and meet you at the house you have for sale. We can discuss this and come up with a solution."

Finbar, not a man for many words, only said, "Come on, Tom. But meet me at my pub in Kenmare, County Kerry. We can have a cuppa and come to some sort of an agreement."

When I met Finbar at his pub, it was the first time both of us had seen each other face-to-face. He bought me a cup of coffee and we talked at length about the sales price. "Finbar, this is my final offer," I said. "I'm offering a total of two-hundred, twenty-one thousand euro."

"But Tom, it comes with most of the furnishings," Finbar countered. "Those are worth at least five grand."

"Finbar, I don't need the furniture," I said as I looked down at my empty coffee cup, which was an outright lie. "All I want to buy is the house."

Finbar ordered us both another cup of coffee and we started arguing about the final price. "Look, I'll pay another five hundred quid but that's my final offer. Now do we have a deal or am I outta' here?"

I stuck out my hand but the cheap Kerry man wouldn't shake it. "Tom, the house belongs to my wife, Rose. I'll have to phone her so that she can make the final decision."

"But Finbar, you two are married! The house is yours, too!"

I could see by the twinkle in his eye that he was only stirring the Irish shite. He took out his mobile phone and I watched as he pretended to dial. He walked away from me and talked into thin air for about ten seconds. Pretending to hang up, he stuck out his hand and we both shook.

"The deal is made!" Finbar exclaimed. "It's just after one so how about a pint of Guinness and we'll toast the success."

Which is just what we did. I reckon that J.J. saved me well over one-hundred thousand euro through his way of negotiating with Finbar Quill. Years later, I learned that most Kerry people are 'tight as a fiddler's arse'. And it's true! So if you're ever buying something from a person from Kerry, be sure to negotiate as hard as you can for a fair price.

A number of months later, after I had moved into the home on 12 November 2010, Carm came down for a visit. Looking around the house and out at the views, she told me that she wasn't certain that she could ever live there. She pointed out how isolated it was from any real shopping. But, later that day, I received a phone call from Finbar who invited me down to his Woolen Shop in Kenmare for what he called "A Lucky Penny".

I asked Carm to come along with me and when we walked into the Quill Woollen Shop, Finbar explained that a Lucky Penny was a traditional piece of Irish Luck. "See, Tom?" he said, "Carmel, your partner and girlfriend know this. But first we spit into the palm of our hand like this." When he did it, I did it too. "Then we shake on the deal," which we did. "And now, since you've paid me for the home in Eyeries, and it was a good price, I give you and your lady a Lucky Penny and that's an Irish blessing for me and for you two."

I finally understood what he meant. When he led both of us to the first floor, I looked around at all the men's woollen clothing that he had for sale. I explained that I had many, many items of clothing, some of which I'd purchased at Quill's. Determined to give one of us a Lucky Penny, he took Carm to the lady's section and led her to all of the Hiking Boots lined up in a row.

"Carmel, if you ever move down here you'll need a great pair of boots," Finbar said. "Try a few on and when you find one that's comfortable let me know and, well, they're free to you and Tom."

Carm did exactly what Finbar suggested. Having found a pair that were fully comfortable, she insisted on keeping them on when we left the shop.

"Tom, these boots are wonderful!" Carm said as we climbed back into our pickup truck. "And that Finbar Quill. What a saint of a man. Have you ever met his wife, Rose? I bet she's a saint of an Irish woman."

"No, I've never met Rose but someday I hope we both can."

And that's the story of how Carm and I came to live in our Main Street, Eyeries Village home. It's a wonderful home and I hope, if you're looking for a similar house to buy, you can find one just like we did.

One last thing. Only the other day, I heard that Rose Quill had died of some sort of terminal illness. I suspect a heart attack or cancer. My heart goes out to Finbar, they're children and grandchildren and all of the staff at Every Quill's Store in all of Ireland. May I ask you another favour? If you're shopping in Ireland, try Quill's. It has great woollens with many patterns and at a variety of good and fair prices. If you tell them that Tom Richards sent you, who knows? You might get a Lucky Penny from a Kerryman like Finbar or a Kerry Angel like Rose.

Blessings to Rose and may you be happy and content as many of my good friends and relatives are now.

Chapter Three: The Outrageous Prices of Homes – and Just about Everything – in Today's Ireland (and no, it's not a Joke!)

Today's Ireland is even more expensive than when I first move here in 1982, or so most people living her say. Here, I'll do my best to indicate how much homes cost not only in Dublin but also in Rural Ireland (it's usually less expensive, let me tell ya'.

Home Prices – a New Bubble?

If you're truly considering buying a home in Ireland, and unless you're earning a fortune, I'd avoid Dublin City Centre at all costs. Even suburbs of Dublin? Homes cost a very pretty penny.

For instance, right now on www.daft.ie, I see a 5 bed, 2 bath semi-detached home with garage in Stillorgan, County Dublin. The asking price? □875,000! I couldn't afford that home and most people wanting to come here, or even local people, can't afford it either.

Go a little farther away from Dublin City and you'll find that some places are somewhat more affordable. For instance, my son and his partner recently bought a three-bed home in Lucan, County Dublin. They purchased that house, which needs quite a bit of work, for about□350,000. Including all of the renovations that need to be done, their total investment will be just over a half-million euro. A lot, some might say. But for a place like Lucan, right near the M-4 Motorway and with quick access to the City Centre, many motorways and Dublin Airport, that's an outstanding investment. Home prices are rising astronomically again!

Now if you look in RURAL Ireland, things are somewhat different. Take County Cavan, as an example. About 90 minutes' drive from Dublin, I've been there any number of times. The entire county is filled with lakes and many people love fishing there. In the Town of Cavan there's a new 4 bed, 3 bath two storey home for sale with an asking price of €325,000. You could buy a 2 bed, 2 bath apartment for €129,000. Now that's not bad at all. And yes, this location is rather far from any large city but the savings are massive compared to many other places.

Now let's look at where I live. As I illustrated in the last chapter, my home has soared in value over the past 13 years. This is due to the fact that because it's right by the sea, getting planning permission to build a home here is quite difficult if not impossible. For that reason there's a housing shortage.

Fortunately, if you're looking to move to Eyeries, there are a few new builds still available. Just up the road from me, a brand-new line of terraced homes were built only a few years ago. I have two good friends living there and they like their home very much. So, if you go to House for Sale in Eyeries | 5 Ard Cuan | Sherry FitzGerald you'll see that a 3 bed, 3 bath modern cottage is for sale at €249,000. A great price for this location! There are a few other homes for sale near me and also in Castletownbere, County Cork, which is only five miles south of here. For a list of homes, go to www.daft.ie. Filter that by the location that you want and have fun finding a place to buy!

But what about other prices such as energy, food, transportation, and similar? I've covered much of this in A Survivor's Guide to Living in Ireland (see well below) so I won't go through all of the prices. Instead, let's just look at some as an indication of how expensive Ireland has become since I first came here.

I'm going to keep all prices in Euro even though, back when I moved here in 1982, our currency was the Irish Pound, or Punt as it was called by all Irish citizens.

Let's start with a weekly figure. Each week, my then-wife spent about □25 per week for our ENTIRE family (that's me, Bernie, Kristin and Cathy, who were both very young, as well as Jonathan who was an infant). That weekly cash, which was so difficult to earn, had to buy everything from bread to eggs, diapers and baby food for the infant, some medication, meat, a very few sweets and everything else that we needed to get through the week. That did NOT include cash for: petrol (so I could get to work), house payments (which were about □140 per month and I could barely afford it); home insurance, fuel like coal and wood, electricity, or the $30 I had to send to UCLA every month to clear my student loan. I felt back then like we were paupers, living from hand to mouth each and every week.

Fortunately, things have changed for the better since then because disposable income for most people is much higher than for Irish citizens in 1982. But now, prices are on the up yet again and for many of us here it's become a huge struggle again just to make ends meet.

As a recent Irish Mirror article stated: "Ireland food prices soar by fastest rate on record as cost-of-living crisis escalates."

The article states that Ireland's households face a huge spike in the cost of basic foods by over □1000 per annum. Grocery price inflation soared by to a new record of 16.3 percent.

Let me give you some examples: the cost of 6 fresh eggs bought in my local shop is now one euro and 50 cent higher than they were only 3 months ago. A loaf of white bread is now two euro rather than one fifty. A litre of milk is now one euro fifty cent rather than one euro 30 cent. Butter has increased by a similar percentage. A six pack of Coke has gone up so much that I now refuse to buy it. A six pack of Pepsi is now a much better deal at about one euro when it's on sale.

I talked about house prices going up but this has been exacerbated by the surge in new employment. The high demand for housing created by the likes of Google, Pfizer and many other large companies has meant that they are actually building apartments for their new employees to live in, particularly in Dublin. For many employees of these companies, it's a new 'perk'. They're charged much less than market rate for their monthly rent.

Food prices, housing prices, all still on the up. But what else?

Not too many years ago, say in 2014 and only ten years ago, a very good 3-course meal with my partner Carmel would cost just over ☐30. Including a tip and a few extras like desert, it would cost a little over ☐35. But now? With Carmel gone, I usually go out for a meal at least 3 times a week because I don't like eating alone. A good 2-course meal including a tip at a really nice restaurant near where I live now costs me ☐40. Often, I'll decide on something that's 'Cheap and Cheerful' so I'll go out to my local take-away restaurant. Most people order take-out food but I'll usually sit there to enjoy my meal. The cost of a double-cheeseburger or a Kebab or a pizza for one is only ☐6.50 to ☐12.00.

All this means that you pay for what you get. There's now a tremendous choice of foods from many different countries and cultures than when I first moved here. Back then, you could only get fairly standard Irish fare like good roast beef with potatoes, gravy and veg. The price of something like that - a good Sunday lunch - would set me back just under 6 euro. Or, we could get a take-away from our Chinese restaurant in Navan (it's still there by the way and the owner still works most days. She's been there for what seems like forever and now owns a few great Chinese restaurants and take-aways all over that part of Ireland). The cost for a family of five, with too much for everyone - spring rolls as a starter, a large portion of chips and curry sauce, beef with cashew nuts, chicken with honey, and three large portions of rice) would cost €25. But today? The price has soared because the cost of all fresh ingredients has gone up. Owners who rent their premises have seen huge rises in rent and insurance. So much so that many places, just like the States, are having to close down. But what's the cost of the same meal today for a family of five? Just under €50.

It's outrageous but how about petrol prices (gas in the US).

Here I'll have to do a number of calculations.

In Ireland, we buy 'gas' in litres, not US gallons. 1 litre is equal to about one quarter of a US gallon.

The cost of a litre of Petrol today is €1.75 (that's the cheapest I've seen it).

So a US gallon of gasoline is equal to 4 x €1.75. Right? Wrong! Then we have to convert the currencies

A US dollar is about equal to .92 euro.

So now the final calculation.

.92 x €1.75 x 4 = $6.44 per US gallon.

It's outrageous and it is! The reason? Ireland taxes almost everything. In this case the government places huge taxation on Petrol, just over 70 percent. The high price is also due to the war in the Ukraine and in Gaza. Excessive profit-taking by oil companies and some Petrol forecourt companies. And the bloody, bloody fact that the government keep increasing taxation on Petrol and will for years to come!

I like to think that I'm something of an environmentalist. I try to offset all the carbon I burn (I think of the many times that I have to fly or the coal and wood that I burn to stay warm, or the oil that

I burn for the same reason) and do my best to offset that carbon footprint in any way possible. In Ireland, many politicians, including those with the Green Party, are convinced that if they keep increasing prices on petrol, diesel, aviation fuel, coal, fuel for trawlers and fuel for farming tractors, they'll reduce the demand for products made from oil. But that, in my opinion, is so silly and stupid! Some say that the advent of the electric car will help us to reduce carbon in Ireland. But when I asked my local mechanic (who knows a great deal about all types of cars) all he can do is shake his head.

"Tom, Electric Cars are so stupid! Where do they get their electricity from? Off the grid! In Ireland, some of our electricity is generated by solar and wind power but we still make electricity using generators running on oil or buy it from England which is way too expensive.

"And how much does it cost to make one of those huge lithium batteries or get rid of them when they expire? The cost in energy just isn't worth it.

"And my final point. Many companies and politicians want the Irish to by EV cars. But in rural Ireland? We've very few charging points down here. The time it takes to charge a vehicle can take hours, not minutes. If I run out of electric juice, I'll be stranded someplace and the only option I'd have would be to call a tow truck which runs usually on diesel fuel."

So what's the solution? Many years ago, back in the early 2000s, I had a good friend who was a scientist and an engineer. I well remember him saying, "What we need to do is create Hydrogen powered engines. All they need is water in the tank and some sort of catalytic converter. The same things that many space vehicles use to power their electrical systems while in orbit. Hydrogen power splits H2O into two parts: hydrogen and oxygen. Anything left is only steam which is water!"

He was right, of course. But it will take humanity years to develop a Hydrogen engine. Which means that once again we're off course. Companies and governments across the world are continuing to develop the electric vehicle. The millions of dollars that they're spending is ridiculous. They could all siphon off just a bit to develop the HV or Hydrogen Vehicle. That could well be a game changer for the entire world. We're unlikely to run out of water in most places.

And all you need is water to power an HV.

The Financial Benefits of Living in Ireland

I've discussed the 'bad'. Now the good. I've covered many of these points in the Survivor's Guide, well below. But let's cover some of them again.

- Education - in Ireland much of a child's education is almost free. In primary school (elementary school to those in the US) all you need to do as parents is buy books and school uniforms. You may have to also buy a small Notebook for a primary student depending on the school that they go to. Most schools here are run by the Catholic Church. This means that Religion classes are part of the curriculum. But if you don't want your child or children to learn Catholic religion because you're not of that faith, most schools will let your child sit somewhere else to study another subject. But what about High School - called secondary school here?
- Secondary School - in this case kids go to Secondary School sometimes for 7 years. This includes a Transition Year. They'll have to study like mad for their Junior Cert, which is a very difficult exam taking place over a few days. This covers everything they've learned in the previous years. At the end of Secondary School, in their Seventh year, they again have to study like mad for their Leaving Exam. This HUGE exam covers everything they've

learned in the last Seven years. When I first came here and my kids had to sit these difficult tests, I was appalled! All we had to do in America was study for each and every exam. Our Grade Point Average and say an SAT or ACT, as well as a few recommendations from teachers and a long essay on why any college or university would accept us was all we had to do back then. In Ireland, it's very very different. I've changed much of my mind about the Exams that Irish Secondary School kids must take. While it's very difficult, their teachers and parents help them study for it. That's what I did for each of my three kids when it was time for them to take the Leaving Cert. I helped them to create a schedule on an Excel Spreadsheet. A half-hour or so for each subject every day, and maybe 3 or 4 subjects each day. So they worked about 2 hours a day for their exam. They took Sunday off and all of our kids did quite well!

The Irish educational system is much more than superlative. It's basic education covering maths and sciences, history, geography, English and - of all things! - As Gaeilge, the Irish Language. Two of my children found Irish very hard and needed extra help to pass any of the exams. But my youngest son Jonathan started the Irish language when he was only six-years-old. He's now fluent in the Irish Language as well as English and holds a PhD in Irish literature. Working as an Assistant Professor at a large University in Dublin, I often ask him to translate English phrases for me into As Gaeilge, which he does with no problem at all! The Irish language isn't for everyone but it's a lot of fun to try to learn. One of the most ancient languages in the world, I still find it difficult to wrap my tongue around almost any word. Take Milk, for instance. That one is easy: Baine. Or Sugar. Sucre. Or Teacher: Muntuir. But anything else? Forget it, almost. Try learning 'Thank you' or 'You're welcome' in Irish. Thank you is: go raibh maith agat. Which, believe it or not, is pronounced: Gara - meeha - maha - goot. Or how about 'You're

welcome'? That's: tá fáilte. Which is pronounced ta faltche. And that Irish phrase for 'You're Welcome' means something like: a thousand welcomes.
But how about going to college or University? I won't go through all the options. But here are a few:

- College and University - is once again almost free compared to the United States. When each of my three children when to University at exceptional Irish schools I budgeted about (in US dollars for a change) $12,000 for each child for each year. That included all tuition, room and board, money for books and food, and some beer money. Each of my kids also had a job while in University which helped. No matter where you go, college is one of the most expensive investments a parent can make in their child's future.

It's become much more expensive for kids to go to College or University than it cost me and my then-wife back when my children went to school. Due to the higher costs of almost everything, especially apartments or dorm rooms (for room and board), and having talked to parents that are currently paying for their children's college education, the approximate price is $22,000 - $30,000 per annum depending on what they're studying.

A few points: first, you have to be a resident to get lower tuition fees here. If you're not, and as a foreign student, you'll pay a multiple of that price. Of course, there are grants available even for foreign students, and some of these students get a work visa and a job to mitigate their large expenses.

But if you're a resident here and want to study medicine? If you can get into medical school - and it's very, very competitive - the price is about what you'd pay for any graduate degree in Ireland. I won't go into detail, but in talking to doctors and medical students (who worked their way through university and have taken out some loans) the average price per year is about $50,000 or so. And that's for one of the best medical degrees in Europe or anywhere in the world.

Compare all of those prices to what you have to pay in America. The costs are now staggering. One year of Medical School in the States can cost, I gather, much more than $200,000. Yes, you can get loans for your years of education, but the interest and loan payback schedules can lead to large headaches even for successful surgeons and doctors.

But let's say you don't want a 'profession' but only want a trade? Here that's also easy and very inexpensive.

- Trade Schools - Ireland has many, many Government supported 'Trade Schools' that can help you train for a very good and well-paying job such: plumber, electrician, construction, business, home help and many more. Usually, there's a very, very small fee involved and a person taking one of these courses may have to travel to it for a number of years until they obtain a Qualification or Diploma. Often, these students will be employed as an Apprentice which will offset their various expenses. Or, if a person is already employed the employer's company might well pay for those courses that lead to a relevant qualification. For more information go to: https://www.citizensinformation.ie/en/education/further-education-and-training/training-courses/

As I say above, the cost of going to almost any kind of school in Ireland is 'almost nothing' compared to many other countries.

But what other benefits would you have if you came to Ireland?

High Personal Taxation but Oh, the Tremendous Pay-off When a Taxpayer Retires!

Yes, Ireland has very high levels of personal taxation. We have any number of thresholds and pay both PAYE (Pay as You Earn) and PRSI (rather like Social Security taxation in the United States). We also have something called UI tax (Universal taxation) which was put into place by the Irish government only a few years ago.

Here are the latest tax rates and rate bands:

Tax rates and rate bands

Rates and bands for the years 2020 to 2024

Personal circumstances	2024 €	2023 €	2022 €	2021 €	2020 €
Single or widowed or surviving civil partner, without qualifying children	€42,000 @ 20% Balance @ 40%	€40,000 @ 20%, balance @ 40%	€36,800 @ 20%, balance @ 40%	€35,300 @ 20%, balance @ 40%	€35,300 @ 20%, balance @ 40%
Single or widowed or surviving civil partner, qualifying for Single Person Child Carer Credit	€46,000 @ 20% Balance @ 40%	€44,000 @ 20%, balance @ 40%	€40,800 @ 20%, balance @ 40%	€39,300 @ 20%, balance @ 40%	€39,300 @ 20%, balance @ 40%
Married or in a civil partnership (one spouse or civil partner with income)	€51,000 @ 20% Balance @ 40%	€49,000 @ 20%, balance @ 40%	€45,800 @ 20%, balance @ 40%	€44,300 @ 20%, balance @ 40%	€44,300 @ 20%, balance @ 40%
Married or in a civil partnership (both spouses or civil partners with income)	€51,000 @ 20% (with an increase of 33,000 max), balance @ 40%	€49,000 @ 20% (with an increase of €31,000 max), balance @ 40%	€45,800 @ 20% (with an increase of €27,800 max), balance @ 40%	€44,300 @ 20% (with an increase of €26,300 max), balance @ 40%	€44,300 @ 20% (with an increase of €26,300 max), balance @ 40%

Note: The increase in the rate band is capped at the lower of €33,000 or the income of the lower earner. This increase cannot be transferred between spouses or civil partners.

BUT, just like the United States, at least a little, you can REDUCE your personal taxes like this:

Tax credits, allowances and reliefs

Credits, allowances and reliefs for the years 2020 to 2024

Personal circumstances	2024 €	2023 €	2022 €	2021 €	2020 €
Single Person	1,875	1,775	1,700	1,650	1,650
Married Person or Civil Partner	3,750	3,550	3,400	3,300	3,300
Widowed Person or Surviving Civil Partner with dependent child(ren)	1,875	1,775	1,700	1,650	1,650
Widowed Person or Surviving Civil Partner without dependent child(ren)	2,415	2,315	2,240	2,190	2,190
Widowed Person or Surviving Civil Partner - bereavement year	3,750	3,550	3,400	3,300	3,300
Widowed Parent 1st year after death	3,600	3,600	3,600	3,600	3,600
Widowed Parent 2nd year after death of spouse or civil partner	3,150	3,150	3,150	3,150	3,150
Widowed Parent 3rd year after death of spouse or civil partner	2,700	2,700	2,700	2,700	2,700
Widowed Parent 4th year after death of spouse or civil partner	2,250	2,250	2,250	2,250	2,250
Widowed Parent 5th year after death of spouse or civil partner	1,800	1,800	1,800	1,800	1,800
Single Person Child Carer Credit	1,750	1,650	1,650	1,650	1,650
Age Tax Credit if single, widowed or surviving civil partner	245	245	245	245	245

But there are other deductions, too:

Age Tax Credit if married or in a civil partnership	490	490	490	490	490
Home Carer's Tax Credit (max.)	1,800	1,700	1,600	1,600	1,600
Employed Person taking care of an incapacitated individual (max.)	75,000	75,000	75,000	75,000	75,000
Employee PAYE Tax Credit	1,875	1,775	1,700	1,650	1,650
Earned Income Tax Credit (max.)	1,875	1,775	1,700	1,650	1,650
Incapacitated Child Tax Credit	3,500	3,300	3,300	3,300	3,300
Incapacitated Child Tax Credit - income limit of child	0	0	0	0	0
Dependent Relative	245	245	245	245	70
Dependent Relative Income Limit	17,404	16,780	16,156	15,740	15,060
Blind Tax Credit - single person	1,650	1,650	1,650	1,650	1,650
Blind Tax Credit - one spouse or civil partner blind	1,650	1,650	1,650	1,650	1,650
Blind Tax Credit - both spouses or civil partners blind	3,300	3,300	3,300	3,300	3,300
Guide Dog - allowance	825	825	825	825	825
Rent Tax Credit - single person (max)	750	500	500	0	0
Rent Tax Credit - jointly assessed married couple or civil partners (max)	1,500	1,000	1,000	0	0

On average, most working class to lower-middle class people pay about 20% income tax. Then, it depends on if you're poor or wealthy. As you can see, the top rate of taxation is 40 percent (not including PRSI, of course, which is an additional 2 percent). Actually, that's not bad. When I first moved to Ireland, the top rate of taxation was over 60 percent! Now that's a lot! It drove many wealthy people to other countries where they would pay far less taxation on their income. The Irish government has become much, much smarter. While we pay a great deal of tax from all sources, we also get a super benefit when we retire.

Using Tom as an Example of a Retired Person

I started to receive my Irish Government Pension when I turned 66, just about two years ago. I have what they call a 'contributory pension'. This is just like the United States and many other countries. As I earned, I collected what the Irish still call Stamps. For every few old Irish Punts or modern Euro I earned, the government took taxation from me. Over the many, many years that I worked in Ireland, and including the taxation that my company had to pay when they employed me, and also including VAT (Value Added Tax) which I won't go into here (it's rather like sales tax in the US) I reckon I paid over $1 million which is a GREAT DEAL OF TAX.

But, get this. As I've said in many memoirs and online, my father Bill Richards was a retired Pilot for United Airlines. He paid a great deal of tax on every penny that he earned. When he retired in 1979 from the airline due to a heart attack, he was earning about $75,000 per annum. While he used a tax accountant, and used every deduction possible, Dad still paid about 20 - 25 percent of those annual earnings to the US Federal Government.

Even in retirement he paid high levels of taxation not only on his dividends and interest that he received from his bank and stockholdings, but also on his Company pension. He made a GREAT deal of money over the years until he passed away in 2022, and he paid about 20 percent of this to the Feds.

And his US government pension when he received it? Just over $1,900 per month. Which is a great deal of money and very fair because he filed tax forms with the IRS ever since he started working.

Now, let's look at Tom. As I say, I retired when I turned 67. And I was SHOCKED at what I received in my Irish government pension. Below is a breakdown:

- Weekly pension: €334.24
  The above includes: FREE TRAVEL on Irish railways, buses, trams, and certain ferry companies; the Living Alone Allowance which I receive because, due to the fact that my partner Carmel is now in a nursing home, I now live alone; a Fuel Allowance which provides me with more cash to heat my home.
  This does not include occasional Government support for Electricity and an occasional Cost of Living Increase (which for many of us means that our pensions have gone up every year for the past 3 years by about 4% per annum)
- Bonuses: everyone earning a pension receives an occasional bonus at Christmas and if the Government can afford it: About €700 per annum
- I no longer have to pay the Dreaded TV License Fee which I never understood anyway (as of this writing, it seems the government is going to SCRAP this fee, finally!)

If you add it all together, I think I earn almost €20,000 per annum which is NOT TAXED AT ALL. If you include tax at 20 percent (and Dad, like most pensioners in the US, had to pay tax on his government pension because he earned a great deal of money from other sources), this would mean, IF I HAD TO PAY TAX ON THIS, that I'd be earning €24,000 per annum! But it IS NOT TAXED so YIPPEE!

Now go back to Dad's example. He earned $1900 per month or so. That's equal to $22,800 per annum. Assuming that he was NOT taxed on this, I'm earning just about what Dad is right now if you take into account the present currency exchange rate.

I always assumed that my Government Pension would be far less than my father's. But I was wrong. And those aren't the only advantages of being retired in Ireland.

Tom also has a Medical Card! Usually, taxpayers in Ireland get a Medical Card when they turn 70. But because I had a heart attack recently, I only had to apply for it and I received it about 6 months ago. This means that I now pay:☐1.50 for EVERY prescription that I require. And pretty much ZERO for everything else. This means that if I have to go back into hospital for more surgery or a hip replacement, I pay NOTHING to the hospital, the surgeon or anyone else. Nor do I have to pay for a bed.

The downside is that like many companies, Ireland has huge waiting lists for many procedures. I'm currently waiting for an MRI at my local hospital. However, there's a long waiting list and I probably won't get an appointment for another few months. This is why I also have standard Health Insurance. In the even that it takes an inordinate amount of time to get an appointment, I can use my Health Insurance to cover most of the costs, at the standard deductible.

Yes, Ireland can be very expensive. It is, after all, one of the most expensive places to live in Europe. Yet, it was recently rated as one of the top destinations for tourists and one of the Happiest Countries to Live In. Only the Nordic Countries and some other beat us out. We are a happier place to live in that the United States and the UK, that's for sure.

Why? For many of the reasons listed above. But as I will write about soon, the Irish people are happy simply because we often have a less stressful lifestyle. Here in Eyeries on the Beara Peninsula, life is usually tranquil and very, very peaceful. If I get stressed out again for some reason, all I have to do is take a walk or simply listen to the waves crashing onto the rocks below my home.

As I've always said, this little island is magical and as for Eyeries and Southwest Ireland?

Magic personified.

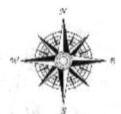

Chapter Four: What You Have to Do to Visit, Work or Live in Ireland (and for many foreigners it's a real Mess)

Are You a Citizen of India or Some Other Countries? Trying to get any kind of Visa into Ireland can Sometimes be Impossible!

For many people wanting to visit (or stay in Ireland permanently) getting a Visa is no problem at all. If you're a citizen of any country in the European Union (and there are many of them), or from the United Kingdom (which is no longer part of the EU), or from the United States, Canada or many other countries, getting a Tourist Visa is no problem at all. In fact, there are many, many countries where a Visa lasting 3 months isn't required. All you have to do is book your ticket to Ireland and bring your passport.

But for SOME citizens of other countries, getting even a Tourist Visa to enter and stay in Ireland for even TWO WEEKS is almost impossible. That list includes but is not limited to: much of South East Asia, much of Africa including Egypt and Saudi Arabia, Jamaica, Peru, the Russian Federation, Venezuela, Vietnam – and – Pakistan and India.

Getting a Tourist Visa for Pakistani's and citizens from India seems simply when you look online or call the Irish Embassy in India, or phone the Department of Foreign Affairs in Dublin, Ireland. But I assure you: IT IS NOT! As an example: I employ four people part-time in my company, Storylines Entertainment Ltd. At one point, I was trying to get a Tourist Visa for a new Marketing Executive that I employed who comes from Mumbai, India. I had met this intelligent, experienced woman when I visited Mumbai on business. The Woman, let's call her HRG, and I got online and did our best to follow the rules. That page published by the Irish Embassy in Delhi, India (the capitol of the country) seemed to say that both HRG and I needed to fly to the Delhi Irish Embassy to finish the application. Which we did because we were forced to. It's a rather expensive flight round trip from both cities but we decided to do it in one day.

When at the International Airport in Mumbai, we took an expensive taxi to Embassy Row and asked our driver to wait because I thought it wouldn't take long at all to finish the application (HRG and I did much of it online). The guard at the Embassy allowed both of us in and, when we arrived at reception, we were asked by the receptionist if we had an appointment.

I told that nice staff person "No, we didn't. The application page only said that we had to come to Delhi." She told us to wait while she asked the Irish Consul to come to see us. When he FINALLY showed up, he stood and looked at me with his arms crossed.

"Mr Richards and HRG, I'm sorry but there is absolutely nothing I can do for you, nor anything that the Irish Embassy can do for you. You must finish the application process online. Only then can we begin to process the Tourist Visa application for your new employee."

I looked at HRG and she looked back. Fuming mad, I didn't say a word to the Consol but only shook his hand and smiled. When we left the Embassy we took the taxi to the City Centre. There, we shopped a bit and had a meal. When it was time to go to the airport for the trip back to Mumbai, we took yet *another* taxi.

As I say, it was a relatively expensive trip. In that I paid for it in Indian Rupee, by Western standards it wasn't that expensive. But the point is this: the Irish Government is absolutely useless when it comes to helping those of us needing assistance. Back in Ireland, I wrote a frank letter to the Irish Ambassador in India with the complaint that the Consol was not helpful to an Irish Citizen, nor was he helpful to HRG, or to many other people that I subsequently met who were Citizens of India and trying to get an Irish Tourist Visa. The Ambassador, of course, never replied. Nor did any of the Irish politicians whom I emailed asking for help with this matter.

I needed HRG to get into the company for 2 or more weeks to help me plan marketing strategies for my company. My hope was that, having proved to the Irish Government that she was now employed full-time, I could get a work visa for her which means that she could stay for well over 3 months. Of course, when I complained to the Irish Department of Foreign Affairs and told them that I had hired HRG full time despite the fact that she was still in India, they wanted more proof than I could give them. Even when I sent them the company contract between my company and HRG, signed by both parties, they still wouldn't accept that as proof.

When I phoned them, finally seeking an appointment to see them in Dublin, the person at the end of the line told me that there was no one available. "Are you saying that there is no one in the Department of Foreign Affairs or the Department of Justice to help me get this employee into the country?"

"No sir," the woman said. "I'm sorry, but we are very very busy with other problems right now. Look, the easiest way to get a woman into the country is if you were to marry her."

"Great! But I'm already married!"

"Sorry, sir." Then the line went dead.

As I write this, I finally hired a team of immigration lawyers in Dublin to sort out this mess. They promise me that, while it will take some time and may be somewhat expensive, getting HRG into Ireland should be no problem at all.

My point this time is this: if you're from certain countries and want to come to Ireland on a short-stay visa, get a qualified firm of immigration lawyers to help you. Irish officials charged with helping certain nationalities get into Ireland on a short-term visa?

ARE NOT HELPFUL AT ALL. MOST OF THEM SHOULD BE FIRED OR ASSIGNED TO OTHER JOBS. OH THE LIFE OF BUREAUCRAT!

As one woman I phoned recently, again from the Department of Foreign Affairs told me (and I phoned them again only the other day, BEFORE I hired the above Immigration Lawyers):

"Mr Richards, the rules are the rules and that's it!"

Haha! So bend the rules a bit in certain cases or make the laws regarding immigration fairer and more transparent. The law, it seems, is not equal to everyone. One last point: We have many, many nurses and doctors (as well as other professionals) working in Ireland. Why do they find it so easy to get a permanent visa when an employee for my company can't?

And how about this: one person I talked to who employed Indians at her company stated to me: "Tom, occasionally many people from my company must go to the UK for important conferences. Our professional workers can't come because getting into the UK is also impossible."

The laws must change. Oh, why are there borders on this planet? Borders are invisible, after all. They are placed there to protect various cultures and its citizens. But wouldn't it be better for everyone if those who would cause no harm were allowed into every country in the world without the frustration and expense of trying to get a simple short-term Visa??

How to Get a Work Visa

I've written about this extensively in A Survivor's Guide to Living in Ireland. The rules have changed slightly so I'll let you know what I know about getting a long-term Visa to work and stay here.

First, let me say that there are a number of ways to come to Ireland permanently. This is just one example.

Let's say that you're a Professional or a Person with a Trade who wants to live and work in Ireland. Then here's what you have to do. First go to the following Website for a List of Ineligible Occupations for Employment (in other words, Ireland has enough people to fill the vacancies for these jobs): https://enterprise.gov.ie/en/what-we-do/workplace-and-skills/employment-permits/employment-permit-eligibility/ineligible-categories-of-employment/.

Having decided that you're eligible to apply because there's a shortage of skilled workers in your field, you must do the following (and the Citizens Information Page is somewhat confusing. Go here to view the page): https://www.citizensinformation.ie/en/moving-country/working-in-ireland/employment-permits/work-permits/

So these seem to be the steps:

1. Find an employer in Ireland willing to hire you (you can use a variety of websites to find jobs in Ireland that will also let you apply online. Go here for an example of one of these. This webpage by www.indeed.com posts jobs that require Visa Sponsorship from Employers. So these Employers are looking for Foreign nationals. Just today, I see that they're posting for a Registered Midwife, Registered Nurse, Support Workers, Accounting Technician and over 300 other jobs): https://ie.indeed.com/q-ireland-visa-sponsorship-jobs.html?vjk=1f0c03dceb86b62f
As I say, you must apply for a work visa (and perhaps a visa to enter Ireland, once again, depending on the country you now live in)

2. Having done the above, and if you are successful in landing a job, you must register with your local registration office in Ireland. Having done that, you'll receive an Irish Residence Permit.

3. Following 1 year, you can then bring your family to Ireland to live with you.

In my case, when I finally moved to Ireland, I had to go to the local Garda Station in Navan once a month. There, they would look at me and say, "Tom, you're still here?" Then they'd stamp my registration card and initial it. As I remember, I had to do this for over a year.

I must say that the rules, and the positions you can apply for, to live and work in Ireland have changed dramatically in only the last 5 years. So do look at the above pages to make sure you are eligible to apply for a job here.

Other Methods

As one webpage I just read said: "Moving and staying in Ireland can be a long and complicated process". And for many people, it is. Of course, if you have family here then it's easy: you can get a visa in a snap! But for others?

Remember, there's always the Grandparent rule (see https://www.dfa.ie/globalirishhub/archive/sport-culture-heritage/claiming-irish-citizenship/#:~:text=You%20can%20become%20an%20Irish,on%20the%20Foreign%20Births%20Register.) This is very simple. If your grandparents were Irish citizens, you have the RIGHT to apply for – and receive – that same citizenship. Or, of course, if you have Irish parents you have the right to the same thing. When my children were born, I applied for United States citizenship for them. It was very, very easy. All I had to produce was my Birth Certificate (in my case, from Chicago, Illinois) and They're Irish birth certificates showing that I was their father. They received US citizenships instantly. And then, they're U.S. passports.

In the recent past, when Ireland was struggling economically, there were a number of Investor programmes that encouraged non-EU nationals to move here and invest in their own business, thereby employing Irish people. However, now that the economy is booming again these programmes have been cancelled.

That said, do remember this: if, for example, you are a US citizen you can live here with a long-stay visa for 1 year. Then you'll have to go back home for a few days or weeks. You then re-apply for your 1-year visa. And then you do the same.

After 5 years you are then eligible for Permanent Residency. That's my understanding. But the rules on moving to and staying in Ireland permanently have become very, very complex. Contact the Irish Department of Foreign Affairs or go here to start the application process for a Long Stay Visa: https://www.visas.inis.gov.ie/AVATS/OnlineHome.aspx

Note that the best thing to do is to contact your local Irish Embassy or Consulate near you. There are many of these in the United States, alone!

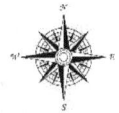

Chapter Five:
In Eyeries, County Cork,
I 'Made My Stand' for the Rest of My Life

If you're really considering moving to rural Ireland, take a deep breath and think about it. That's not what I did. I'd always wanted to live somewhere out in the country.

When I lived with my parents in San Ramon, California, back in the 1970s, the entire area was filled with farmyards, walnut groves and vineyards. I used to ride my bike up a long hill, along a four-lane road, only a half-mile from our home there, and when I got to the top all I could see was a vista of light brown fields (in the Summer) and in the distance, low-lying hills. Turning to the north, I could gaze at Mount Diablo (which years later, near the town of Danville, my eldest Daughter was born). I fell in love with the entire area instantly. In some ways, it reminded me of the Wild West. That area, and the Seattle, Washington area which I lived in from 1955 - 1964, sparked my interest in 'rural' areas.

Of course, things have changed almost everywhere. I visited the area around my parent's home not that long ago (they sold in in 2000) and looked once again around the area. Now, all I could find were huge neighbourhoods and light industrial factories. The traffic is horrible. There's smog settling against the Diablo Hills like there wasn't before. And the price for a home? Astronomical now! I had trouble financing one in 1982 when I lived there with my Ex-wife. When I visited the last time I realized I would never be able to afford to live there again.

When I first visited Eyeries, back in the mid-1990's, I decided to move here for a number of reasons. First, the place reminded me of Seattle only without the trees. The islands, the sea views, the white water crashing onto the rocks. The clouds. The moderate temperatures. The friendly people of the village. All encouraged me to buy what is now and will always be our Eyeries home.

Of course, life in Eyeries wasn't without its struggles. How well I remember talking to Carmel, my partner, when she came down to visit me not long after I moved in. I told her back then that I wasn't sure if I'd made the right decision. And to be honest, I was seriously thinking of selling and moving again.

"Carm, many visitors to the Village have told me that the place is too remote. I like 'remote' but this is almost too far from anywhere. It takes over 2 hours to get to Cork City and, to visit you or my children in County Meath, you're talking an almost 7-hour drive!"

"Tough," she said to me with her hands on her hips. "You made your bed and, like my father Tommy always told me, you'll have to lie in it. Tom, if you sell the house now, you'll lose a fortune! You've only lived here for just over a year now."

"But I miss you, my children and the friends I have in the Navan area."

"Tough again. I'll be down to live with you soon and your children can always visit. It's not that far a drive. And, like me, they can always take the train and you can pick them up in Killarney, County Kerry."

I was stumped because I knew that Carm was right. If I sold the house now, I'd lose about ☐30,000 which I couldn't afford to do. Besides, I rather liked living in that beautiful cottage.

"What I could do is rent it out and then rent something in Trim," I replied. "I rented an apartment in Trim before, you know, and you practically lived there with me."

"Yes, Tom. And what happened to that apartment and the apartment block it was in? The entire damned thing burned to the ground with you in it!"

She looked at me with fire in her eyes then, walking up to me and giving me a huge big hug, kissed me on the cheek.

"Tom, it's time to make your stand. You've lived all over the United States and a number of places in Ireland. If you truly like it here, why not stay here? When I come down permanently, which won't be too long from now, we'll make it a home, not just a house."

Which, of course, is exactly what happened. When I look back at the years I was in our home with Carm, I know how fortunate I've been. While only one of the children and her family visited me recently, I am fairly confident that my other children and their families will visit me soon. Too, I realize now what a stroke of luck I had when I bought the Eyeries Village home. It came completely furnished and had almost everything Carm and I needed to live here. Plates, Cutlery, almost 30 euro in a jar that the previous owners had left, even meat in the freezer. Needless to say, I kept the house.

Over the years I've done a bit to make it our home. I changed the back garden completely and used Liam O'Neill's advice to do that. Now, rather than a flat piece of ground, I put in two raised planters, a very large rock garden, then put in any number of plants, small trees, flowers and vegetables. I also had a good man here, Cormac Sullivan, put in a lower back deck as well as a large Upper shed. The only other thing that I did was to buy a smaller shed to hold my lawnmower and garden tools.

With Carm gone and so much time on my hands, two years ago I made the decision to make the home much more comfortable for her, or any visitor, as well as much safer. I've replaced the wood on the lower back deck with slates that have been cemented into the ground. The old shed that Cormac built is still there as well as a tool shed. Because Cormac was so busy, I hired a man by the name of Richard Doran as well as his son and a small team of construction workers. They've built: a garage made of treated wood in which I've placed most of Carm's clothes as well as our Christmas Decorations. The other day, I finally took delivery of an old Saab as a second car which is now in the outdoor Garage.

Richard has also built me a Large Wood Shop in which I now have most of my hand tools as well as my power tools. I still have a few things to buy for my hobby (I like to turn wood and need a lathe and some of those tools) but other than those, that task is now complete. (Carm would have loved to have come out and tried her hand at something. Her father, Tommy, was always building things with his hands).

The last shed was what I call, "Carm's Cabin". I'm renting it out now for about ☐50 per night (it fits two people in a standard double bed complete with everything a renter needs: the bed, warm bedclothes, battery powered lights, a Primus stove, cutlery, plates and similar). The price will go up in the High Season and every penny that I raise from that, our Tent Camping (which I now manage alone - Carm managed it ever since we started it in 2011), and the sales of my novels at our home will go to defray the many, many costs that I have - and will have - over the coming years to take care of Carmel when she finally comes home.

Richard and his team are now working on a large final project. Years ago, I'd promised Carm that I'd put an extension on the home which would be a new Master Bedroom. The current Master that we use is way too small and has no closet space. The one that Richard is building for us will have just shy of 300 square feet to the house and will be large enough for not only a double bed but my writing desk and a filing cabinet. Just think! I'll no longer have to use my attic to write in. Instead, I'll be able to give out of a huge glass window to see the views of the sea and the nearby Islands.

The new addition, when it's complete, will be the perfect bedroom for Carm and me. It will also add significant value to our home.

The price for all of the above was quite small compared to the quotes that I received. So a Big Thank You to Richard Doran, his son Ritchie and the rest of his Team for making this home an even better home.

Just like Carm told me, this home in Eyeries Village is 'My Last Stand'. There is a large possibility that because of her horrible illness, Carm will never be able to live here again. But I take heart - Carm is in every crack and crevice of our home. She's here in the pictures of her and me that I've hung on the wall. She looks down at me as I write. She is the 'ghost' of Christmases Gone By and the 'Ghost' in some ways of Christmases yet to come.

She will always be my wife and this home will always be our home. But, as she also advised, sometimes life is cruel and treacherous. I'm THINKING about moving much closer to my children in County Meath. After all, and as a child of mine said to me recently: "Dad, you're 68. If you move nearer to us next year, when you're 69, you'll almost be 70! It's time to be nearer to all of your children and grandchildren.

Of course, she's right. So what I'm considering is this: I could rent this home for say 4 months over the summer then come down here for the rest of the year. Just the other day I talked to JJ O'Sullivan, the agent I originally bought this home from. He told me, and get this, that if I rented this home for the High Season, I'll receive:

One-thousand, four-hundred euro for each month! That's about $1600 - 1700 dollars a month! That's astronomical! But it's enough to let me rent a nice place somewhere in County Meath, or maybe, which is more likely, somewhere in County Cavan which is only a few minutes north of my children and is much, much less expensive.

Renting or Buying 'Rural' is Again What I'm Thinking - and Here are some examples FOR YOU!

Should I decide to move for four months out of the year, I suspect that my options will be somewhat limited. As that day approaches, I'll do much more research into what I can rent in Counties Wicklow, Louth and Cavan. I won't look at County Dublin - it's far too expensive for me. But let's say I decided to rent today somewhere in the above counties? What would that cost for four months or so?

I don't, really, have many requirements for the kind of house I rent for the summer nor do I have any real preference for the location. I'm near the sea here in Eyeries so if I'm in the hills, and landlocked, that's fine by me. I would like to be within an hour or so from the sea and I'd like to be near a golf course. Too, it would be nice if I was a relatively close drive from an airfield (as you know, I also love to fly when I can afford it). So let's see what I can find.

Just now, I'm looking at www.daft.ie again. I'm looking at places in County Wicklow. And for the most part I can forget it! Holiday homes in this part of the country rent from a low of about ☐250 per week to a high of over ☐13,000 per week! Fine, if you're sharing those large, expensive homes with a number of families. But because it's just for me I must find something much, much cheaper.

Now I'm looking at County Cavan. I've driven throughout the county many times. There are two holiday homes that actually make sense to me. One is in the small town of Belturbet right near the beautiful River Erne. I'm sure that I could rent a boat of some kind and do some fishing on it. The town also has a good Golf Club a few miles away. This is a 3 bed / 2 bath terraced house which means I'd have quite a few neighbours. Completely furnished it has a large back garden.

Then there's the holiday home at River Run, Lough Doo, in the same town. I remember that home when it was first opened many years ago. It's in a line of similar homes and sits right next to the Erne River. I actually waved to a couple who had rented it and asked them what it was like to live there for the summer. The husband told me it was a fantastic place for a few months. So, if something like that is available when I move away from Eyeries for a few months, I'd definitely take it! And the price is the same as the one above: about ⌑250 per month! (Unless they have a typo on their listing which I doubt). What I also like about this location is it's only a little over an hour from my kids.

I didn't, of course, go into the prices of buying a home here. But maybe you'd like to come over a rent a holiday home in Ireland before you make the decision to buy one? I limited my search to two counties, but you can do much more depending on where you want to be located for a few weeks or months. Some places on the West Coast and the Northwest Coast of Ireland are also quite inexpensive. Go to www.daft.ie and filter for the home that you want.

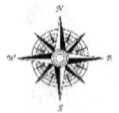

Chapter Six:
Why I Choose to Stay in Ireland

Over fourteen years ago, when I left my wife and our home just outside of Navan, I had a choice to make. I could easily have gone back to live with my Dad in Sun City Florida or - and another big decision - stay in Ireland.

But my children and a grandchild was in Ireland and I thought to myself: "Tom, you can never, ever leave this country. You've been happy in Ireland and if you go back to the States, you might see your children and my grandchild Sam only once or twice a year."

I had visited Eyeries two times at that point and had a photo of Scariff Island as the wallpaper on my laptop. The place seemed to call to me. About a year later, well after I met Carmel Murray, I bought our home here and I'm truly happy that I have.

Now and then, here in Causkey's Bar or in Castletownbere, I'll run into an American tourist or an American who has chosen to move here. We'll start talking about living in Ireland and they'll always ask me,

"Tom, would you ever move back to the United States again?"

I always answer "No" which is not what I would have answered even ten years ago. You see, you who are now reading this, I've always been a very, very proud American. As I say in the first Guideline of A Survivor's Guide to Living in Ireland, like most Americans I have many different lines of Ancestry: English, Scot, a bit of Irish, German, Welsh and native American (Micmac as we spell it in English). My German ancestor left Germany many, many years ago. His last name was Pethtel which is my mother's maiden name (mind you, the spelling of that name has changed many times over the years - it can be Pethtel or Pedal or Petal, but it's all the same bloodline). A few years after he arrived on the East Coast of the United States - and that's back in the late 1600's - he met and married a Bradford, a granddaughter of William Bradford who set sail for America on the Mayflower and became the first Governor of the Plymouth Colony.

I love my ancestry and the mix of peoples that I have in my DNA. Sometimes, I still long for the States but usually that's only for a few very good friends, a few relatives I have left there, the food and some of the holidays like the 4th of July. I no longer have any real good reason to go back to Florida. Mom and Dad have both passed away. My only sibling, Cindy, is way out in Southern California. I have one Aunt left in Ohio (leaving in a small town near East Liverpool where my mother was born) and a few cousins who live quite near her. I also have a number of cousins on the East Coast of the U.S. but I've lost touch with them. (If anyone who reads this know Kathy Vasquez - she lived on the East Coast of Florida and was a Sheriff there) or Nancy Arkis (she's now married and I cannot remember her married name!) do please let me know. I'd love to visit them again and it's been far too long.

So when it comes to relatives and except for my Aunt and my Pethtel cousins, I have no reason to ever go back. Of course, I do still keep in touch with my great, great friends living near Chicago. Bill Arnold, Michelle Lesley, Al Ah and the rest of the crew out there. I'd like to go out and visit them this September 2024 when they're holding what might be our last High School Reunion near our old high school, Rolling Meadows High School. But even that great crew is starting to pass on or fade from view.

So many people that I know well and count as great friends have died over the past few years. And so it is for many of us who are in the last third of our long lives.

So yes, I'll visit the U.S. many times before I finally take my leave of this planet. I LOVE the geography in all the States of the US as well as Canada and Mexico. The last time I counted, I'd visited or lived in about 30 states. I want to go see New Mexico, Arizona and Texas as well as North and South Dakota as well as Montana. And I'd like to go back to see Yosemite again and also Yellowstone National Park and the Grand Canyon. I've never been to those places and would love to.

Dad, who has an airline pilot for much of his life, used to describe what it was like flying over the deserts of the United States. He told me that when the sun went down, it flashed like god on the sand and turned the hills and mountain tops to a startling colour of red. He was the one that got me interested in Geology which I almost majored in when I was a Sophomore at Illinois Wesleyan University.

So yes, I'd also go back as a tourist. I'd also like to go see the Chicago Cubs play again in Wrigley Field and then go to Fenway Park to see the Boston Red Sox play. Both of them are great cities.

But why else won't I go back to live permanently in the United States? To be honest, it's a rather extensive list.

First is the divisiveness that was never present when I last lived there. I'm now a certified, fiscally conservative Democrat who believes in good social programmes. When I first voted in a presidential election, I voted for Jimmy Carter. Then, because I believed the Democrats had lost touch with most of their constituents, I re-registered as a Republican. A REAGAN Republican. I then started to vote for the candidate that I thought was best. I voted for Bill Clinton (and would have voted for Hillary Clinton). I also voted for Bush senior and junior. I voted for President Obama and was so very proud to do so.

Last time, I voted for President Biden. I'll vote for him again this year. I will NEVER, EVER vote for that scoundrel Trump or any of his acolytes. This year, when I receive my long Physical Ballot from Florida for the Presidential Election in 2024, I will vote Straight Democrat. Again. Many of the powerful political leaders in the U.S. are now Republicans. But they're like no republicans that I've ever seen before. They, as well as their Master Trump, have changed the Republican Party so much that I no longer recognise it.

The big problem is this: if Trump wins again, he will jeopardise democracy not only in the United States but all over the world. He'll support Putin and North Korea's little Rocketman. He will no longer support the Ukrainians in the war against Putin's Russia. Trump could even instigate a Nuclear War which, as many retired U.S. Generals have said in TV interviews, is entirely possible.

To reiterate: if you're an American and a Trump Republican, you'll be very, very welcome in Ireland. However, if I were you I wouldn't talk about politics. Many of the Irish dislike Former President Donald Trump with a fervour that approaches hatred.

If you do get into a discussion about Politics with an Irish person, be very, very careful of how you argue your points. Most of the Irish are highly educated or have extensive knowledge of Politics across the world and watch most news channels, or read newspapers, every day. Many of the Irish fella's may look like farmers or fishermen to you and some just might be, as are some women. But, and a big but, some of these are millionaires or self-sufficient but you wouldn't know it. Most will argue you around the bend and use a Socratic method to make their points. They'll listen to you carefully but then will use your logical English sentences against you and win the Argument! Often, to rattle you, they might talk in Irish! What a way to make a point using sentences that most of us will never understand.

Here's my take on chatting with a Trump Republic. A number of months ago, when I was in Lisdoonvarna on a needed break, I ran into a couple from Texas. The wife was a conservative but open minded. The husband was a Trump Republican and all he wanted to do was argue about Trump winning the next election. When I tried to argue that Trump's global policies were causing a great deal of job losses and suffering in Ireland, all the man could do was turn his back on me and walk away. He knew that I was right but wouldn't admit it. As for his wife, she quickly apologised and shook my hand. See? If you can't argue your point well, all you can do is turn your back and walk away from any Irish citizen who just might do his or her best to embarrass you into admitting that you're wrong. By the way, if you're a Christian Evangelical Trump supporter, the Irish may very well give you the URL to buy the Official Trump Bible. They'll laugh at you if you click on it because, let's face it, it's not Trump's Bible at all - it's God's Holy Bible. Some here say that Trump things that he's actually God the Father and I sure do hope it's not true! We have enough problems in Ireland and want to pray to a God of Eternal Power and Understanding, not a Trump-God dressed up in disguise as the God of the Ancient Hebrews. But here's the URL just in case you need to buy Trump's Bible. Bring it into any pub in Ireland and most likely, many Irish will ignore it and maybe even you! Go to: https://www.ebay.com/itm/395312787304?itmmeta=01HVNQN65RSDG58VWG24Z8WC4R&hash=item5c0a7a6f68:g:M7kAAOSwaiVmDFeY&itmprp=enc%3AAQAJAAAA8DwgH1CC0bcCYrrY79g3QaNdIIKd8Asx1qk5K25soooKDS0bgzfRY5IsNfsUF%2FBUZFHorELfGa5c8ouhwLynfHWaQ9SoTL0G67JoBcDTESw0N9jXcP2gQQtZW0Y0%2FGBYxA3pDSkyAM6Kmz72RwXLMAqB2IdKCzerR76EkHuteUg%2BUD8jr4xs3UovZO6fvT0Ky6EoHK5%2Fjk%2FIdZBol5hnCMMxTsdbysEYEPU6xCn68ZIjtw7VJqShCIrflYI%2BFt9wdzMzfAcNo6z0jU0DnPINrNXEPyS19ktB15Tn7J0hlmCiocUkIHKBsOOgsKb1RLtl4g%3D%3D%7Ctkp%3ABFBM-uLUt91j It's only $104.00 on eBay. And just think, if you buy it, you can help to pay for his many lawyers and defray his legal expenses (I have the King James version. I think I'll pass on this one).

In Ireland, we talk about politics all the time but we never, ever fight about it. Ireland has one of the most stable democracies in the world. As I've written in a chapter above, we have a Social Welfare programme like few other countries in the world. We have 'safety nets' which means that should you lose your job you won't, in all likelihood, be tossed out of your home anytime soon. Here, I feel comfortable and for the first time in my life, I feel more Irish that American. And why not? I've been here permanently since 1982. That's a long, long time. I've learned to love the place – the people, the scenery, the food and the Pints. I've learned to talk somewhat like an Irishman (though I'll always have my Chicago accent).

Why else will I stay here for the rest of my life? Let's move onto the next chapter and I'll tell you why.

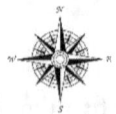

Chapter Seven:
A Welcoming, Stunning & Peaceful Location

When I first came here and stayed at Anam Cara with a group of other artists and writers, we all piled into Sue Forbes-Booth's SUV and she took us first to Allihies, one of the most Westerly villages in Ireland.

Below is a Free Map of the Beara Peninsula. If you're visiting this area, start at Letter D on the map which is the town of Kenmare in County Kerry, only a 40-minute drive from where I live.

This is the part of the Wild Atlantic Way – a drive that takes you almost completely along the West Coast of this country. I've not done the entire Wild Atlantic Way drive. Only some of it. But when my children were young I took them to County Donegal and the beaches there were some of the most beautiful I've ever seen.

Over the years since I've been living in Ireland, I've driven much of the Wild Atlantic Way. About 8 months ago, in September 2023, I drove up to Lisdoonvarna and joined that absolutely wild event! I visited two matchmakers just to see what they were like. They didn't charge much and over the few days I spent there in some great hotels and B and B's, I danced the nights away with some of the best female dancers who love Irish Western Music as much as I do.

Lisdoonvarna, during the Matchmaking Festival that they have each year, isn't for everyone. But if you like music of all kinds, particularly Western, ceili or many other types of Irish music, this could well be the Festival for you. Too, if you're lonely and looking for a partner, the price of that isn't very much at all. Just sign up with one of the Matchmakers and, if you're lucky, they'll get you a date and maybe, just maybe, you'll find your everlasting partner for your whole life.

But back to the map:

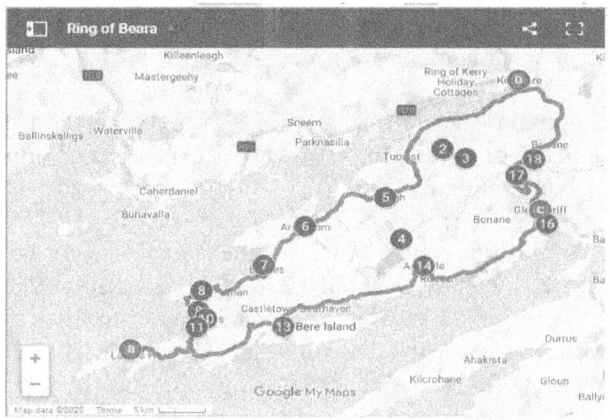

Allihies is Number 8 on the map above. (Go to https://www.yourirelandvacation.com/ring-of-beara/ for a complete

description of each of the Map's Numbers) That's where Sue's group of artists drove to. The day was beautiful! As we drove over the hill toward Allihies, Sue pulled to the side of the road. Getting out of the car, most of us took out our camera's. In the near distance were the Skellig Islands - all of them at once - lit in the warm sunlight. Sue pointed out Skellig Michael, now made famous by a recent Star Wars Film.

Just above is Skellig Michael which is the inspiration for the magical island of 'Solas Mor' in my novel *Dolphin Song* (soon to be a Major Feature Film).

This is only one reason why I continue to live in Eyeries, which is on the Beara Peninsula, about a 20-minute drive from Allihies. If you want inspiration for your paintings, novels, pottery, woodworking, or just about anything including music composition, all you have to do is take a walk or, in my case, look out a window or stand on our back deck. From right here, I can see the island of

Eyeries (which the Village is named after), the large whale-like island of Scariff (which inspired me to move to this Village), and the island of Inishfarnard (which is just below and gives you almost the same view I have from my back deck in my home of Solas Mor, which I named after the magical Island of Skellig Michael). As you look at the photo here, and to the left, you can see the Mountains of Mishkish, which are the spine of the Beara Peninsula. To the right, and out of shot, is the small peninsula of Kilcatherine and just beyond that, the Ring of Kerry which Carm and I visited any number of times.

A simple Warning: If you want to drive the Ring of Kerry (which starts in Kenmare for those of us living in this part of Cork County), don't go in the High Summer. Carm and I did one summer and the traffic was so bad we decided to turn around and head home. The roads were filled with Tourist Buses, Caravans and large Campers. Instead, we stopped in Sneem where we had a wonderful lunch and went for a hike on the beach right near that wonderful small town.

This part of Ireland is a wonderful place to live. But what are the other reasons I choose to stay here? Okay, inspiration is one of them. Many of my books and novels (like this one) are located at least in part here. Too, I've met many other novelists and artists, as well as local potters, who get their inspiration from the local area or the various legends and history of Ireland.

So another reason to stay??

The Many Legends of Ireland

Do you believe in Leprechauns or the Tua da Danaan? Well I do and for a very, very good reason. They truly are real! All you have to do is ask anyone who lives here and they'll tell you that they've met at least one. They exist when Rainbows appear: for the Crock of Irish Gold, the King of the Tua da Danaan (which are Leprechauns in the days of yore) that big pot of Golden Coins, is buried right beneath the Rainbow's end. The problem, of course, is if you walk toward a Rainbow it will always back off. So you can never seem to get your hands on that King's Crock of Gold.

Finian's Rainbow. Now there's an Irish Crock of Gold! Haha! What a great film and if you ever get a chance to see it (and I've seen in any number of times) you'll see how you can occasionally catch the King of the Leprechauns! Take his kingly wee Crown and then you have magical leverage. You can bribe that small King to give you his Gold in exchange for his Crown and Royal Throne! (But don't do it! The King's Crown is the most valuable thing of all. If you take the Crown and keep it, you'll be allowed three wishes. Then, if you're very careful for what you wish for, all of your wishes will come true, forevermore!)

Yes, Ireland is full of Legends and even Ghosts! For instance, as I think I mentioned, Carmel and I have allowed Tent Campers (including Backpackers, Motorcyclists, Bikers and many more types of Campers) to use our back garden on which to pitch their tents. We've had the privilege of hosting people from all over the world: from as far away as New Zealand. In the summer, we often host Americans who are hiking or taking the car toward Kenmare, Dublin or the far east of this small country.

Now, if you're American don't become offended. But Americans can often be rather naïve and so Carmel also agrees. Just beyond the cement wall of our back garden, and very close to where the tourists sleep at night in their tents, there's an old stone ruin that used to be a tile covered two roomed house where a poet slept in one room and cows and pigs slept in the other. After the poet, who was also a famous Irish Seanachai died, that house was turned into an Abattoir which, if you're not familiar with the word, is a slaughterhouse. In there, pigs, sheep and cows were butchered and sold to the highest bidder. The butcher, who had a shop in this village, concentrated on pigs because they got the best price of all. Now, here's the thing and this is what I tell to Americans who stay with us, particularly young women:

"Beware of the Abattoir because at night the Ghosts of pigs come out and they'll squeal at you."

"What," the young women will say. "What are you talking about?"

"Ghost pigs," I'll answer. "Beware of them because they'll squeal and when they do, come into the home and hide in the back room with the lights out."

They women will laugh at me. "Ghosts aren't real," they'll say. "Ghosts? Who cares about ghosts?"

"You'd better care about Ghosts," I'll say back. "If you hear them squeal, they're on their way to BUTCHER YOU!"

At that point they'll usually start laughing again but all I'll do is frown. "Okay, don't believe me. But at midnight, when the cock crows once and then again, be prepared for the Ghost Pigs to MURDER YOU!"

Sometimes, one of the women will dive into her tent and come out with a big knife or even a machete. I'll look at that huge long weapon and smile.

"But they're Ghosts, Susan. Ghosts don't care if you have a weapon."

"But this is a Ghost Machete," Susan will reply. "It can kill all the Ghosts that try to attack us. Even Ghost Pigs."

"Really? Ghost Pigs too? Where did you buy that big weapon?"

"It's a secret," she'll say, smiling. "Actually, I bought it at Walmart. It was on sale in the Ghost Section at Halloween."

Then I'd start laughing. "Prankster," I'd laugh. "Ghost Machete or not, beware of the cocks crowing and the Murdering, Butchering Pigs."

One night, a few years ago, I teased a woman like the one directly above. Her name was Dawn and she was on her own. At midnight, I was in bed upstairs in the cottage and she was asleep in her tent. Through the open window I could hear a cock crow twice, then the distinct cries of a Ghost Pig screaming it's bloody lungs out.

In the morning, I asked Dawn if she'd heard anything last night.

"Yes, I did. I heard something crowing and then screaming so loudly it woke me up. I did what you told me to do. I ran into the back room and turned out the light. Then I hid beneath the dining room table. After a few minutes that damned screaming turned into something howling as if it was being killed."

"Was it howling like a pig being murdered?" I said as I ate my breakfast of eggs and rasher. "Was it a horrible howl, a blood-filled howl, or more of a hoot-howl like that from an injured owl?"

She looked up from her plate of egg and rasher. As she lifted a piece of rasher, she gazed at it. "Like this strip of bacon," she said reasonably. "After it was finished howling I went back outside and saw the shadow of a pig cross in front of my open tent. I just knew that if I'd stayed outside, I would have been butchered and murdered, just like you told me yesterday."

So there you go, all. Ghost Pigs really are real. So says Dawn, the American tent camper, and I really, really believe her.

Don't you?

A Place to Heal

I'll start with a German camper I met two years ago, right after I lost Carm to Alzheimer's. He didn't have a reservation but our camping site was empty of any other Guests. He rode in on a big Grey BMW motorcycle, the kind I've always wanted. Taking off his helmet, I could see a man with a broad smile on his face. He was built like a wrestler or a boxer with short grey hair and grey and white stubble on his face.

"My name is Hubert," he said in his German accent. "I am hoping you might have room for me for two nights."

Shaking his hand, I led him around the back garden just like Carm would have done if she'd been here to welcome him (she loved to welcome our Guests. After all, she was - and in some ways still is - Manager of the Solas Mor Cabin and Tent Camping facility.

If you want more information on us, you can find Solas Mor Tent camping by using Google Maps. Find the Beara Peninsula then Castletownbere. Just north of there, you'll see Eyeries. Zoom in on the Village and you'll find Solas Mor Tent Camping. You'll see a number of reviews and our Phone Number. Do phone if you want to make a reservation which we suggest you do in the Summer High Season).

I told him that he could pitch his tent anywhere he wanted but, desiring to be near the back door of our home, he pitched it right next to the wall and the short climb to the back deck.

Then, when he was finished, I showed him where to charge his phone (in the back shed) and that he could help himself to a tin of beer if he was thirsty from his lengthy bike trip.

"I drink very little," Hubert said as he took off his black leather biking jacket and placed it on the outdoor deck to dry. "As my father taught me, moderation in all things."

"I drink just a little too," I replied. "When you're ready, why not share a tin of lager? I have German lager, as it happens."

"That would be fun!" Then I led him into the back room and told him how Carm had named it the View Room because of the spectacular views we had from the back window.

"A good, good name for a wonderful room," he said. When I showed him the small downstairs bathroom that the campers used, I also showed him how to turn on the shower. Looking into the tiny cubicle, he laughed again.

"I will enjoy my large fat body in a small shower like that. Is the water hot?"

"It's always hot!" I laughed back.

After he finished with his shower, we shared a bottle of lager and Hubert took out some pretzels he'd brought with him from his homeland. As we snacked on those and drank our lager in the shed, I showed him the framed pictures of Carm that are screwed into the wooden walls of the shed.

"That is your girlfriend?" he asked. "Why, she is beautiful in an Irish kind of way. She reminds me somewhat of my daughter who is home in Germany."

Then we talked about his family and mine. Of how I had moved here to this home after I'd left my wife. How I had met Carm and all the happiness she had given me. And how she was now gone due to Early Onset Alzheimer's.

"Not gone forever," Hubert said as he smiled and winked an eye. "Even those with Alzheimer's remember the happy times. I know. My grandmother died of Alzheimer's. But she always smiled when we visited her and told her about the wonderful, happy memories we had with her throughout her life."

Then he said something that changed my life. "You know, Tom, I have not been feeling well either. I have learned something very valuable. At our age, we must learn to take things Slowly. Very slow. Like S L O W."

"Slooowwww," I repeated as I broke into a smile. I felt my cheeks and realized I'd been silently crying again. "Hubert, that's great advice. I tend to try to do things all at once. And, without Carm, I have trouble coping."

"Slllowww, Tom," he said as he slowly waved a big hand toward the ground. "Slow, or you could have a heart attack or grow ill."

So that's what I started to do even after Hubert left the next day. As he put away his tent and got ready to leave, he explained that he'd decided to drive toward the west coast, then back up to Cork where he would take the ferry back to Europe.

"Let me take a picture of you before you go," I asked as he signed our registration book. But I forgot to do that.

So in my mind's eye, I'll always see that huge smile that Hubert wears even now. I do follow his advice and take things slow. It was too late to prevent my Heart Attack, but now life is much slower and more manageable. Too, I've learned to Keep Things Simple, which I really try to do.

Every now and then I phone Hubert in Germany. I've managed to get through to him once or twice. I'll remind him about moderation and he'll remind me to take things Slow and then we'll both laugh.

The last time I talked to him he explained that the real reason he left our camping ground early was because he'd been diagnosed with cancer. It had already metastasized. The day he left he forgot about the West Coast of Ireland and instead biked directly back to Cork and then onward to his home town in Germany.

"Tom, when I met you I chose not to tell you that I had cancer because I wanted to forget that for a few good weeks," he said on his mobile phone from his home. "I have decided to quit working. I want to spend the rest of my life with my good wife and my daughter. I take things slow all the time now because I have trouble walking today. I knew that the trip on my BMW to Ireland was the last long bike trip I've ever taken. Take things slow, Tom. And we all say blessings to you and Carmel from Germany."

Then he hung up. That's the last time I talked to him. I haven't tried to phone him since because I worry that he may not answer in which case the cancer has beaten that huge man from Germany who became a very close friend in one single day.

Why do I stay here in Eyeries? That's another reason. Occasionally, I'll meet someone like Hubert - be that person a man or woman. They'll stay one or two days and we'll share almost everything.

Here in this small Village that overlooks the pristine waters of our Bay, it is always peaceful. Here is a good place to heal from whatever troubles you. We've had campers here who have suffered terrible problems and issues: things like open heart surgery, divorce, children dying, parents and families dying, and many other problems.

My last story is of a man named John. He came here with his wife two years before Hubert did and well before Carm became so terribly ill.

His wife, Jane (they are also American) was a wonderful woman. Jane and Carm hit it off instantly. After I helped my partner settle the two campers into the back garden, I went back to work upstairs. When I came down for a break, I found Carm standing in the View Room, crying.

"What's wrong, Pook?" I asked. "Is it the campers?"

"That man!" she said as she stopped crying and wiped her eyes. "He's a pig of an American. He orders his wife around like she's his slave. He ordered ME to go get him tea, which now I'll never do. If they hadn't already paid, I would have kicked him out. His wife could have stayed in the tent and for all I care he could sleep in the bushes."

"What's wrong with him?" I asked as she came into my arms. "He seemed like a nice guy when he was putting up their tent."

"I have no idea. He's a cruel bastard of a man, that's all I know."

Later that evening, after we all had had dinner, I went outside. Watching that man John order around his wife, I decided to finally confront him and tell him that he was not welcome to stay any longer.

When I told John what I thought of him, he broke down and started to cry.

"I'm so sorry, Tom. And when I see her, I'll say the same thing to Carmel. You see, a month ago my only brother died. He had a heart attack and he was a year younger than me. My only brother is dead and I loved him very much."

Then he broke down and began to sob. His wife ran up onto the deck and took him in her arms. Leading him to their tent, they entered it and zipped up the flap and I guess went to sleep.

A moment later, Carm came back out onto the deck and led me into the shed where we both had a cigarette. When I told her what John had said to me, she only nodded.

"I heard what he said to you through the open window. I'm sorry for him but I wish he'd stop behaving like he does."

"I do too. Maybe, someday with some time ..."

"A lot of time, Tom. Sometimes, it takes years to get over the death of someone you love with all your heart."

And it's true. John and Jane left the next day, just like they'd planned. He was in much better form that morning as they packed. You see, when Carm and Jane were asleep, John woke up and came back up onto the deck. I was having a tin of Guinness in the evening twilight and offered this upset man one. As we both sipped our pints together, he told me more about his brother and how close they had been. But now, he had said to me, life would be much harder without him.

"But this is what I know now," John said to me as we continued to drink in the late evening sunset. "My brother will always be alive inside me. Tom, what you and Carm have done for me is to make me much more aware of my behaviour. I don't mean to get angry or fly off the handle, or order people around. Jane has been after me to go to grief counselling. When we get home, I'll make an appointment. Maybe I'll never get over my brother's early death, but this peaceful place has given me the chance to think about him and to thank the Stars that he was my brother. It's a wonderful place to grieve." Then he shook my hand and went back to bed.

What I've learned about this home of ours and our village (even with Carm gone) is this: this village is a wonderful place to grieve in. It's a place to forget your sorrows and all that bothers you, or me, too. It's a place where, no matter what the weather, I can look up into the dark spaces above my head and thank God for people like Hubert, Jane, John and Carm. So to all of you and keeping in mind that many of you may be grieving like me and many of the people that I've met here, I'll end this chapter with Hubert's simple advice:

"Keep Things SLLLLOOwwwww."

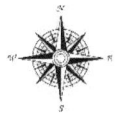

Chapter Eight: Touring this Area and What to Bring with You. Don't Forget about the Irish Weather.

As I've written a number of times above, one of the best ways to get to know this country is to come to visit at least once here. That's what I did in 1980 just after I'd graduated from UCLA in Los Angeles. My intention then was to take a tour of the southern part of England and perhaps go up to the Lake District in Scotland. But that's not what happened to me! I was on a really good Volkscycle which looks rather like a racing bike. I bought paniers and a front bag before the trip and rode around my apartment in Westwood until I felt that I was fit enough to accomplish that trip that I'd been planning for a number of years.

Landing in Gatwick Airport on a Freddie Laker flight, all I wanted to do then was explore the legends of King Arthur and his Knights and visit all of the Cathedrals, Museums and ancient Monuments that I could. The plan was to stay in England and perhaps Scotland for perhaps 4 weeks. I had been saving for that trip for a number of years and with about £2,000 in American Express Travellers Cheques in my bag, I set off to discover England.

That was the start of a journey of discovery, let me tell you. When I found myself in Anglesey, Wales, I had a decision to make: do I go right to Scotland or left to the ferry that would take me to Ireland? For whatever reason, I turned left and found the ferry, the Avalon - King Arthur's Holy Ferry - ready to leave for Dun Laoghaire, just south of Dublin, Ireland (ready for a lesson in Irish Pronunciation? The name of that large town is NOT pronounced

DUNE LOUGH, as I originally pronounced it. But rather, it's pronounced DONE LEERIE. Some here pronounce the name DUN LEER).

The story of how I married Bernie Richards nee Smythe was covered in *A Survivor's Guide to Living in Ireland* (you can read about the story of how we met and married below). So I won't repeat it. But, just as the tagline to that first memoir states, *I came for a visit and stayed for a lifetime.*

Having now lived in Ireland for 43 years, I've had the good fortune to visit most counties, cities, towns and many villages in both the Republic of Ireland and Northern Ireland.

So if you're coming on a visit – or more than one – where would I recommend that you go? Let's start North of Dublin Airport. I'm assuming that you'll rent a car. There are many, many rental car companies in Dublin Airport. The price is still rather expensive but not as expensive as it was when I first moved here.

A HINT: in Ireland, we all drive on the LEFT-HAND SIDE of the road, not the right! I highly suggest that you sit in your rental car for a few minutes to get 'the lay of the land'. Unless you're renting an automatic, and even then, it can be quite confusing when you first start to dive here. The stick shift is on the LEFT of you. You sit in the Right seat. The rear-view mirror is above and to the left, not the right. The hand brake is to your left. The side mirror is to your right.

Take your time and get used to the vehicle. And when you first start to drive out of the airport, go SLOW and if you get lost Stop and ask for directions. The Irish love to help people who are visiting here. Be careful of our round-a-bouts. They're also confusing. At the airport, ask any official for a copy of the 'Rules of the Road'. We don't have a 'free left or fight' at a stop light, for instance. In rural Ireland, the roads can be QUITE NARROW, so give-way to those vehicles that are approaching you. Find any kind of lay-bye and pull over. When a vehicle passes you, put your thumb or index finger up and wave a bit. Smile! And the other driver will think you're an Irish citizen, and a local resident, too!

Now, where do I suggest you go?

The Newgrange Monument, County Louth

First, assuming that you're going somewhat Northwest of Dublin Airport, stop at Newgrange, the Megalithic Monument that's older than the Pyramids of Egypt. It's older than Stonehenge! The OPW (Office of Public Works) has built an absolutely lovely Tourist Centre there. Go in for a cup of tea and a 'Cuppa'. Then take the tourist bus out to see the Newgrange Monument. It's a stunning place! The front of it has white quartz mineral stones that glitter white and a bit silver in the sun (if you get any – but no matter, that's Irish weather for ye). The bottom of the Monument is made of Kerbstones – huge lozenge shaped boulders that were pulled there aeons ago but the men and women who built it. The Tourist Centre has a large exhibition of how Newgrange was built. If you get REALLY lucky you may be able to go into the Monument itself on Winter Solstice. You'll see the sun come up through the door of the Monument and into the Roof Box. The entire interior of the Monument lights up. I've never had the opportunity to visit this astounding structure on the Solstice. But if you can, do it!

I used that Ancient Monument (which, I gather, was also something of a fortress) in my first novel for young adults, "The Lost Scrolls of Newgrange." When I was doing the research, the Gate Attendants (and there was an entry gate just a few meters from the Monument back then – they charged a pittance to see this extraordinary structure) allowed me to literally crawl all over that magical structure. They let me walk onto the top of the monument and all around the base, and also inside. If I had any questions, the gate attendants answered them as best as they could.

So before I forget, a big CALL OUT to the OPW again! Thanks for letting me in to see that Monument for absolutely FREE! I didn't have much of a job at the time, and saving that few pence really meant something to me. My novel above went to Number Three in the Irish Times Young Adult Best Sellers list in 1995. What a way to start a career! If it hadn't been for all of you back then, that novel would never have been written!

For more information on the Newgrange Monument, opening times and similar, simply Google The Newgrange Monument, County Louth, Ireland

Belfast, Northern Ireland

Now for the second stop on our brief tour. Take the Motorway up to Belfast, one of the best cities on this Island. Today, it take only two hours or so rather than the 4 hours that it took me years ago when I had to drive there from Navan. I've been to Belfast a number of times and love that city! The streets are fairly wide, the architecture is stunning, the shopping a treat and the people! Well, they're all Irish too so they'll also welcome you with open arms - particularly if you have ancestry from their part of the world.

I first went to Belfast during the dreaded years of 'The Troubles'. I had employed a wonderful woman up there as part of our expansion of Direct Concepts, the first marketing agency that I'd set up in Ireland. Claire was a Catholic and we did business with Coca Cola who employed both Catholics and Protestants. Back then, pitching to a company run by Protestants could be trouble. Claire and I visited a Northern Ireland Gas Company looking to land them as a new client. When the marketing manager came out - a big man with a firm handshake - the first thing he did was to ask Claire where she'd gone to Primary School and Secondary School. When Claire told him that was the end of our meeting. We never did land that company as a client.

When we climbed into her car and drove back to the Belfast City Centre, I asked her why the man had asked about her schooling.

"He wanted to know if I kicked with the left foot or the right foot," she explained in her soft Northern Ireland accent. "He wanted to know if I was Protestant or Catholic."

It was only then that I realised the extent of the bigotry in the North and what was really behind the so-called 'Troubles' that had resulted in so many murders and atrocities to the people of both the North and the South. Thank God, is all I can say, for the Peace Process that has resulted in a lasting peace to this Island. No longer will citizens or visitors have to duck when they see a soldier running at them with an Automatic Weapon poised to shoot us. No longer will we all have to pray for the souls that have been lost - though many of us still pray for the hundreds and hundreds of people lost to this 'war' caused in great part by religious persecution. Instead, people from the North and those from the Republic visit each other just as neighbours should.

The last time I visited Belfast was only a few years ago. I took my partner, Carmel, up there to see the Christmas Festival. I'm so glad we went! It still is one of the best memories I have of the two of us enjoying each other's company so very much. Belfast was decked out in Christmas lights. A Festival was underway featuring a tall Ferris Wheel also decked out in Christmas Lights. A number of Christmas trees lined the main street and we strolled through the city, shopping in all the stores, and eventually had dinner in a very good Belfast Restaurant. I went into a rather small shop where I bought Carm a Fossil Bag and Purse, which I still have because she no longer needs it in the Nursing Home. Still, it's something else I'll always treasure. The bag has disappeared but the purse is still here, worn out with years of use. I take it out occasionally and remember how she held it when searching for some coins or a few notes. That little purse also reminds me of how much we loved our time in Belfast, just as you will, we're both sure. And of how much I still love her. I took the Fossil Purse out a few minutes ago and also the bag that I keep it in. It's filled with older jewellery: unmatching earrings, a few that match and that I'll soon send to her. A few parties rings. I bought many of those over the years and I'll keep them all to remember how she once was. Too, I found 50 cent piece and a 10-cent piece. She left them in there and forgot about them. I put the 10c piece in my pocket. The 50c piece I'll hang somewhere in the shed where we spent so much time together.

Whenever I travel to many of the places that I'll soon describe, I'd always have Carm at my side. I hope that when you visit here someday soon, you'll also have some one that you love and treasure to accompany you.

The Northwest of this Irish Island

I won't tell you about all of the places that I've visited in this part of Ireland. Some of them include: Portrush and west along the coast all the way to Malin. Take in the lighthouses along that rugged coast. Go to Giant's Causeway and marvel at the octagonal rocks created by volcanoes and the tides so many millions of years ago. Make sure you go to Derry (I've not had the opportunity to go there yet) and walk in the heart of that small city. By the way, some people still call it Londonderry, not that it makes any difference anymore.

Travel further west and you're in County Donegal and back in the Republic of Ireland. Now County Donegal and points west? Yes, I've visited there many, many times particularly when my children were younger.

They all went to Gaelic School Bunbeg. We'd all climb into the car – Kristin, Cathy, Jonathan, Bernie and me – and head west from Navan. When we finally drove into this amazingly beautiful county and started to look for the right road (this was many years before Google Maps), my ex-wife started to notice that all the road signs were in As Gaeilge.

"What does that say, Jonathan?" Bernie asked our son who was studying the Irish Language in elementary school. When he translated the sign into English, it was too late, of course. I'd already driven past it and, with a lorrie (the word for 'Truck' in Ireland and the UK) just behind us, had no choice but to continue on the wrong road toward the west. Sometimes, Jonathan couldn't translate the Irish sign at all. So we ended up doing loops all over Donegal.

If you haven't been to County Donegal, make sure that you include this in your visit. The beaches are stunning, the food decidedly Irish and the language? Most people speak Irish. All of my children went to Gaelic school there to work on their Irish. They stayed in a home right next to the beach and studied there too with a number of wonderful Irish speakers.

Galway: the Oldest Chartered City in Ireland, Galway has to be one of my favourite cities in the entire country. Filled with narrow streets and buskers, the shops will make you 'shop 'til you drop'. They also have fine restaurants, a variety of hotels, and if you're tent camping like my family did many years ago, you'll find a place to set up your camper, tent or trailer just west of the city, which are often found along a fine strand. You'll see a small white tower with a red roof which a diving board on it. If you like to dive into the sea (like I do) then try it! Just be careful because in the Winter or when there are storms coming in from the West or North, or even the South, there can be riptides off the beach that can take you out miles to the West.

Galway is sort of the Gateway to the far West of Ireland. Drive to Connemara which, to me when I first saw it, looks like the back side of the Moon. The fields are littered with large boulders and smaller stones that were brought here forever as part of the huge Glacier that covered much of Ireland in the last Ice Age. Often, you'll see small 'valleys' which are called 'Glacial Moraines' that are the result of the immense weight of the ice.

Too, you may see fields of soft ground which are often filled with tiny lakes. These are also the result of the Glaciers. You see, back thousands of years ago Ireland was covered with dense forests. Oak, fir and other indigenous species. When the Glaciers covered the land, the trees fell and died and were buried by tonnes of ice. Over the next thousands of years most of them turned into peat. While much of that peat has been used for heating homes or factories, or turned into Garden Peat (rather like very dark, wet compost), some patches of peat can still be harvested for fuel. You may see Irish people digging into the ground with a flat spade. They're actually taking out 'sods of turf'. The harvesters will stack them in 'Tee-pee' shapes and allow those sods to dry in the wind. After taking them home, they'll build a turf fire which makes any home smell as sweet as any place on Earth.

Of course, the Irish government is beginning to ban the collection of turf as it is now a scarce resource. But you can still buy those very dark sods or purchase 'peat briquettes' at the local shop. If you stay at a hotel, BnB or walk into a pub in the Winter months, you can see the fire roaring and smell that Earthy aroma of burning peat. I use it when I can and, after the fire dies down, the result is very fine ash which is easy to clean out and can be used as a sort of fertiliser in the garden.

Connemara is also one of the locations where John Ford's The Quiet Man was filmed. You can still visit the Pub where John Wayne put up his Dukes and had fisticuffs with the locals. And you can see the small cottage built on the glen where the Duke and Mareen O'Hara lived when they were married, and she made dinner of boiled potatoes for her brother, her husband and all the hard-working men who helped to farm and fish in the area.

The Aran Islands: if you have a little more time take the ferry (or an airplane) from the mainland to one or two of the Aran Islands. I did that too and it was an experience that I'll never forget! On the voyage across that local bay toward the Aran Island of Inishmore, we saw a huge pod of dolphins as well as a number of

Basking Sharks (Basking Sharks are often thought to be some sort of Whale but they're not! They're the biggest Shark in the seas though they eat only Krill and other small fish. These Sharks are the ancestors of similar sharks that lived in the ocean Millions of Years ago.)

We visited two of the Aran Islands but I'll focus on Inishmore. This island is in the Irish-speaking Gaeltacht and its people are all grand. Take a walk all over the Island because it's rather small or hire a push-bike. When we were there back in the late 1980s, there were very few cars and no taxis of any kind. Walk to Dun Aonghasa (Dun Aengus) and you'll be amazed, the same way as I was. First built in 1100 B.C. when rubble was piled against large upright stone pillars, and added to over the years, the triple wall defences were constructed along the fort's west side. That fort is named after the Irish God of the same name described in Irish legends (for more information about this fort, go to: https://en.wikipedia.org/wiki/D%C3%BAn_Aonghasa

What I remember best about visiting Dun Aengus was walking up the steps on the very West side of the fort. I stood at the top and looked down where, hundreds of feet below me, the Wild Atlantic Ocean crashed against that small island. I looked out to sea and in the distance could see trawlers catching fish with a number of seagulls squawking madly for their lunch. Beyond those fine vessels, I could barely make out a freighter heading West toward the Americas. I wondered what it was carrying and where her crew were from and wished, just for a moment, that I was part of that long voyage. What an adventure it would be to live on a great vessel as large as a freighter, steaming West to where the sun would soon set. As I say, and if you have time, the Aran Island are certainly worth a great visit. (I also remember wishing that my family and I had more time. I would have rented a BnB on that Island and experienced the life of those who lived and worked on Innis Mor.)

Lisdoonvarna, Lahinch, Doolin and the Area: if you're bound for Shannon Airport, or even if you're not, make sure that you take a tour of this area. I've already discussed my trip to Lisdoonvarna (do remember, if you're single and looking to find a partner, the Matchmaking Festival is the place to go!) When I was in Lisdoonvarna, I took my Ford Ranger Pickup Truck (called The Beast by Ford Motor Company and it is! The best truck I've ever owned) all over the area. I played pitch n put in Doolin then had lunch in Lahinch. Following that I continued driving to the Burren, a fascinating area and home to plants, birds and insects not found in the rest of Ireland.

In the Burren area are a number of megaliths that I just had to see. I parked in a local parking lot (for free) and, along with a number of other visitors, walked a short distance up a gravel path to view an ancient Wedge Tomb. Made of ancient shale, some covered with lichen, a Capstone sits atop three other stones that act as 'walls' for this Ancient Buriel Place. We were allowed to take photos of this fascinating structure but we were not allowed to approach it. The Director of the Tour told us that many other tourists - as long ago as the 18th and 19th Century - had carved their initials into the walls.

When it began to rain I went back to my great hotel in Lisdoonvarna. What a magical time I had! I very much recommend that you, too, try to visit this area. (I HIGHLY recommend the Knockaguilla House Bed & Breakfast. Only 2 miles from Lisdoonvarna, the rooms were brilliant, the owners very friendly and helpful and they had a huge Breakfast Room where you could help yourself to anything that was in the refrigerator: eggs, rasher, milk, vegetables and more. You could also drink as much tea and coffee as you wanted as well as fresh Juice, and make your own Toast in a large family Toaster, or help yourself to fresh Brown Bread. I stayed 3 nights there: the price was outstanding! For more information about this wonderful Hostelry Google: Bed and Breakfast, Lisdoonvarna, County Clare, Ireland. Look for the above BnB's listing on Booking.com.

The Ring of Kerry

Before I start to bring you back to Eyeries, let's go Northwest again, and back to County Donegal. I have a good friend from High School, Karen Segal, who told me recently that I needed to take 90 days off and go somewhere peaceful to recover from the continuing absence of Carmel. Karen, if you're reading this, taking 90 days off is highly unlikely. I just have too much left to do! Too much writing, too many highly stressed actions that I must take. So how's this as a peaceful alternative? Yesterday, I booked 3 nights at The Sanctuary of Saint Patrick in Lough Derg, County Donegal. It will be a LONG drive up - about 8 hours from the village (I tend to take my time. If I was in a rush it takes 6 hours and 30 minutes). It's such a long drive that I'll probably stop in Galway City and go exploring again. Or somewhere else along that route.

I've always wanted to go to the Pilgrimage of Saint Patrick's in Lough Derg. I'm staying from 31 May thru 2 June, 2024 and intend to pray a lot and try to get some rest too. The way it works is this (and you don't have to be a Holy Nut to do this). Over the three days, you take one day and stay up an entire 24 hours for the Vigil. During that time, those who want to will be offered the Eucharist, Reconciliation and the Way of the Cross. In your bare feet, you walk across the rocks and pray for all of your intentions and those of the people you love and know. There is also extensive Fasting: we'll all be allowed one meal per day of dry wheaten bread and toast, oatcakes and tea and coffee (no sugar or milk). During the three-day Pilgrimage, there is time for personal Reflection on Day 2 and Nine Station Prayers over the 3-day period.

I'm sure that this will be good for me. I need the exercise and I'm also trying to lose some weight, and I certainly need time for prayer and personal reflection on what I need to do with my life. My only real concern is that I may not be strong enough to stay up the entire 24 hours. I'm sure if I get truly sleepy due to my many medications that they'll let me get some sleep. If worse comes to worse, I can always leave and come back another time.

The cost of this 3 day say on an Island in Lough Derg is □80.00. This includes everything. Too, it helps to support the structures and Priests, and other people I'm sure, who live on the Island all year.

But back to the Ring of Kerry. Carm and I have visited the southern side of the Ring a number of times. The first Christmas that she was gone from our home due to Alzheimer's, on the spur of the moment I decided that I had to get out of the Village. I simply couldn't stand being alone anymore.

On Saint Stephens Day 2022, the Day of the Wren, I took off in my Beast of a Ford Ranger Pickup and made my way to Portmagee, County Kerry. I'd booked it for 3 nights two days before I left. The price was excellent for a room and breakfast every day of my stay. As I went past the places that Carm and I had visited, I became so sad again. But I brightened up as I approached this small town which sits on a wonderful harbour. Prior to checking in, I went to see the Lighthouse at Valentia. There I had a tour and it was absolutely super!

Walk up toward the walls that surround the lighthouse and stand next to huge, immense, yellow painted Sea Buoys which are used to mark a harbour's mouth, for navigation and to measure the height and directions of the sea when the storms come in toward Ireland. Entering through a door in the wall, I found that I was one of the only people visiting and had the entire Lighthouse almost to myself. I was able to climb up all the way to the top of that immense building and from there I could see the whitecaps on the Wild Atlantic Ocean. Too, I watched a Lighthouse Keeper come in and climb up to the Lantern where he switched the Light on and off a few times.

After that, I went down to the Lighthouse Museum where a few members of the Irish Coast Guard showed me around. They let me talk on an old Telephone, the type that you have to crank to get an operator. They also showed me the old bedroom and the sitting roof of a typical Lighthouse Keeper and his family. I was even given a small biscuit that they made there which illustrated what that family would have for an evening snack.

At the end of my tour I went to check in at the only hotel in Portmagee, the only one that was open that winter: The Moorings Guest House & Seafood Restaurant. (For information about this outstanding place, go to: https://www.moorings.ie/.) It was off-season and, as I remember, the price including breakfast was only ☐85 per night. What a great hotel! I had the room all to myself (not that I wanted that): two huge double beds, extra blankets and plenty of towels. In that the town's other restaurants were closed in the winter months, I ate downstairs at the fine restaurant and also had a drink at the bar. The food was stupendous (over the 3 days I must have sampled their entire menu), the staff amazingly helpful and they even had a smoking room where you could sit with those staff members who were having their break.

Portmagee is a large fishing town and also has Boat Tours to the Skellig Islands. Once again, I recommend this lovely Port to anyone who wants to visit the Wild West Coast of Ireland.

Home Again

Killarney and Kenmare are two of my favourite places around here. Killarney is a large city with Quick Access to the Killarney National Forest. You can take tours from the centre of the City (try the Train Station to find one that isn't engaged with other tourists) all the way to the Lakes of Killarney. The City has any number of Good Hotels (Carm and I have stayed in a few of them over the years. We both recommend Killarney Towers. A wonderful place, great food, two bars, a swimming pool and exercise room. Get more information here: https://www.killarneytowers.com/?utm_source=mybusiness&utm_medium=organic

Killarney also has any number of shops, restaurants, take-outs – pretty much anything a person could want from such a big city.

Now let's start home. Down the N22 toward Cork City and then a Right turn at the road that takes me toward Kenmare. I'll stop at a small forest where I always stopped when Carm's Dog Jack was with me. I still stop here when my little puppy Bluebell is in the back seat and needs to pee. Then I'll keep going down the R569 (a very wide and safe 2 lane road) and perhaps stop in Kilgarvan where I might fill up the Truck or have a light lunch. Then direct to Kenmare.

When Carm was with me we might stop there for the night. Kenmare, a great working town but also known here for its many tourists across the year, is another location that I highly recommend. Great shopping (try Quills Woolen Shop - I bought our home from Fergus Quill so a quick Call out to Him and his wonderful wife, Rose. Rose passed away recently and I sure wished I'd met you. What a wonderful couple, and Rose is sadly missed by her many, many friends and family) or any of the shops there. The restaurants are incredible and, for the most part, are great value. Try the Chinese Restaurants (there are two in the town), the Kenmare Brewhouse (I eat there all the time!), Davitt's (Carm and I have stayed in this Boutique Hotel and always went to the restaurant there), Tom Crean Base Camp (the original home of the famous Irish Antarctic Explorer), Poffs (I'm going to RAVE about this little restaurant for a moment. Carm and I usually ate breakfast there when she was with me. Now, I usually have breakfast there or a late lunch. But they do breakfast all day! The menu is wonderful! I'll often have Eggs Benedict or pancakes with real Maple Syrup, but they also serve salads and more standard lunch fare. A truly great and beautiful staff who are always helping visitors to Kenmare. Need I say more? Go if you can! They open fairly early but usually close at 5PM. See their Facebook Page for more info: https://www.facebook.com/poffsfood/).

So, after a brief light lunch in Poffs, we all climb in the car and head toward the Beara Peninsula. We'll climb some tall mountains (tall by Irish standards) then head down the far hill to Lauragh where I'll stop and have the first cigarette of the day. Then, out of

Lauragh past the Josie's restaurant sign (Carm and I always laughed about that sign in that Josie is Carm's mother) and into the small village of Ardgroom. If I'm with another driver who doesn't drink, I'll stop at the Village Inn for a Pint of Guiness. Then back in the car and onward to Eyeries which is now only 10 minutes away.

Down the hill again toward Ballycrovan and then a left at the sign for Eyeries. Up the hill and then a sharp right corner. Over some other hills and past the old schoolhouse that's being converted into a home. Down the hill again and then we can see the Mishkish Mountains come into view and, as I always say to Carmel when she's with me:

"Darlin', we're home!"

"And Tom, Thank God for it! I'm so tired and so glad to be home at last!"

(And I pray to God the same as I pray every day, someday soon you'll come back to our home and into my arms, just as you always do).

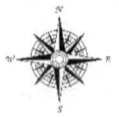

Chapter Nine:
What Do All Irish People Constantly Talk About?
Why, <u>The Weather</u>, of Course!

It's inevitable. Meet anyone, and I mean ANYONE AT ALL in most places in Ireland and, if they don't know you or have nothing else to talk about, we'll all start with some sort of comment about the weather.

It's no secret that for the past two years (at least!) the weather in Eyeries and this part of the world has been Miserable. And when I say Miserable, I mean it! We've had two of the worst years that I can ever remember since I started living here.

This year, and it's now the 14th of April, 2024 as I type this, we've had 4 straight months of nothing but rain, wind, gales, overcast skies, a few thunderstorms, some hail mixed with sleet and a little snow and very, very few dry days.

So another small warning for those of you visiting or moving here: learn to wear Layers of clothing.

Most people here, and I'm talking about most men, wear: a T-Shirt, thick socks, underwear of course (and sometimes, thermal underwear from the waist to the ankles), trousers (thick jeans or, if it's really cold, I bought a pair of black thermal hiking trousers that I use), a good thick Jumper (I own a number of them), some sort of thick jacket with a hood (or a Parka), perhaps a scarf and gloves and always, always a hat of some kind. On my feet, if it's truly miserable outside, I'll wear a good pair of hiking boots and some thick socks.

Layers of clothing? You know it. Many of the women here dress the same as the men. When the weather is really bad and it's pouring so bad you feel like a Duck, no one cares what they look like so long as they stay warm and dry. Yes, sometimes we'll all have to dress up to go to a wake, a funeral Mass, a wedding or a Christening, but even then we'll all wear a good, waterproof, warm overcoat of some kind.

So do yourself a favour. If you're coming to Ireland bring layers! Or, when you get here buy yourself a few things. Most of the clothing items above aren't that expensive and can be purchased in Kenmare as I described in the last chapter, in Killarney or in all larger towns and cities. Here, I usually go to Castletownbere where Carm and I have often bought all of the above (try Wiseman's at the top of the town for good Runners and Boots) or in the town go to the Indigo Boutique (owned by a good friend of ours. This boutique sells a variety of fashion items for women), Loop-de-Loop for jewellery and a whole range of health items), or try Hartnet's for a wide range of reasonably-priced men's, women's and children's clothing.

The History of Aran Jumpers

When I first moved to Ireland I didn't have many friends. Carmel had not moved down here full-time yet and I had to fend for myself. Soon, however, I met a number of men and families in Causkeys Bar and as the months past and I came to know them all better, we became very good friends. There was a group of us who would get together most weekends. Bill and Bernie were a great deal of fun. When Carm came down to visit, the four of us would take part in a Table Quiz held periodically in that Bar. Then there was Jim and Mary, a fine couple who lived down just past Kilcatherine Church and who eventually asked me up to visit them in the wonderful cottage that they'd fully restored. Jim was a retired boxer and he taught many young men how to box and let them use all of his weightlifting and boxing equipment in the shed that he'd converted into a workout room.

The couple I want to focus on right now, however, is Jamie and Carol Dixon. Jamie is originally from Canada and we grew close because I have Canadian ancestry. Sitting with him, Carol and Micheal (Jamie and Michael have both passed on), the two men would recount the many tales of how they fished in Coulagh Bay to make a living. They fished from a small fishing boat with nets and a couple of fishing poles and when the gales blew up, sometimes that tiny boat would swamp.

One day, Michael recounted how an unexpected storm had swept in from the West and swamped their fishing boat. Jamie fell overboard and Michael, being a very strong swimmer, rescued him and took him ashore. Jamie was okay, as it turned out, but was very cold and both men were soaking wet. As Jamie said to Michael, "My friend, you saved my life once or twice," in his soft Canadian voice. Michael would wink at both of us and nod. "Yep, I sure did. And isn't it a good thing too! Jamie, the next pint or three is on you, not me."

That single conversation made me realise how dangerous it was to be a fisherman back then, and how all types of men – and women too – went fishing to keep food on the table even when they all knew that unexpected gales might blow in.

As for Carol: at that time, they all lived in a really lovely old-fashioned 2-storey cottage and, over time and as they could afford it, added a number of extensions to it. (By the way, and for the record: today, Carm and my great friends, Fleur and Kevin, live there when they can take time off from work. Fleur is Jamie and Carol's daughter and Carm and I would have a fine time going over to see them and sharing a bottle of wine). To make ends meet, and assuming I remember what she and Jamie told me, Carol learned to make Aran Jumpers in her home and supplied many shops around here. The demand for those homemade Jumpers increased so much that she had to hire a number of women in the Village. She and her team of craftsmen developed their own brand and, using very strong thread, made some of the best Jumpers to be found in County Cork and most parts of the West of Ireland. At that time, during a period of high unemployment in our area, many local families depended on the salary that they received from Carol's business.

Too, a stranger could walk into the small shop and buy what had been made, if it wasn't already sold. Or, Carol would measure that person and take their order, and promise to have the new Jumper ready in a few days.

Oh, that I'd lived here only 30 or 40 years ago. I would have dropped in to see Carol and would have ordered at least 2 of her Aran Jumpers. And the price? Not much by today's standards, nor is anything!

Aran Jumpers have a long history here in Ireland. Born on the Aran Islands, and the starkly self-sufficient lives of the islanders who fished and raised a few sheep, women learned to knit as part of that Island Tradition.

When in 1934, U.S. Filmmaker Robert J Flaherty released 'The Man of Aran' (which I highly recommend), the documentary created a huge demand for Aran products in the United States and a small industry was born on that group of West Coast Irish Islands which supplemented the income of those courageous Islanders.

But what about the patterns that are knitted into those now-famous Jumpers? Do that have a meaning? The answer, of course, is YES! And courtesy of Blarney Woolen Mills (which has many, many wonderfully large shops dotted around this country and with an incredible selection of goods), here is a photo of an Aran Jumpers and some meanings of the various patterns and stitching:

Blackberry - Represents the thickets of blackberry bushes around the islands. A reminder of nature's riches.

Diamond - Frequently, matched with moss stitching. This represents the hope of future wealth.

Basket - Represents the angular squares of a fisherman's basket and the hope of bountiful baskets of fish to come.

Tree of Life - This depicts the tendrils of family and clans and past generations.

Moss - Represents the carrageen moss which lines the stone walls of the islands. Often knitted as a diamond 'filler!

Honeycomb - Represents hard work. A testament to the busy bees of the island.

Cable - Represents the fisherman's ropes and hopes for the day's catch

Zig Zag - A half a diamond. It represents the cliffs of the islands.

Trellis - Represents the fields of the Island.

(Go to their website for more information https://www.blarney.com/?gad_source=5&gclid=EAlaIQobChMI2ueYyMTGhQMV55FQBh0LmgA7EAAYAiAAEgLUp_D_BwE)

Carm and I have a number of these Jumpers. Some of them are rather expensive. These are usually the Handmade Woolen Jumpers. I tend to buy Manufactured Aran Jumpers. They're much less expensive and, for me and how much I work in them, are almost as good as the handmade ones.

Aran Jumpers are a great gift for friends and family. Sometimes, you'll find Specials for these Jumpers: a 30% reduction off the usual price or a 2 for 1 sale. Enjoy them! Depending on how tightly knit and what kind of wool the weavers use, they're almost waterproof and quite, quite warm!

A number of years ago I walked into Weavers, another great woollen store located in Glengarriff, County Cork. I bought SEVEN Aran Jumpers: one for each member of my family, which also includes Carmel. What a wonderful Christmas present and another great memory of my life living on the Beara Peninsula. And, boy did the sales clerk give me a deal! She threw in a pair of earrings, too!

To conclude with this small chapter about the Irish Weather and what to bring with you or buy here: do remember that this is a Moderate climate. We are fortunate to have the Gulf Stream a few miles off the west coast of the Beara Peninsula.

In the Winter, it can get somewhat cold here. Temperatures can range from just below freezing to a high of the mid-40's (in Fahrenheit). In the Spring and Autumn, temps can vary considerably. Most often, as it is right now outside, the temps can have an overnight reading of the low 40s and in daytime, in the sunshine, it can hit the high 60s. In the summertime, if you're very lucky, our temperatures can range from the high 60s at night to the very high 80s! That's when this tiny village can look somewhat like Greece! The sun sparkles from the still, light blue waters of Coulagh Bay. Seals bask in the sun. Seagulls, sparrows and swallows zip through the air. The Swallows have always been special to Carm and me. When the Swallows migrate back to our home in Eyeries Village all the way from Africa, the fly low across the garden looking for insects. We might hear the cry of a corncrake or see a pheasant or two in our back garden. We know that on mid-summer's day, the nights will start to get longer. And as the sun slips beneath the far mountains of the Ring of Kerry, just as it's doing now, maybe this is a good place to bring this chapter to an end.

Oh! And do remember that it rains all the time in Ireland, and I mean all if not most of the time. As an American tourist asked me many years ago, "Why does it rain so much in this part of the world?" I could only shrug my shoulders and reply:

"It rains all the time to make the fields green. That's why we have forty shades of green in Ireland. Would you like it, my American friend, if the fields of Ireland were brown?"

"No," she replied. "I'll take Ireland as it is."

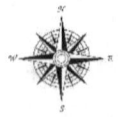

Chapter Ten:
Taking Ireland Just as It Is.
The Lesson I Learned Many Years Ago.
And If You Come Here,
You Should, Too.

The Title of this Last Chapter says it all: if you're going to visit, or live in, Ireland, to survive here all you have to do is learn to accept that this culture might be *very different* to what you're used to at home.

Back when I first came here, I couldn't get so many things that I considered 'basic'. Things like Peanut Butter or a working Telephone. Or a TV that didn't cost the price of a small used car. But things are different here. Not as different as when I moved here in 1982, but different nonetheless.

The words people use here, while they may be in English, often have different means or sound different. See the book of Irish words and phrases at the very end of this memoir. It took me years and years to understand what some of them meant. And, by God, I'm still learning.

Ireland is, to me, a wonderful place to live. And as for Eyeries: I'll never sell our house. And that's Never! I've come to love it here. Yes, I might buy another home near Trim, County Meath so I can be near to Carmel. She is, after all, one of the biggest reasons I've stayed in this country. But without her here at our home? I'm not sure anymore what to exactly do.

Today, on this 16th day of April 2024, we have our first camper of the Season, Cyril from France. It's so good to have a camper here tonight. I'm sure I'll enjoy his company and now, in mid-April, I can look forward to other Campers and Cabin Renters to visit me. It used to be that they'd come here to visit Carm and me but oh how life has changed. And it will keep changing, I'm sure.

This is a very short ending to a rather short first memoir and travel guide on *How an 'Auld Yank Learned to Survive in Southwest County Cork* but it won't be the last edition. Over the next year, I'll start taking more notes and meeting more people and, I'm sure, visiting other parts of this country - or other countries - that I've not been to before. The Philippines comes to mind, for instance. I'm hoping that Dolphin Song, the feature film, will start shooting this year or next. If so, then I must get me little arse over to those beautiful Islands to help with that shoot. And if that happens, why not visit other countries in the area? The entire South Sea will be right there at my doorstep.

When Carm and I were driving anywhere away from this small village, we'd always look out the windows and I'd turn to see her sitting to the left of me with a wide smile on her face.

"Carm, can you imagine? This stunning area: it's right at our doorstep."

Then she'd look at me and her smile would turn into a grin: "It surely is. Which is why we'll never, ever leave."

Things don't always work out as you want them to. That, I've found, is the hard truth. Carm isn't here to share the ride in our Pickup anymore. Nor is my friend, Jack the Dog my favourite Bejong. All that's left is me, my little puppy Bluebell and our old cat, Sasha.

And for now - just awhile - well, all of you who are reading this - I guess that's enough. Don't you?

If you'd care to join me to find out more about this area of Ireland, go to my website: www.storylinesent.com and click on the link to my blog.

Or, you can go directly to that brand new Blog by clicking on: https://ayanksurvivesireland.blogspot.com/

To all of you who want to survive Ireland as I have for well over 40 years, I can only wish you God's Speed. Maybe someday when you least expect it, this older Yank will come up to you in a bar somewhere near our home. I'll stick on my hand and welcome you here to this fairytale of a small Irish village.

And when you finally leave the pub, having consumed a few pints, I'll follow you out of that welcoming place, stick out my hand, and just as the Irish do say to you:

"Slán agus beannacht Dé!"

Which means in English: Ahaha! This time I'm not going to tell you. You'll have to meet an Irish person to translate!

Slán, everyone. And God Bless you!

And that, my friends, is my final hint.

The End

(Until the Next Edition of this Memoir and Travel Guide for those who want to Visit here, Work Here, or Come to Ireland to Live)

All my best to you, Good Reader, and Carm and I appreciate the fact that you've now read this)

(Why did we use the   Compass Rose, you might ask, at the top of Every Chapter? It's there to give us all a new direction in Life. While Carmel isn't here right now, I'm trying to learn which New Direction to go in? North toward Kenmare or Killarney? West out onto the Wild Atlantic Ocean in a brand-new sailboat, heading toward the far western Horizon? South perhaps to Africa? Or East to Europe, Paris and India? It's rather nice to have choices now. On some levels anyway. We so much you all have similar choices in your lives today. God Bless you again and keep you and your families safe. Rely on someone Larger than You to help you make your decision. After all, a Higher Power of some kind made the compass that helps us travel straight to our final destination).

Acknowledgements

This page or two is usually used to thank those who have contributed to this book. I've mentioned all of those people who are, or were, important to the writing of his Memoir and Travel Guide either on the Dedication Page or in the Text, above. However, let me name some of those people who have, and continue to, help me Survive in this stunning part of Southwest County Cork:

To Simon, my close friend and neighbour, who is always there for me and those that he loves and likes. To Carmel Murray, my partner, who stands at my side as I finish this book. To all of the employees of Storylines Entertainment Ltd including, but not limited to, Larry Power our Financial Director,Toqueer, Sami, Ahmed, Frank, Erica, Harsha, Divya, Rinka and her good husband, Zach, as well as Tony (the final 3 people are the Team directing and helping to Produce Dolphin Song, the Feature Film, which should be released sometime in 2025 or 2026 - it takes a very long time to create a Global Feature Film!; to my good friends in Eyeries including Frank, Liam Sullivan, Elvee who passes right by my home here most days to take care of her huge farmyard and garden right below my house; to all at Beara Oil who makes sure that they deliver oil when I need it to keep our home warm (thanks guys - as you know, I often forget to dip the oil tank and you go out of your way to deliver what I need right now!);

To Richard Dornan and his son Ritchie, as well as the rest of Richard's construction team. You're in the process of building a brand-new extension which we can use both as an office and a bedroom. Thank you so very much!)

And of course, to my family who made surviving this country for well over 40 years, not very hard: to my Ex, Bernie; to my children, Kristin, Cathy & Jonathan; and to my grandchildren and those grandchildren who are meant to be here: Sam, Dylan, Robyn, Val; Toby, Ally and Jack as well as to my in-laws who have also passed on to sunnier days: Luke & Kathleen and the all the rest of the extended Smyth family.

And to all of those that I've met along the way. Friends and foes alike. Those who have helped me to survive here and those who have ignored me when I needed you most. To all of you, particularly my next-door neighbour, Claire, her brother and her three grown dogs - thanks so much for being there when I've needed you. I won't ever forget.

And finally, to those who have passed on to another good life somewhere high above us:

To Patrick, James, Ritchie, Marie, Michael, Liam, my Dad and Mom, my many relatives, my good teacher Ron, David Stolzoff, Bob Smith, Alison Vesely, Mr Fred Schimmelman, Mr Robert Burda, and perhaps (and I sure hope not) Dr John Ficca.

Many of you helped me to learn to write or act or sing. Many of you were my good friends in High School or College. Most nights I do my best to remember you in my prayers and I know that you're all here somehow. Right here! Like my Novel and Screenplay, Dolphin Song, it's the basis of my everlasting faith. Miracles do occur, you know. Even in modern times. You're all with me when I need you the most, and I thank you for it! And do my level best to laugh when I need to and cry when I need to, and simply live a good and honest life.

Goodbye for now, everyone. Be well and enjoy life! As the Hebrews often say, L'chaim and To Life!

May all good things come to all of you, and may your prayers bring back my good woman, my wife, Carmel Murray and place her in my arms where she belongs.

Tom Richards and, if she were REALLY here beside me and at my elbow, nicely criticising my words, Carmel Murray.

Slan again!

A SURVIVOR'S GUIDE TO LIVING IN IRELAND BY TOM RICHARDS: AN IMPORTANT NOTE FROM THE AUTHOR: please remember that the following book was written in 2021. Therefore, MUCH OF IT, PARTICULARLY THE CHAPTERS ON HOME PRICES AND HOW TO GET AN IRISH VISA are now inaccurate. Things have greatly changed in these areas and other areas. USE THIS MEMOIR FOR REFERENCE ONLY. Much of this, however, gives you additional background on what it was like for a Crazy Yank to come to Ireland in 1982 during that huge recession when many other Irish people were escaping this country for job opportunities all over the world.

ENJOY this free Memoir! I so much enjoyed writing all of the editions as I did the above NEW Memoir and Travel Guide. Tom 17 April 2024.

A Survivor's Guide to Living in Ireland

Tom Richards

2021 Edition

Storylines Entertainment Ltd.

A Survivor's Guide to Living in Ireland

2021: the eleventh, and final, edition

Come for a week - stay for a lifetime! That's the lure of Ireland.

2021: A Forward for this Edition

The world keeps spinning 'round despite a pandemic and, as it revolves, a bit of light rises over a far horizon. In Ireland, as elsewhere, vaccines are making an appearance as the war on COVID continues. Ireland's government is implementing wholesale distribution of these life-savers across the country. In the meantime, our citizens hunker down, as they do across the globe. Unemployment has skyrocketed. Visiting our country is now almost impossible. Yet, hope brings thoughts of a future. The cruelty of the virus will be conquered. Life will return to something approaching normal. It may well be that our hopes and prayers won't be answered this year. But soon, this old world of ours, and those that live here, will again know a bit of peace.

Even now, as people across our planet wait for the virus to be vanquished, many are dusting down the dreams they have been forced to put on hold. Some are making the commitment to turn those dreams into reality when the world again spins toward a familiar orbit.

For months, particularly during the brouhaha of the US 2020 presidential election, I received many missives from those asking how they might move to Ireland or come here for a prolonged stay. If you're once again examining an aspiration to live or work here (or both), this book could be for you.

In 1982 this American, clutching a brand-new graduate degree from UCLA, took a four-week holiday to Ireland. I've been here ever since. This 2021 edition — the eleventh and final volume — speaks to the concerns expressed by many who long to move and work here: How do you learn to fit in to a culture not quite your own? What are the chances of getting a work permit and a job? How do you become an Irish citizen? What opportunities does this country offer to those who want to immigrate here?

In this small tome, I do my best to relate how I overcame the culture shock of living in the Auld Sod, learning to twist my middle-class American thinking into a more European point of view while managing to pay the bills at the same time. Along the way, I've learned some practical lessons:

From how to understand the Irish to how to drink a perfect pint; from finding a job to how to get a work permit; from purchasing your first dream home to learning to take soaking walks on a soft Irish day.

In this 2021 edition, I do my best to show you that to survive in Ireland, all you have to do is discover the magic of this wonderful country for yourself.

A Survivor's Guide to Living in Ireland has sold more than 25,000 copies. With it, you can learn to Talk like the Irish, Drink like the Irish, and Live like the Irish.

I like to think it is essential reading for anyone considering either a visit or move to this fabulous country.

A Survivor's Guide to Living in Ireland

ISBN 0-9550212-0-0

© Copyright Storylines Entertainment Ltd, 2005 - 2021. All rights reserved

The moral right of Tom Richards to be identified as the Author of this Work is asserted.

Conditions of Sale

All rights reserved. Except for brief passages quoted in newspaper, magazine, radio or television reviews, no part of

this book may be reproduced in any form or by any means, electronic or mechanical, including scanning,

photocopying or recording,

or by any information storage or retrieval system

without prior permission from the publisher.

Set in 9 pt Palatino, and 9, 10 & 14 pt Arial

First published in 2005 by

Storylines Entertainment Ltd.

This 11th edition published March 2021.

Many of the names in this book have been changed to protect the innocent and ensure that the author is not slugged in the nose.

Cover Design: Paul Tierney, Avalon Print & Design,

Dunshaughlin, County Meath, Ireland

Editing: Michael Scott

To contact the author email tomrichards@earthnet.ie

Dedication

To all who dream of living in Ireland

and to the fervent wish that your dreams will come true

as mine have;

To Mary and Bill Richards,

parents and friends: and Mom, on whatever cloud you now call home I know you're still singing.

To Kristin, Cathy & Jonathan, and my 5 grandkids, the surprising result of a summer's cycling trip;

To Bernadette,

Still my wild Irish Rose.

And to Liam O'Neill, filmmaker and best mate.

A Covid victim, he was taken much too early for any of us.

Rest easy, my dear friend.

Ireland 2021:
Thoughts of optimism

A *Survivor's Guide to Living in Ireland* has been part of my life since 2005 when I wrote the very first edition. In most years since then, I've done my best to update the text to reflect an ever-changing Republic. This year, as I sat down to write again, it dawned on me that I've said much of what needs to be said about this wonderful country and my experiences here - though in the next edition I'll write about what it's like to live on the Beara Peninsula, one of Ireland's remotest locations. But as with all of the past editions, this one too will deal with the fundamental questions so many have asked me:

What's it like to live in Ireland? Why did you immigrate in the first place? If I wanted to, what do I have to do to immigrate so I can live and work in Ireland, too?

I've always been surprised at how many people would like to live in Ireland. I shouldn't have been, of course. It's an absolutely delightful place to make a home.

Today, answering the above questions is, of course, more complex than it was twelve months ago. Since the updating of the 2020 edition, COVID 19 has ravaged the world. Ireland is no exception. As I write in early February, over two-thousand people are in Irish hospitals with this dreadful illness. Almost two-hundred are in ICU receiving life-giving treatment. To date, over 175,000 in Ireland have contracted the disease. The country has experienced

2,536 deaths since the first case of the virus was reported in February, 2020. I'm afraid that final statistic includes my best friend, Liam O'Neill, another Yank who immigrated here many, many years ago. He caught it, was put on ventilation for three weeks, and finally passed away in late May 2020. My heart breaks when I think of him and the wonderful family he was forced to leave behind.

As with many countries, we're fighting back hard but at great cost to our people and this economy. Ireland has been hit with a series of lockdowns. Today, the only establishments open are essential services. Unemployment has moved to twenty-five percent or more. Ireland is once again taking on a mountain of debt as its war against the virus continues: most of our newly unemployed are entitled to a PUP – the Pandemic Unemployment Payment. This ranges from between ⬜203 to ⬜350 per week per person. Many businesses are receiving financial aid from our government in hopes of staying above water until such time as they can again re-open.

The Irish government has imposed mandatory two-week quarantines on visitors arriving from Brazil and South America. Furthermore, anyone arriving into this country from any foreign destination are now required to have a negative result from a pre-departure COVID test taken within 72 hours of putting a foot on Irish soil. Even tighter travel restrictions will, I'm sure, soon follow.

Brexit has compounded this country's nightmare. On Christmas Eve 2020, the UK government finally negotiated a deal with the EU on its divorce terms. If you're confused about Brexit, that's completely understandable because the process has taken forever. While the UK voted to leave the EU in 2016, it officially left the trading bloc on 31 January 2020. Between then and 31 December of last year, trading rules were maintained as the parties engaged in often acrimonious negotiations about the terms of the British departure. For a few months, it looked like a so-called 'hard Brexit' could result. If that had occurred, Ireland would have suffered further woes because the border between the Republic and Northern Ireland would have once again become 'hard'. Those traveling between the two countries would have faced customs and passport control while business activity would have crumbled. Many thought that a re-imposition of such restrictions could again give rise to the brand of violence that haunted the island of Ireland for so many years.

Fortunately, a hard Brexit has not come to pass. However, the new trade and travel restrictions between Britain and the EU are already leading to higher costs of goods, while a plague of red tape has slowed distribution. Irish companies attempting to import or export goods to and from the UK are facing a tough time. As for Irish consumers: we've already noticed that some of our favourite British foods are not as readily available on our grocery shelves, while SKY cable television has axed transmission of some programming into Ireland because, it is reported, the business refused to purchase the EU licenses making such transmissions into European Union countries legal. In these early days of post-Brexit reality, we've only seen the tip of an iceberg loaded with trouble. There's bound to be more trouble ahead.

God alone knows that this country is due for some good luck because we've already had our share of the bad. If you'll remember, for a long number of years starting in 2008, Ireland suffered one of the most horrific economic meltdowns in its one-hundred-year history as a free Republic. During the years of the Great Recession, the citizenry of this country was hammered. Families lost their jobs. They lost their homes. They lost hope for both themselves and their children. Many emigrated across the world to salvage a future, repeating the stain of migration that has plagued this country for hundreds of years. They went to England, North America, Australia, and New Zealand to name but a few. The country was declared bankrupt for the simple reason that the Irish treasury could no longer finance day-to-day expenses. It had lost the capacity to borrow on world financial markets.

Fortunately, starting in 2012 or so, our economy came roaring back. Unemployment plummeted. Irish citizens who had escaped to far-off destinations came home. The economy was once again skyrocketing into the stratosphere. And then ...

Like every other country, we were hit with the pandemic. And like everywhere else, our ever-growing recovery was put on ice. That said, I view the future with optimism. COVID will one day be defeated. On that day, Ireland will resume economic growth. When that happens and assuming, as I do, that past trends continue, this country will need more people with more skills.

The IT industry was crying out for software and service engineers. It will again. Pharmaceutical companies, many of which are seeing growth even during the pandemic, will once more be looking for scientists and other staff. Doctors, nurses, and related medical practitioners have already been called from abroad to shore up a healthcare system in dire need of their talents as we battle against the coronavirus. That trend will continue as Ireland allocates even more money to the healthcare sector.

Upward pressure continues on the building industry. While most construction projects are on hold due to the virus, I suspect the industry will experience unrelenting expansion due to pent up demand when the country finally reopens. Ireland will be awash in construction sites as crews create new housing, factories, and needed infrastructure. So, if you swing a hammer or have construction in your blood, you could be in luck.

These are only some of the skill-sets that will again be in demand when we all return to something approaching normal. Mind you, I have a fond sense of confidence in the people of this country. For centuries, they have beaten impossible odds as they journeyed to create an Ireland hallmarked by growth and kindness.

This June marks the thirty-ninth year of my unplanned stay in this country. Somehow, I managed not only to survive but to discover a way of living I will never leave.

To all of you who consider living the Irish dream as I have, know I wish you well. Plan ahead, and if you're of a mind, make the leap over here as I have. This Yank managed to survive Ireland. Based on that experience, allow me to lean over to your side of the planet and whisper in your ear:

'Trust me. If I can do it, you can too.'

Tom Richards

Eyeries, Beara, Bantry
County Cork, Ireland

March 2021

P.S. I write an occasional Blog that answers even more questions. Feel free to visit: http://survivingireland.blogspot.com.

Map of Ireland

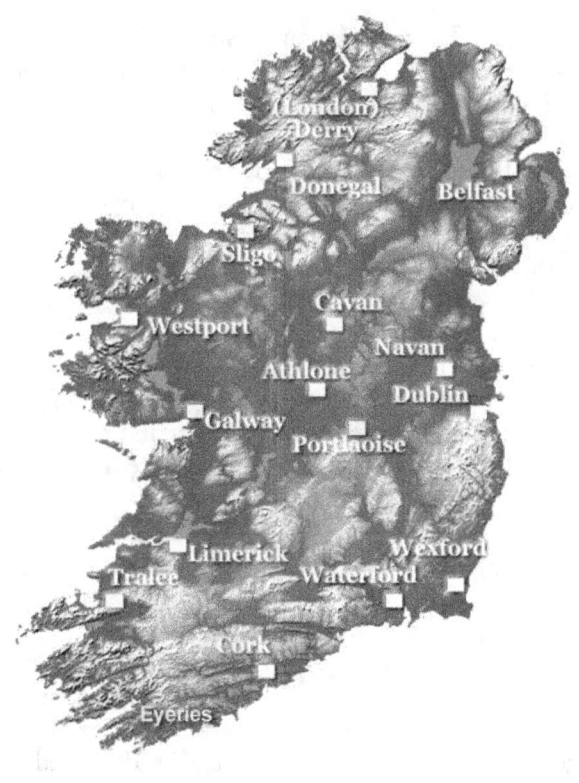

Preface: Notes from a Long-Gone Yank

If in a moment of uncertain insanity you have ever thought of abandoning the rat race by throwing an obnoxiously composed letter of resignation onto your boss's desk, then packing your spouse, children and dog into a forty-foot container and drifting across the sea to the green fields of Ireland for either a prolonged stay or the dream of actually living (and perhaps dying) in this far-flung location, then this book is for you.

A Survivor's Guide to Living in Ireland gives you the information to allow you to start the process of achieving that crazed dream. This book tells you how to: understand the often misunderstood Irish and the magical country within which they live; get a work permit; get a job; find a house; buy that house; understand the locals; fit in with the locals; educate your children; experience the wonder and mystery that is a pint of Guinness; and otherwise enjoy the exceptional experience of living in a country that is populated by a tapestry of people who are some of the most welcoming in the world.

This book is based on my personal experience of living well over thirty years in this country. Except for a very few creative and crazed liberties that I have taken, this is not a book of fiction: it is fact. It is not even a memoir but could possibly be described as one person's descent into insanity and the upward journey toward subsequent salvation. Whatever it is I hope that you'll find it useful.

While I have done my best to ensure that all figures and statistics mentioned in this small tome are accurate please don't take my word for it. Check things out for yourself. At the back, you'll find a series of references. Use them. Online resources and your local library is also a good place to start. I'll not have the fate of a would-be immigrant on my conscience particularly if you make the decision to move here based only on the ranting of this insane American expatriate.

I hope you enjoy these few words as much as I enjoyed writing them. And I hope that they give you some idea of the magic — and occasional disaster — that can befall you should you choose to stay in this delightful country.

Prologue

Chicago, Illinois   August 15, 1982

Dear Tom,

Have you completely lost your mind? Whatever possessed you to move to Ireland? You know what I taught you in history class. You will undoubtedly find the country and its people impossibly backward, impoverished and xenophobic.

Ireland is a tribal nation. As a complete outsider, you will undoubtedly be stabbed in the back at the first opportunity. I must say that I understand you even less than my son —and Robert has chosen to join the Peace Corps and has gone away to Peru of all places. I suspect that your parents are as equally disturbed with your decision as I am.

For Heaven's sake, grab that Irish wife of yours (another ill-made decision that I intend to discuss with you in the near future) and come back home immediately. You are wasting your life. Write back at once. You know how I worry.

Fondly,

Ronald

    The above letter was received by me almost forty years ago, now, penned by my old high school history teacher whom, as you can tell, was somewhat perturbed by a major decision that I had taken at the time.

The stream of events that Ronald alludes to can be summed up thusly:

In 1980 while on a bicycling holiday through Britain, I decided to make a left turn rather than a right at a particular crossroads in Wales. Had I turned right I would have cycled through the Welsh countryside, then turned north to Scotland, made a right back to London, and then caught the Freddie Laker flight home to San Francisco and to my waiting, if uncertain, fiancé. Inevitably, I would have followed the path of other young bucks my age: a career hellbent on achieving vast sums of disposable income, a house in some faceless American suburb, and a lifetime spent commuting on a mind-numbing freeway entombed in metal and plastic while listening to the *Eagles Greatest Hits* over and over again.

I don't think so.

Instead, I turned left, which in turn led me to a small ferry port in Wales, which subsequently led me on to Ireland. I crossed the Irish Sea despite impending seasickness and finally docked in the small Irish port of Dun Laoghrie, just south of Dublin City. From there, I cycled north to Dunleer in County Louth, and having been brought by fate to this lovely small village, met a beautiful woman whom I impetuously proposed to exactly three days later (she says five days, by the way) in a swimming pool surrounded by a group of innocent mentally handicapped Irish children. Though my parents, friends — and Ronald — thought that I should be immediately committed to the local asylum, and despite my wife's parents' feelings that this was some sort of fanciful summer romance soon to be forgotten, we were married the following December.

My Irish wife Bernadette, an absolutely stunning young blonde with beautiful flashing green Irish eyes, had not thought-through what it might mean to be married to someone from a country vastly different from her own. Nor had I, come to think of it. I saw myself as her victorious American knight, and determined to take her home to the United States and away from the seeming backwardness of 1980's Ireland. The thought of setting up home in her country had never even crossed my mind. After all, why would I, a newly minted college post-graduate with a bright future before me, *ever* think of living in Ireland, of all places? With my new bride at my side, we climbed onto an airplane bound for San Francisco and toward a life that could only come up roses.

As I said, at the time I had not thought things through. In that I was only twenty-six back in those impetuous days, however, I have long ago learned to forgive myself.

Eighteen months later my wife, having just given birth to our first daughter — and missing her Irish life to no small measure — decided that she was homesick and pleaded with me to take her home. As it happened, my bright future wasn't working out: I had just been given the sack by Avis Rent-A-Car. My uncaring boss telephoned me in the hospital minutes after Bernie had given birth to Kristin and informed me that my job wasn't really all that important after all and would I kindly leave at the earliest convenience, which happened to be the next day.

We were already behind on our mortgage, America was in recession, and the prospects of finding another job seemed more than a little remote. After thinking it through for exactly one day (I was a little precocious back then) I made a decision.

We sold everything, loaded a couple of bags and our then three-month-old daughter on board a draughty charter jet and left for Ireland. Had I thought about it, I possibly would have changed my mind. At that point in history, the Irish were emigrating in droves the other way. It seemed that I was the only American — or other foreigner — crazy enough to think that I could possibly survive in Ireland. But I didn't think about it, and one fine day found myself standing in Shannon Airport and quickly came to the realisation that perhaps I had indeed lost my mind.

I've been here ever since.

For almost forty years, since July 1982, I have called Ireland — sometimes reverently, sometimes reluctantly — my home. Every now and then I get a phone call, letter, or email from a friend or colleague who is hell-bent either on immigrating here or coming for a prolonged stay. Each one, barely concealing their envy, asks me, "What's it like to live there?" And each one is surprised when I lay things on the table, bare my soul and crassly destroy the myths they have of the place.

Ireland is not *The Quiet Man* let me tell you. At least not any more. When I tell them the reality of living here, I usually hear a static-filled pause as a lifetime of carefully constructed illusions are flushed down the toilet. It usually goes something like this:

Friend (in alarm): 'You mean that everyone has a car now?'

Me (trying to be patient): 'That's right. Sometimes two. Maybe even three.'

Friend: 'Three cars? But what about the donkey carts? The ones on all of the tourist brochures?'

Me (getting more frustrated): 'The carts were burned when they put in the new motorways, right after the government bought all of the farmland in a compulsory order, and for all I know the donkeys are now retired and living a life of luxury in Majorca.'

Friend: 'But that's horrible! Ireland is supposed to be so quaint!'

'Quaint'. Now there is a word that I have come to abhor. Years ago, I also believed that Ireland was quaint. But let me tell you something: Ireland has changed. Today, it is a sophisticated, growing, European country populated by some wonderful, if at times rather obstreperous, people. Yet so many of the world's citizens, especially the Irish, try to deny that fact.

But when I try to explain this new mind-set to my friends, they usually think that I'm either still insane or am living in some sort of isolated monastery and don't really have the right to an opinion on the matter.

Having been asked so many times what it's like to live here and how I survived almost thirty-nine years and more in Ireland, in 2005 I finally decided it was high time that I put down on paper what I know about this country and its people. My thinking then, as it is now in 2021, is, if nothing else, it saves me the bother of having to rewrite it every time I get a phone call from some long-lost friend asking me to tell them how to move here, how to get a job, what to bring, what not to bring, what to expect, where to go, and what to see when they get over here.

And, of course, I won't have to expand on what it's 'like' anymore nor grow hot around the collar when friends relate their 'quaint' views of this country. I'll start thusly, and remove immediately some of the most popular misconceptions of this country. To wit:

After half a lifetime of mishaps, mistakes, mad escapes, conversations both riveting and infinitely boring, hope-filled wanderings through potholes both large and small, contemplative walks through misty rains, wild dashes through thunderous downpours, and careful — sometimes drunken — philosophical observations of both this country and its citizenry, I start by imparting some riveting knowledge of what Ireland *isn't*.

Ireland *isn't* a part of the United Kingdom (suggest that to an Irishman and you'll find a balled-up fist under your gob), nor is it a country governed by a federal democracy such as the United States (it is ruled by a parliamentary democracy modelled on the United Kingdom). Ireland is no longer an agricultural society, although a significant portion of its exports are still agricultural-based. It is not a twee mystical world full of little people or faeries, pushbike riding businessmen, or horse-pulled trams.

Ireland is absolutely *not* a country devoid of trees, Coca-Cola, personal computers, hotdogs, pizza, coffee, fast freeways, international airports, digital telephones, hot water, indoor toilets, cell phones, big screen plasma televisions, central heating systems, dishwashers, exterior and interior house paint that comes in colours other than white, tile roofed houses rather than falling-down shanties wearing thatch caps, fancy cars owned by most of the populace, Tablet Computers, iPhones, out of wedlock childbirth, divorce, black people, brown people, Asians, Africans, Americans, Italians, French, Germans, Poles, Russians, Swiss, and other peoples of the world, decaffeinated tea and coffee, low fat milk, or any of a thousand things and peoples that my American friends, in their unfortunate ignorance, believe to be central to the character of this country. Mind you, when I first moved here in 1982 many of the material items mentioned above were decidedly absent.

No one says 'Top of the morning to you!' on a cold and blustery autumn morning. Thatch cottages, except for an occasional bed & breakfast or as part of a tourist trap, have made way for two-storied red-tiled suburban housing. And the people, though still some of the most welcoming in the world, have begun to develop the cynical attitudes present in America, England, and much of the rest of the West. If you think that Ireland is still a land of milk, honey, and the occasional leprechaun, you'll have a hard time surviving here.

So, what is Ireland, then, exactly? Well, that's a good question. It's what I'm always asked, come to think of it. And I've never been able to properly answer in a sentence or two. The Ireland of 2021 is much different from that of 1982. In the intervening years, I have watched as this country has attempted — sometimes successfully, sometimes not — to become part of the modern world.

Liken it to a tapestry still in construction: a wonderful fabric woven together with small 'quaint' villages clogged with modern traffic;

folklore and mystical tales cobbled to twenty-first century technology; miles of country lanes, many still sporting large potholes that can swallow entire cars; crazed drivers that don't yet understand how to navigate traffic congestion; stupendous sunsets that have not yet surrendered to Western pollution; maddening weather that everyone talks about despite everything because the weather is one subject which we all have in common; cruel taxation that the government says is getting easier to swallow — but none of us believe anything the government says; and with the country again in recession due to the virus, we all know damned well that it's going to get worse, and soon. Any negatives, of course, are offset by the best pint of stout this side of heaven.

Ireland is an anomaly. It is a quickly changing society that is trying to drag itself further into the new millennium with much gnashing of teeth in the process. If you are planning to venture out this way for whatever reason — on vacation, as part of a work assignment, or pursuing a personal dream of permanently settling here — you had best be prepared for the challenge. Maybe I can help.

I've survived in this country for almost forty years. And if I can do it, so can you.

Guideline One:
Don't Believe Anything You Have Read, It Probably Isn't True

Chicago, Illinois   May 1, 1980

My Dear Tom,

I am absolutely delighted to have received your letter. Your decision to take a short vacation to Ireland is absolutely correct, particularly after the rigors of graduate school. You will find the charm of its ancient people warm and invigorating, if somewhat pre-modern.

I am certain that you will love the country and its history. That said, avoid Northern Ireland at all costs in that you will undoubtedly be shot as a gunrunner.

As you know, Ireland has no trees. These were borne off by the English when constructing their great fleet in defence of the Spanish. Nor will you find indoor plumbing other than in the largest cities, telephones that work except in government buildings, or adequate heating systems except in the Ambassador's residence. Do make certain to bring along your woollies.

It has been over fifteen years since I last trod the broken roads of the Irish countryside during a sabbatical to that far-off land and I suspect that nothing has changed. Nor is it likely to, at least not in our lifetimes.

Fondly,
Ronald

I should perhaps explain that I have no Irish blood whatsoever running through my veins. My ancestry positively excludes Ireland but is instead littered with a hodgepodge of other immigrant nations who made their way to North America and the United States in hopes of finding a better life.

French Acadian, German, and English genes have undoubtedly managed to screw up my DNA makeup to no end. Rumour has it that we even have a little Native American kicking around in us somewhere. Along the line we picked up some Welsh and Scottish blood, which perhaps gives me some sort of predisposition toward the Celts. Maybe that was the genetic magnet that called me toward Ireland. But I don't think so. The warring factions in my genes, even without the benefit of Irish-ness, have in all likelihood made me crazy enough to consider just about anything.

The Richards' on my father's father's side, the Buote's on my father's mother's side, the Pethtel's on my mother's father's side, and the Scott's on my mother's mother's side, were solidly North American. Some first settled in Prince Edward Island way up in the Northeast corner of Canada and then, having been kicked out by the English, moved to wild outposts around Boston. Others purportedly came over on the Mayflower and took up residency, eventually fighting the British in the Revolutionary War, then each other in the Civil War.

My kin helped to settle the Ohio Valley, fought in World War I, World War II, Korea and Vietnam. Back then, these adventurous ancestors were honest-to-God pioneers and loved America to bits. They really enjoyed packing into some Godforsaken corner of the world and hacking out a little place in the wilderness they could call home. Growing up in the 1950's, '60's, and '70's as I did, much of the wilderness in America had already been overrun by fast food joints, strip malls and super highways. Though I never intended to be a pioneer, perhaps my genes insisted that I should locate a new wilderness in which to make my mark. A place to chop down a tree or boil the locals in oil, something like that.

So, God only knows what my ancestors would have thought of their great-great-great-great grandson who decided to turn his back on all their hard work and head east rather than west. I've probably made them all turn in their graves.

My point is that nothing prepared me for, nor gave me cause to consider, a lifetime of living in Ireland. Perhaps the genetic need to roam the world and conquer other lands is still buried somewhere deep inside me. I'm not sure. What I do know is that when I finally decided to come to this ancient land of saints and scholars, I was completely unprepared for the experience. I was naïve, uncertain, unaware, and believed everything that I had ever read or heard about this country which, to be frank, wasn't much.

Big mistake.

Most Americans — and may I say, peoples from many other nations even if they make a blood claim to Irish ancestry — seem to possess no sense of Irish history whatsoever. I admit a similar ignorance though perhaps I have some excuse in that having no Irish heritage I was totally unaware of things Irish. What I knew about Ireland was gleaned from watching John Ford's classic film *The Quiet Man* every St Patrick's Day — not quite the education one would seem to require if intending to blend in with the locals. I did attend Catholic school near Seattle, Washington, when I was eight, and Sister Raymond Francis taught us to sing 'When You're Irish, Come Into the Parlour', but that was about it.

Prior to coming here, I thought the entire country was full of peace-loving people who had spent the past three-thousand years growing turnips and potatoes, and who occasionally took out their frustrations at not having won the hand of the local beauty by beating each other senseless. Then I discovered that the potato didn't arrive in Ireland until the 16th Century, a piece of information that continues to baffle me.

Therefore, and assuming that many others desire to up-end their lives by moving to, or visiting, this part of the world, perhaps it is best to start with a short discussion of the history of this small island. Ireland, as it turns out, has a wonderfully colourful — if bloody - history that, if I had bothered doing a bit of research, should have given me some sort of warning of what to expect when moving here.

The world has known about this country since people first started writing things and creating maps. The Greeks were the first to mention Ireland in an obscure text by Festus Rufus Avienus, based on another text (plagiarising began early it seems) with its origins in the sixth century B.C. Ptolemy, the map-maker and geographer, even illustrated a pretty good likeness of the island in the form of a cubist-looking map dating from seventy A.D. or so. It is so bizarre looking that Picasso possibly used it for inspiration.

What with a map on how to get here, Irish tourism of the bloody kind began early.

Ireland has always been invaded by races both mythical and factual — Nemedians, Fir Bolg, Tuatha De Danann — but at some point or other the pre-historic Irish were conquered by the Celts and that's when all the trouble started. From that point on, it seems that every country with a bloodthirsty army to support it had designs on Ireland. They either wanted to trade with it or conquer it. Even back when people ran around in small boats and waved short swords at each other, everyone wanted a piece of the small little country shaped somewhat like a mystical Teddy bear.

The Romans didn't bother conquering the country — they considered it the End of the World and besides, they had enough trouble trying to keep the warring English tribes under their thumb. They did, however, do a little trading with Ireland, which managed to keep everyone happy.

As the Roman Empire started to fall apart, Roman rule in England went to hell and some of the Irish kings got together and decided that England — just over the other side of the Irish Sea — would be a perfect spot for a little rape, pillaging, and kidnapping. So that's exactly what they did. I doubt that the Irish raiders made many good friends in England, and when the tables were turned and the English invaded Ireland, I suspect that every John Bull decided that it was high time to get his own back.

One of the many people the Irish brought back in chains was the man who later went on to become Ireland's patron saint: the Welshman — of Roman extraction — known as Patricius, or Saint Patrick to you and me. Life in Ireland became even more stressful with the coming of this saintly man. In my opinion, Patrick (God bless him) did more to ruin Ireland than any throng of invading Viking hoards. He not only brought Christianity to Ireland but also paved the way for the establishment of the Catholic Church (not the Roman Catholic variety, however, in that this particular brand of Catholicism had not yet been invented). The Church was hot into property acquisition in those days and one of the first things they did was to divide up the country for themselves. The Irish Kings, thinking they were in danger of being damned for all time (and perhaps being condemned to a hell even worse than the miserable Ireland of the first century in which they lived) played along.

The result was that the Catholic aristocracy kept a tight grip on the entire populace of this country. The Irish have trembled in their boots, bowing before any cleric that looks strangely at them, right up to the last twenty years or so. I shouldn't, of course, be too unkind or snivelling regarding the Catholic invasion. The teachings of the Church and its priests and monks did, after all, help to preserve small things like the written word and basic education. If it hadn't been for them, all of Europe (and the rest of the world, perhaps) might have devolved into savages with the coming of the Dark Ages. It seems that the light of knowledge was kept aflame in this out-of-the-way corner of the world, making Ireland briefly The Land of Saints and Scholars. Eventually, the Irish priests let the word out and helped to fan this tiny spark of Irish custodianship into a first-class Renaissance.

That said, the Church also managed to inflict a great deal of damage on the Irish population including rape, fraud, collusion with the enemy, and a general feeling of insecurity and harsh feeling. You might not guess it, but many Irish are fundamentally guilt ridden and insecure. Over a thousand years of iron-fisted Church rule does that to a civilisation, doesn't it? I've often wondered what would have happened if Patrick had been executed at a stake by some ill-mannered pagan Irish King who thought Christianity to be nonsense. We could, of course, now be communicating by heathen drumbeats but I suspect that the Irish might be a little happier all the same.

Then the Vikings blew through in the seventh century and set up camp for a while. They built a few humble structures along the River Liffey in what is now Dublin, and have since provided occasional excitement in that every time the Dublin County Council digs a new channel for gasworks, they uncover a Viking wall or whorehouse, and the archaeologists run down with shovels and brushes in hand and for a while the locals become happily involved in a great deal of historically interesting work. The Vikings also promoted that wonderful economic activity called slavery, in addition to a little coinage and beer making, and for some time things must have been pretty lively in this country. Little did the Irish know that they too would soon face several hundred years of servitude.

In the middle of all of this, Irish kings kept running their own small feudal principalities with some little success. It seems they took out most of their frustration at being conquered all of the time by attacking each other, which makes perfect sense.

Maybe that's where Irish begrudgery got its start. If a relative, friend, or the King next door had grown above his station, the local neighbours started saying that he was a twit. Soon everyone recognised this fact, and so a fellow who might be completely innocent of anything could suddenly find that everyone in town hated his guts and would begin throwing verbal abuse. The other option, of course, was to attack him with a vast army and stab him with a short sword.

The fact that Ireland was next conquered by a mean-spirited group of English tyrants also has something to do with the country's general psychoses. In 1175, an Irish twit by the name of Dermot MacMurrogh, the King of Leinster, was kicked out of his kingdom. To get even he asked England's King Henry II for some help. Henry decided to recruit an army of Norman knights for a little adventure and the result was the establishment of an English beachhead in Ireland.

Thereafter, and for a few hundred years, it's back and forth as the Irish try to get the upper hand on the English and vice-versa. During that period, the English did what they could to drive home Anglo rule including the declaration that all of Ireland was a mere province of a new English empire. Needless to say, many Irish didn't like the idea and the short wars got only worse.

However, in 1649 an English fellow by the name of Cromwell decided that he'd had enough and decided to pay a little visit himself. He also brought along a vast armed force complete with sharp swords and a thirst for Irish blood. The Irish didn't stand a chance. The result was almost complete English domination for the next four hundred years or so.

The lot of the Irish was made even more difficult when, in the mid eighteen hundreds, a farmer suddenly realised that his entire potato crop looked more than a little constipated. He sent out a general alarm but it was too late. The potato blight had hit and what seemed to be every potato in Ireland was lost. The fact that the Irish depended on the lowly potato for most of their nutritional needs meant that Irish folks died in droves.

At the start of the blight, over eight million people called this wee island their home. A few years later, following starvation, death, and immigration, only three million souls remained. So, if when travelling through Ireland you see a ramshackle, deserted, falling down shanty, it could well be the ancient home of a family who died of the Hunger or chucked it all in for a new start in America or Australia. Chances are that they never survived the trip. When you see those old falling down walls, say a prayer. Those long-ago occupants might need it still.

England, their foreign masters, hardly did anything to help the fate of their Irish subjects. While it is true that some of the local landlords really did their best to help the Irish keep body and soul together, their rulers across the Irish Sea did little except to set up a few workhouses to call home. For the next seventy years or so, Ireland and its people suffered.

By 1916, the Irish had had enough. A group of seeming madmen, armed with little more than conviction and a love for liberty, decided that the English should be booted across the Irish Sea and back to England where they belonged. On Easter Monday of that year (24 April, 1916 to be exact), all hell broke loose. The heroes of Ireland — including Pearse, Connolly, and assorted brave hearts — occupied the General Post Office in Dublin, attempting to keep from getting killed while the English threw everything they had at them. These valiant Irishmen held out long enough to distribute their proclamation of freedom within the capital city, a proclamation that reads thusly:

Poblacht na hEireann

The Provisional Government of the Irish Republic

"To the People of Ireland ....."

Irishmen and Irishwomen! In the name of God and of the dead generations from which she receives the old tradition of nationhood, Ireland, through us, summons her children to her flag, and strikes for her freedom ... .

We declare the right of the people of Ireland to the ownership of Ireland, and to the unfettered control of Irish destinies, to be sovereign and indefeasible ... ... In every generation the Irish people have asserted their right to National freedom and sovereignty; six times during the past three hundred years they have asserted it in arms. Standing on that fundamental right and again asserting it in arms in the face of the world, we hereby proclaim the Irish Republic as a Sovereign Independent Sate, and we pledge our lives and the lives of our comrades to the cause of its freedom, of its welfare, and of its exaltation among the nations ... ...

The Republic guarantees civil and religious liberty, equal rights and equal opportunities to all its citizens, and declares its resolve to pursue the happiness and prosperity of the whole nation and of all its parts, cherishing all the children of the nation equally, and oblivious of the differences carefully fostered by an alien government, which have divided a minority from the majority in the past ... .

We place the cause of the Irish Republic under the protection of the Most High God, whose blessing we invoke upon our arms ... ... In this supreme hour the Irish nation must, by its valour and discipline, and by the readiness of its children, to sacrifice themselves for the common good, prove itself worthy of the august destiny to which it is called.

Signed on behalf of the Provisional Government

Thomas J Clarke

Sean MacDiarmada

Thomas MacDonagh

P H Pearse

Eamon Ceannt

James Connolly

Joseph Plunkett

      Unfortunately, these brave men were later captured and all shot by the British. But their sacrifice got the ball of independence rolling.

After a great deal of negotiation on both sides, things finally changed when in 1922 the Irish finally got their act together with the formation of a provisional independent Irish government. After a great deal of acrimony between the Irish and English, together with an Irish Civil War and the exclusion of Ulster from the newly formed Irish Republic (an entire quarter of the Island of Ireland as it turns out), everyone seemed to have calmed down for a time. That said, and even today, is it any wonder that a few English people may occasionally be reviled with the polite phrase 'You English bastard!' by some Irish fool? This makes it perfectly clear why some English visitors who are brave enough to walk into a local tavern drink their pints in such a nervous fashion.

The Irish, it seems, have long memories. Based on their unfortunate history you can't really blame them. It also goes a long way to explaining why some Irish men, fuelled to the gills with drink, prefer to end heated discussions with fists rather than a reasonable vocal response.

Fairly recently, however, things started to get better. A 'Peace Process' began in earnest in the mid-1990's. This finally resulted in a bone fide, long-lasting peace. Former enemies now shake hands. Gerry Adams, a past leader of the IRA, together with heroes such as recently deceased John Hume, successfully convinced his bloodthirsty brethren to dispense with the bullet, replacing it with democratic processes. Now retired, Mr. Adams, though still a citizen of Northern Ireland, was for years a duly elected member of Ireland's parliament, the Dáil, which illustrates just how much has changed. Now the English and the Irish, while they might still stare suspiciously at each other, will at least shake hands before starting to yell names and often get along tolerably well. In short, and despite hundreds of years of mutual hatred and violence, this country was fortunate to experience a miracle.

But despite this progress, many of my American and European friends have not yet heard of this astonishing outcome. When visiting the bright lights of New York or the busy streets of London I'm often asked if the Troubles are still as lively as they were heretofore. Without a doubt, the answer is a resounding 'No!' But even back in the '80's, when the Troubles were at their height, Ireland was safer than often depicted in the world's press. Living north of Dublin as I did in those times, and in the geographic corridor that has often been associated with the IRA and their doubtful campaign of hatemongering, I can assure you that my family and I were never in any danger. We were never accosted by any IRA hooligans. We never heard the bang of loud explosives (except once, many years ago, when the film *Omagh*, depicting the Real IRA's bombing of that Northern Ireland town, which resulted in so many deaths, was shot in Navan. On that occasion, what seemed to be the town's entire population trooped down to watch as the film's Special Effects people turned one of the main streets into a land of carnage). In fact, throughout the years of my stay here, we have been as safe as houses.

Yet the perception among some of the world's populace is that murder and mayhem continue to terrify and disrupt Ireland's citizenry, both North and South of the boarder. Don't believe them. Continuing peace is supported by almost everyone on this small island. If you are still in doubt about your safety here, you'll just have to take my word for it: you're safer on Belfast's city streets at midnight than you would be on certain Los Angeles thoroughfares at high noon.

The majority of the citizens of Ireland – Catholic, Protestant, Unionist and Nationalist – have taken a common stand. Except for a handful of thugs from all sides that refuse to accept change, most people here of all persuasions agree that the time for killing is at an end. After hundreds of years of religious and politically motivated bloodshed, the Irish have reached a lasting peace. For that, all parties involved should be truly proud.

Living here has allowed me to immerse myself in the history and culture of this people. But before I moved here permanently, I hadn't bothered to learn much, if anything, about Irish history. In fact, I didn't know too much about the place at all except what I had gleaned from the afore-mentioned *Quiet Man* film, numerous travel brochures, and the rebel lyrics of songs sung by the Clancy Brothers.

In any event, and despite my ancestral predisposition to conquer new lands, and even if I had gone to the bother of reading a complete unadulterated history of the country, I was doomed to learn how to survive in Ireland the hard way.

Guideline Two:
The Economy — a Chink of Light

San Francisco, CA

July 10, 1980

Dear Tommy,

Where are you? We have not heard from you since you sent your last postcard from what I am certain is some miserable little village in the back-lands of Ireland. Don't you know not to trust foreigners? Please don't believe anything you are told. I'm certain they are telling you a pack of lies.

Please, please get in touch with us! I've talked to your father and if you phone collect, he promises not to hang up. I am sending this to your last return address which I gather is some sort of monastery? Are you really considering a career as a monk? Oh God forbid!

Your sister, your father, and your <u>girlfriend</u> wonder where you are, as do I. I miss and love you. Get in touch!

Your Loving Mom

When Mom wrote (and yes, I did get her letter. It seems the Postmen here know everybody and had no trouble tracking down a naïve Yank staying for a time in the only monastery in County

Louth), I had no particular wish to make a home in Ireland. Nor did I have any particular desire to work in this country. In 1980 Ireland why would I? The nation's economy was faltering. In only two years' time it would fall off yet another precipice☐which is exactly when I decided to move here.

In 1982, the year of my return for what would turn out to be a permanent stay in this country, I seemed to be the only idiot travelling east from the United States in hopes of employment. Those living in Ireland were emigrating west in search of a future because the Irish economy was in tatters. However, if you're reading this book it is possible that, like me, you may desire to work and live in this wonderful country. But before I talk of how to get a job here it would seem I am obligated to provide a stark warning:

Once again, Ireland's economy is in tatters. Downward pressure is due not only to the coronavirus but other factors. As I describe elsewhere in this book, Ireland has a wide-open economy. This is wonderful when the good times roll. In 2012, as the world economy recovered from the Great Recession, Ireland's economic fortunes skyrocketed yet again into the stratosphere. The downside of this turn-on-a-dime characteristic is: when the global economy crashes, Ireland's economic fortunes can be driven onto the rocks. Which brings me, in a rather round-about sort of way, to the fallout of the virus, Brexit and the legacies of the Trump administration's policies.

As with most places in the world, COVID 19 has turned Ireland into an economic wasteland and no one is quite sure when the situation will turn around. Most businesses are closed as we again face Level 5 restrictions. Gone are visits to the hairdressers and singsongs in our pubs. Restaurants are closed and deserted. All shops except for those deemed essential (like pharmacies and hardware stores) are shut tight. Hotels, Bed & Breakfasts, and camping sites are shuttered. All schools including colleges and universities are closed. Students and their teachers are having to make due with online teaching. Irish citizens are restricted from traveling more than 5 kilometres from their primary place of residence, except for essential travel to their jobs, a medical appointment, or similar.

Until quite recently, many of these guidelines had little chance of enforcement by the Gardaí because they had no legislative teeth. However, as virus cases and deaths climbed due in great part to the flouting of the rules by a minority, the government came down hard. Today, if you're caught ignoring Level 5 restrictions, you could be fined ☐500 and face a spell in a local prison.

As already noted, new restrictions for those traveling into and out of Ireland are also being enforced as our government attempts to quash the possibility of new virus variants entering the country.

The result of all these necessary measures has been economic chaos. So many of us are out of work. Many sectors of the economy are not functioning right now. The government is once again being forced to take on massive debt to keep the lights on during this crisis. The only bright spot is that certain areas of the Irish economy are performing above expectations. Pharmaceutical and medicinal exports are hitting all-time highs. While tax receipts in to Ireland's public coffers has been hit hard, it has not contracted at the scale many had forecast.

Unfortunately, the challenges we all face from COVID 19 have been exacerbated by the reality of Brexit. Unless you've been living in a cave located somewhere in mid-Saharan Africa, you'll have heard that in June 2016 the people of the United Kingdom voted to leave the European Union. For Ireland this is a very big deal because 35 percent of the total volume of Irish exports is purchased by the UK. In March 2017, the British Parliament invoked Article 50 of the Treaty on European Union which is the legal mechanism by which the UK actioned leaving the EU. Theresa May's government toughened its stance as the Prime Minister tried to negotiate a way forward. Her efforts failed with continuing rejection of possible solutions by Parliament.

This was, as we all know, followed by the often-fraught election of Boris Johnson. Boris promised his Brexiteers that he would do anything and everything possible to again establish the United Kingdom as a country independent of EU law. Tough new negotiations followed in Brussels. On Christmas Eve, 2020, Boris and company got what they wished for: a final divorce.

Unfortunately for many, it seems no one planned on the consequences. While it is still early days yet, the repercussions of Brexit are seeing massive logistical problems across the UK and EU due to new rules that have been adopted as part of the divorce deal. Distributors, hauliers, and truck drivers from all countries involved are now facing a tangle of new red tape. It's been reported that drivers have to sit for hours, and often days, in Larne, Dover, Belfast, Dublin, and many other ports waiting for customs clearance.

Distribution across Europe and the UK was already experiencing difficulties due to the virus. But the added confusion of Brexit is a problem we could all do without. Northern Ireland in particular is caught in a vice. A majority of its population voted to remain in the European Union. Yet, because they are part of the United Kingdom, the country was also forced to leave the EU. The situation for Northern Ireland is exacerbated due to its unique situation: they are the only UK country having a land border with an EU nation, the Republic of Ireland. Ireland and Northern Ireland depend on each other for trade. While Brexit has not resulted in a so-called hard border between these two countries, we're all taking a deep breath, worried about what might be coming.

What is clear is that Brexit has created new difficulties for Irish businesses and citizens dealing with the United Kingdom. While Brexit negotiations avoided the imposition of damaging tariffs, importers and exporters are being hit with new costs as they navigate revised trading rules. Brexit, as well as the virus, has also resulted in volatile currency fluctuations that are hitting Irish exporters' bottom lines hard. Some Irish businesses who depend on exporting to the United Kingdom are worried it will no longer be economically viable to trade with them.

Irish consumers are also being hit with a few unwanted surprises. Many people here order online from companies based in the United Kingdom (think amazon.com.uk). Prior to Brexit, it was a seamless exercise because the UK was part of the EU and subject to the same trading laws. However, today the UK trades outside of the European Union. For that reason, when people here order from a UK company, and though often not mentioned online when they make their purchases, they are hit with additional costs. When the postman or delivery company drops off the purchased goods to the consumer, they won't release those goods until additional VAT and delivery charges are paid. I've heard reports that those costs can be as much as a third of the price of the original purchase.

Of course, it could have been worse. During the months of Brexit negotiations, many of us were concerned that Irish citizens living in the UK, or UK citizens living in Ireland, would no longer have that right, or would be hit with insurmountable new regulations. Fortunately, that has been avoided.

It must also be said that Ireland's economy has somewhat benefited from Brexit. For instance, some banks and other financial institutions, desperate to keep a foot in the EU, have closed their London headquarters, a few moving to the Dublin Financial Services Centre. This has increased the demand for Irish financial services talent, which is a boon to the local jobs market.

Unfortunately, that positive note would appear to be the exception rather than the rule. While the jury is still out regarding the full impact of Brexit implementation, we worry tourism could be hurt because the British, who are one of Ireland's largest single bloc of visitors, are stuck with a devalued Pound Sterling. Their Pound simply won't buy as many nights in hotel rooms or B&Bs, pints of Guinness, and wool jumpers as it did before. Consequently, and until we see a turnaround in currency exchange rates, British tourists may choose to stay away from this delightful country when travel restrictions due to the virus are finally lifted. We all hope that day is soon.

Irish exporters of foodstuffs may also find the going even tougher. In 2015, the UK was the main export destination for Ireland's food and drink industry, that year accounting for 41 percent of all Irish exports. Because these companies trade in euro and the UK buys in Sterling, trading conditions due to volatile exchange rates will continue to make things difficult. To survive, companies are facing two stark choices: either lose market share and trade less with the UK (and hopefully find other export markets for their wares), or cut profit margins to shore up sales. So, even after COVID passes, and due to Brexit, the Irish economy could be in for more of a hammering.

And then, on top of everything, we still face the Donald Trump legacy. First, a fact: well over 85 percent of the populace in Ireland had no time for the man. Most of us breathed a huge sigh of relief on 20 January 2021 when Joe Biden moved into the Oval Office. Joe is a firm friend of Ireland's. More on the new president, below.

But back to Trump. Five years ago, who would have thought this man would be the next president of the United States? Certainly not this writer. Nor did many on this side of the Pond believe Trump would win.

My opinions regarding Mr. Trump do no matter in this book. However, the impact his presidency has had upon the Irish economy does. It is only weeks since the now ex-President left office, and perhaps now is a good time to see how his policies affected Ireland.

One of Trump's most important promises was to bring jobs back to the United States. One of his methods was the promise to decrease taxation on corporate profits, while motivating U.S. businesses to move those profits back to the States, rather than investing hard-earned moneys elsewhere. The December 2017 passage of new tax legislation tried to do just that. The new U.S. corporate tax rate of 21 percent encourages American companies based in Ireland (and throughout the world) such as Apple, Google, IBM, Microsoft and many more to re-gentrify profits from overseas back to the United States. Literally trillions of U.S. dollars will wend their way back to America. While this is great news for the United States and its people, it will leave far less cash to invest in those companies' Irish operations. Recent reports suggest that this flow of repatriated cash back to the States has, in fact, occurred. It is still too early to see what effect this will have on continuing inward investment to Ireland.

Too, U.S. companies who have located abroad have done so at least in part to find tax havens that protect profits. Ireland, with its low 12.5 percent corporate tax rate, is one of these. This low rate has always been a central policy that allows Ireland to attract inward investment from multinational firms. Consequently, with the passage of the new U.S. lower corporate tax rate, Ireland still might be in trouble. This country has long relied on inward investment by foreign companies as a large source of good paying jobs. Today, almost 200,000 people work in Ireland for companies such as these. Trump's policies therefore still pose an enormous threat.

Trump has also renegotiated various multi-lateral trade deals. The president has adopted a protectionist stance regarding global economic relations. His policies have resulted in stiff new tariffs on products imported to the United States from many other countries. Ireland is one of those targets. With additional tariffs, Irish products — everything from whiskey to wool jumpers — are now more expensive to U.S. consumers. Like Brexit, Trump's policies leave Irish exporters with few options: either they cut profit margins to shore up sales and take into account higher prices due to new tariffs, or they maintain current pricing and lose sales.

Ireland is today sandwiched between two economic powerhouses whose policies have the potential to decimate the Irish economy. Should exports and tourism continue to stumble hard, and even after the battle against COVID 19 has been won, a period of job losses could replace the hard-charging job creation that has characterised Ireland's economy until recently. If that happens, a dismal period for Ireland could follow, as it has countless times in the past: exports will fall as unemployment rises, and the Irish government's tax take will descend like an out-of-control elevator. Less taxes mean less to spend on day-to-day expenditures such as capital projects, nurses' and teachers' salaries, new hospitals, public housing, and similar. And with fewer jobs to go around, those wishing to immigrate to Ireland will find it even harder to do so.

However, we're seeing a chink of light in the darkness. First, and as mentioned above, the new conditions we face with Brexit could have been much worse. Britain could well have left in a so-called 'hard Brexit', meaning we would have again seen a true border between Northern Ireland and the Republic. This would have had all sorts of negative ramifications including, perhaps, decimated trade between the two countries as well as a resumption of sectarian violence. Fortunately, the hard Brexit scenario has not materialised.

Then, there's Joe Biden. For those who don't know, Joe is a friend of Ireland. He can trace his ancestry back to Counties Mayo and Louth. He's visited this country a number of times and has made a promise to visit again during his presidency, COVID allowing. In only a few weeks since taking office, he has signed Executive Orders to overturn a number of the former president's policies. However, while Joe is a firm friend of Ireland, he must keep America central to his policies. While I believe he will soften, or repeal, the current trade tariffs that negatively impact Irish businesses, I do not see him loosening measures that incentivise American companies from re-gentrifying profits from Ireland back to the United States. That said, I believe that President Biden will work to encourage global trade, where Trump did not. Should that come to pass, the world will benefit, including Ireland's economy and its job market.

Finally, humanity's war on COVID will end in victory. No one knows exactly when or how long it will take. But eventually, and we all hope sooner rather than later, the world — and Ireland — will return to something approaching normal. When that happens, this economy is again scheduled for a rousing lift-off. Tourism will skyrocket, resulting in a need for more employees in the hospitality sector. Housing starts will leap, and the industry will cry out for new skilled employees. The healthcare and educational sectors will seek more staff. Local manufacturers will again gear up to meet the demand of booming local and global economies. The underlying economics of this country will swing back to growth due to consumer demand which has lain dormant in a time of crisis.

As I write in February 2021, moving to Ireland simply is not possible. But if you've long hankered to live in this country, now is the time to plan. Start your research. Identify how your skills might match the demand for labour in a new, growing Ireland. Figure out where you might want to live. Bone up on what you need to do to get a job and immigrate to this country. Some of these areas are covered in chapters, below.

Ireland has been forced into a long sleep as the virus has wreaked havoc on our population. But when this challenge finally passes — when we beat it and the threat recedes — Ireland will again re-awake with a tiger's roar.

Guideline Three: and a Visa,  *How to Get a Job and Also Survive*

Chicago, Illinois

November 16, 1982

Dear Tom,

I was stung by your most recent letter of the 1st of the month stating that you have decided to stay in that foreign country. I find it impossible to believe that you are bull-headed enough to continue living there while still being out of work! Undoubtedly, you will find it next to impossible to obtain gainful employment in that land of poverty. When are you going to come to your senses and realize that your future is much more important than your dreams of destitution?

Please write back at once. If you need airfare for the trip home, I am more than willing to help in that I am certain your parents are no longer talking to you.

Ronald

(**Note**: for a short-hand list of rules regarding who is eligible to live and work in Ireland see the bottom of this chapter.)

When I breezed back into Ireland in 1982, this time with my wife and child in hand, I thought getting a job would be easy. Why wouldn't it? I was qualified, wasn't I? I had experience. After all, I had an MBA from UCLA hadn't I? My enthusiasm was matched only by my ignorance.

In 1982, Ireland was embroiled in one of the worst economic recessions in its history (only the recent 2008 economic debacle and, of course, the current Covid horror, have been worse). At that time the Irish government had decided to spend well beyond its means (why is it that governments never learn?), attempting to drag itself into the twentieth century by funding massive construction (much of it borrowed from a number of International Financial Institutions) that it could little afford. To pay-off the borrowings it raised taxes. This had the effect of creating inflation, higher interest rates, and a skyrocketing unemployment rate that quickly approached twenty percent of the working population. While new roads were being built, the economy of the nation was being ground into wholemeal. Interest rates reached fifteen percent and more. Ireland of the early 1980s was on its knees.

Despite this, and with his eyes wide shut, this young American confidently stepped into the breach of immigration not knowing what was about to hit him. For the next three months, and without a job or the prospect of same, I carefully studied the local want ads, sending out enthusiastic missives, expectantly waiting for those cheerful responses that would inevitably lead to an interview and subsequent employment.

My wait was in vain. For you see, most Irish companies didn't answer letters from those seeking employment. And as of the writing of this final edition in February 2021, they still don't. I've never understood the reason why. Perhaps it's because the Human Resource people were busy drinking down in the local pub or were trying to pick the next winner at the Cheltenham Races. Or perhaps they had all been fired. What I am now certain of, however, is that all of my letters ended up in the bin next to remnants of cold coffee and cigarette ends.

Consequently, I took to the streets. I plodded the main office blocks, knocking on doors in a futile attempt to ingratiate myself with the local business intelligencia. Unfortunately, I never made it past the reception desk. Most of the sweet young receptionists that

I met took one look at me, nodded agreeably at my Yankee verbal waffle, and told me that the boss was unavailable. Though I left numerous resumes along my journey no one — not one — responded.

Next, I tried the telephone but with the same results. No one wanted to talk to me. In fact, rather than an interview, they suggested that I post in my details but I already knew that my well-crafted letters would head toward the first available bin and sure oblivion.

Then one night in the local pub, with my meagre financial resources running out and my emotional mindset contemplating suicide, I sat literally crying into my drink and mentioned my plight to a local. And that's how I discovered the secret of getting a job in Ireland.

Networking.

We all know the importance of networking when it comes to getting a job. We've long been taught that who we know is much more important than what we know. But nowhere is this simple premise more important than in Ireland. While it was true in 1982, networking is even more important today.

For you see, Ireland is a village. The twenty-six counties within the Republic of Ireland contain just shy of 5 million souls, or so says the most recent government census. Add to that another 1.8 million living in the six counties of Northern Ireland and you can see that all of Ireland could be housed easily enough within the greater Los Angeles area.

But the small population alone does not in and of itself give credence to networking. Other factors are at work here, one of the most important being the art of conversation. The Irish love to talk and they'll talk about almost anything: the state of Irish politics, the weather (a constant source of verbal acrobatics), their neighbours and relatives, the colour of their living room wallpaper, the antics that they got up to on their most recent holiday abroad...the list goes on and on.

This propensity to chat is reinforced by an incredible supply of information sources, a list that I suspect would be envied by some of my fellow Americans living in their reinforced continent. The Irish, a highly intelligent lot, are voracious consumers of news and, considering the size of their population, they have a whole lot to choose from. The Republic alone supports three national daily newspapers, not to mention assorted Sunday papers, as well as countless tabloids and English broadsheets. Many communities are still lucky enough to have a local newspaper. And of course, also add countless Internet sites to the list of written news sources.

This deluge of written words is supplemented by cable television. The Irish also enjoy the thousands of television channels available to many American and European citizens and today have access to any number of news channels including the national stations (RTE, RTE Two, Virgin One and Two, and TG4 - the Irish speaking channel), English stations (BBC, ITV, Channel Four, Sky), a number of American channels (CNN, CNBC, Bloomberg), a wide range of other international news carriers (including but not limited to Al Jazeera, Euro News, CCTV - the Chinese news channel, French channels, and many others), as well as a couple of Arabic television stations.

This stunning range of news coverage is supplemented by a number of 'foreign' language cable television stations (broadcast in languages other than English). So, if a viewer happens to be competent in Spanish, French or German, and has nothing else to do, he or she could be quite content to spend an entire week catching up on those events that make the world go round. The result is that the Irish can obtain any number of competing viewpoints that provide fuel to the fires of communication.

This characteristic — this gift of the gab — means that a verbal account of almost anything can be spread like wildfire, should it be properly kindled and fanned. This gift has been handed down from generation to generation, and most probably emanates from the *Seaneachi* (the ancient Irish for Storyteller) from long ago.

Properly utilised, this propensity to talk about almost anything can be used to land a job.

Too, the Irish truly enjoy lending a helping hand and are some of the most giving people in the world. Has a neighbour's house burned down? Locals will quickly come to their aid with a spirited fundraiser. Is a friend in desperate emotional trouble due to a separation, unemployment, or worse? The Irish will lend a helping hand and have also set up any number of organisations, such as The Samaritans, to assist those going through hard times. Is there a famine in Bangladesh? The Irish will not only send out much needed money, food, and materials but a stalwart few will actually venture there to give hands-on help and experience. In other words, if you're facing disaster, the first reaction by many here is to lend a helping hand. And most greet a cry for assistance as an opportunity rather than a waste of precious time or resource.

In my case, and with time running out, my drinking partner suggested that I talk to one of his relatives. He, in turn, chatted to a neighbour regarding the poor unfortunate who was so constrained by lack of money that his child was being forced to eat yesterday's boiled potatoes.

The neighbour talked to a distant friend who owned an electrical components supplier and who was fortunate enough to be occasionally hired by an industrial weighing systems company. The components supplier, in turn, talked to the managing director of the weighing company (who was a good friend of his) and a week later I was hired as a salesman responsible for travelling the width and breadth of Ireland to twist the arms off local farmers into purchasing expensive cattle weighing systems.

Networking in Ireland can pay off and it continues to do so even with the advent (and subsequent demise) of the so-called Celtic Tiger. Today and even in the grip of COVID, Ireland continues to be a magnet for billions of dollars in inward investment. Any number of renowned IT companies including Microsoft, Intel, IBM, EMC, PayPal, Google, Facebook, and Yahoo, as well as assorted pharmaceutical companies such as Pfizer and many, many others, have now established operations in this country. Ireland is a strategic location used to access the rest of the world's markets, as a location for a variety of tax incentives, and as a resource renowned for its highly educated workforce.

During the period of exponential economic growth (approximately 1996 through 2001), getting a job was as easy as downing a pint of Guinness and many of the methods that citizens of other nations are familiar with often yielded quick results. Employment agencies and executive search firms came into their own. Companies would return calls. Internet employment search sites began to blossom. Everyone was having a grand old time.

Then in 2008, and with the bursting of the global economic bubble, Ireland began to suffer along with every other world economy. Having grown at a double-digit pace since the mid-1990's, then maturing into a pattern of single-figure growth through 2007, the Irish economy (and job market) suffered through one of its worst periods of decline in living memory. Ireland's official unemployment rate rose to almost 14 percent, but many believed it to be much higher – approaching 20 percent. While large international companies continued to invest, Ireland was locked in a period of economic malaise. The result was one of the toughest job markets in the past 25 years. To illustrate the point: about 1 in every 1,000 people emigrated from Ireland in 2011. That's 4,000 people. But anecdotal evidence suggests that this figure rose even further.

However, due to stringent, even harsh, measures, the economy turned around. Unemployment fell to just over 4 percent. Then, of course, the virus marched in to town. As already mentioned, unemployment in early 2021 has blown the roof off of everyone's expectations. However, we all believe this will end and, when it does, employment figures should recover. So, while would-be immigrants to Ireland are blocked from doing so for the duration of the virus emergency, it's a good time to lay the groundwork.

The Right to Work

If you are intending to immigrate to Ireland in the near-ish future, the bottom line is still hard to swallow: getting a job here as an immigrant is tough. Not impossible but very, very difficult.

Are you an EU citizen or a national from Norway, Iceland, Liechtenstein or Switzerland? Then immigrating to Ireland is easy because you have the right to work here. But if you are not a European Union citizen, finding a job is a much harder proposition. Too, if you're from outside the EU and want to live in Ireland, emerging patterns of immigration have had a substantial impact on the Irish job scene. In recent years, the European Union (of which Ireland is a part) grew by another ten countries. Total EU membership now stands at twenty-seven nations, when we include the United Kingdom's departure. Citizens of the European Union have the right to work anywhere within the EU, including Ireland. And many of them — particularly from Eastern European countries such as Poland, Hungary and Slovenia, as well as citizens of non-EU nations including Russia, Nigeria, and other African countries —voted with their feet and during the height of the Celtic Tiger economy, moved to Ireland in record numbers. All of them hoped to grab a little part of the Irish economic miracle for themselves. And many did. And even during the most recent recession, many chose to stay here. When the economy again recovers in 2021 / 2022, I anticipate that more EU citizens will move here.

The Irish government, concerned about the possible political fall-out from uncontrolled immigration, started to turn the screws not too long ago. For years, Ireland was a country of net emigration to the four corners of the world. Then, during the Celtic Tiger years, it became a country that acted as an economic magnet for the world's population, including the disenfranchised, and became a country of net immigrant inflows. And all of these people wanted a job. The Irish, having never dreamed that their country would attract so much interest from would-be job seekers, started to scream in protest. A minority actually believed that these people were going to rob this little corner of the world of opportunity, and believed that wholesale immigration must be restrained, and preferably stopped altogether. In response, the government took the stance of making it as difficult as possible for non-EU immigrants to gain entry to the country.

However, and not even counting the situation due to COVID, job prospects now have grown even more challenging for non-EU nationals. As mentioned above, during the Great Recession, the Irish once again migrated abroad to find work as Ireland grappled with economic recession. That changed as things bounced back. Now, once again, the Irish are returning to their homeland. Which means that if you're born in the United States, Canada, and anywhere outside the EU (including Britain, I might add), you'll have more competition to land a job and stay here. So that's the bad news. And it means that if you hope to move and work here, you should think about it with your eyes wide open.

But if you are still considering a move to Ireland, remember this: I came here in 1982, at the height of that horrific Recession. When I moved here, and as mentioned, almost 20 percent of the work force was unemployed. And yet – I survived. And you can, too. It just means that you're going to have to work a bit smarter and try a little harder to make things happen for you. Too, you must also keep the facts to hand.

First, and unless you are an EU national, or are married to an Irish or European Union citizen, your chances of getting a job and remaining in the country are limited. If you are married to an Irish or European national, you are automatically entitled to apply for the right to work here. You are then entitled to apply for your Irish citizenship after a few years of residency.

Of interest to many: you are also automatically entitled to Irish citizenship if one of your parents is Irish, or if your grandparents were Irish and registered the birth of your parent with the Irish government. In such cases you are automatically entitled not only to live and work here but also to obtain a European Union passport.

If you are American and choose to take up Irish citizenship if you are eligible you will not, fortunately, have to turn your back on the United States. The State Department has changed its rules and now you are more than welcome to carry both passports as a dual national

If, however, and like many, you do not have a recent Irish ancestor at your disposal or cannot find a potential Irish bride or groom that turns your head enough to take that long walk down the church aisle, your journey will be more difficult though by no means impossible.

But, if you're not automatically entitled to Irish citizenship, here's what you can do:

To get a job here you will require a work permit. The rules in this area are rather convoluted but the key point is this: you can only get a work permit by selling yourself to an employer who can't find anyone else in the country with particular skill-sets.

So, acquiring a permit now becomes a two-stage process: first, you have to find an employer with a job whose skills are in short supply. Second, you must convince that employer that you are worthy enough to have him or her go through the hassle of getting you that work permit, a permit that costs that employer hundreds of euro a year and which must be paid if he or she is to legally employ you.

But getting that work permit is becoming more and more difficult. Due to fairly recent immigration and employment laws, the government will *not* quickly give work permits for jobs in a variety of categories because those areas are already well served by an existing work force. Those areas of work include clerical and most administrative positions, many construction jobs (although this is subject to change depending on the market) and many others. People landing jobs with salaries of □60,000 or more per annum are almost guaranteed to get a work permit. For those landing positions with annual salaries of between □30,000 - □60,000, the odds decrease. For those gaining employment with salaries under that, getting a work permit is almost impossible. For more information on obtaining work permits go to:

http://www.citizensinformation.ie/en/moving_country/moving_to_ireland/working_in_ireland/coming_to_work_in_ireland.html.

Skills in Demand: But I have good news too. As of this writing, Ireland is facing a severe skills shortage in a number of vital areas. The government has created the Highly Skilled Eligible Occupations List which features areas of employment opportunity. Right now, Ireland urgently requires: Chemical scientists, mechanical engineers, electrical engineers including chip designers; ICT professionals including information technology and telecommunications specialists, project engineers, business analysts, programmers and web designers; health care professionals including doctors, nurses, radiographers, vascular technologists, social services managers, and laboratory assistants; business professionals including accountants, taxation experts, Big Data analytics specialists, sales and marketing professionals specialising in international sales; and people with multi-lingual skills.

This is just a short-list of the skilled professionals Irish employers are currently looking for. For the complete list and more information go to:

https://enterprise.gov.ie/en/What-We-Do/Workplace-and-Skills/Employment-Permits/Employment-Permit-Eligibility/Highly-Skilled-Eligible-Occupations-List/

Note: for some reason, the URL above changes all the time. If you hit a '401 Not Found', Google 'Highly Skilled Eligible Occupations List.

Of course, just because you have a skill that's mentioned on the list doesn't mean that you'll automatically get a job. Nor does it mean that you have an automatic right to get a work permit. But it does mean that an opportunity exists and that your dream of coming to Ireland could be that much closer.

Students: Another way of getting around the work permit problem is to become a full-time student. If you are studying in Ireland on an approved course, you can legally take up casual employment and work a maximum of 20 hours per week (full-time during holiday periods). No work permit required.

Even with a work permit, you'll have to 'register' every few months with the local police. When coming here in '82, and even though I was married to an Irish national, I had to go through this same process until I was eventually 'officially' registered. And even after that —and for the next fifteen years until I bothered to apply for my Irish citizenship — I had that wonderful pleasure of walking down to the local police station (known in the Irish as the Garda Siochana, and a great group of guys and gals they are too) to register with the Force and let them know that I hadn't yet knocked off the local bank or mugged a little old lady for the contents of her handbag.

As a newly arrived immigrant where do you start to look for a job and that elusive work permit? You could, of course, start by running through the newspapers, walking the streets, or standing on top of a building and begging all and sundry for a job like I did. But I don't think that you'll find those methods very effective.

As already mentioned, the best way of getting a job in Ireland is through networking, of course. Even if you're new here and recently off the boat or aircraft, I can safely advise you that networking in Ireland is easy to do. Visit the local pub (when they finally open up after lockdown). Strike up a conversation. Tell people —beg people — to give you a hand...that you're a poor newly arrived immigrant who loves the country with a passion, who longs to live here. And that you could really use some advice and some contacts.

Scan online for job fairs. If you're in the country make sure you attend, gather some business cards, and keep in touch with your new contacts. Or reach out to executive recruiters. Just Google Ireland job fairs and Ireland jobs for a huge number of relevant links. But make those contacts and start pestering them.

Then keep at it. Follow leads. Use the phone. In fact, if you come over before being offered a job, make sure to buy a local mobile phone. Like the world over, everyone uses them and though the Irish pay higher cell phone rates than almost anyone in Europe it's still a great resource and allows prospective employers to easily get in touch with you. Then enhance your resume (called a Curriculum Vitae or CV over here) illustrating not only your past experience but how your skills can fit into niche areas that are in demand.

Emphasise energy and commitment. It's no secret that Ireland sells itself on its young, vibrant, well-educated workforce. If you, like me, are past your mid-thirties (and I'm well past it at this point), you'll find it tougher to get a job. But be persistent. Understand that in many ways Ireland is still finding itself. It is still developing its skill-sets. You, as a person from another country, possibly possess skills not available here. If you're American or from a larger European nation then you possibly have experience working in huge, sophisticated markets. To survive in those economies, companies and their personnel must develop capabilities to flourish despite stiff competition. If you have such experience and skills —and if you spend some time to see how you can apply that experience to this market — you can make a difference over here particularly if you can provide businesses with export assistance and advice (the Irish economy is a net exporter which has historically resulted in an astoundingly positive national balance of payments). Communicate your skills base correctly and you can prove that you have much to offer. Too, skills with larger companies could be appreciated by many of the country's 'inward investment' corporations such as Microsoft, PayPal, and so forth. Many of those companies are also looking for a wide range of foreign language skills to support their Irish-based European sales and customer support activities. So, if you speak Spanish, French, German, or other foreign languages, you'll have an edge.

And don't forget to use Internet social networking strategies. Join LinkedIn. Join Facebook. Use them to connect with Irish-based companies and their people. Dig deep into relevant Irish websites and blogs. Then start tunnelling to ferret out the employment opportunities that exist here.

Having found that employment opportunity, bug the hell out of the employer to get that work permit. As mentioned, it will cost your future employer not only time but also money to employ you, so (nicely) beleaguer the poor person with stories of your experience, intelligence, and willingness to work.

And finally, if all else fails, consider establishing a business here (see below for possible opportunities). Potential immigrants who set up their own businesses and who create jobs — and subsequent taxes — for the Irish economy are entitled to apply for their own work permit and have little difficulty in obtaining one. Though Ireland is small, it can be a land of opportunity. Small and medium-sized businesses, as with the United States, England, Australia, and throughout the EU, have been the engine that has driven economic growth in this country over the course of many years. If you have an idea, go for it. Having become your own boss in what is now a land of entrepreneurs, you'll never again have to go looking for permission to work or stay here.

And then, of course, you pay tax.

Having landed a job, you will — naturally enough — look forward to your first paycheque. If you're working for a company, you will quickly discover the absolute horrors that many of us go through when payday finally rolls around. In short, prepare yourself to be staggered by the amount of tax that you're going to pay to the government for the simple pleasure of working for a living.

Some time ago, *Money Magazine* conducted a survey of taxation levels within all EU countries. Their 'tax pain barometer' noted that, despite contrary opinion, Irish citizens do not carry the highest level of taxation burden in Europe. That dubious honour went to the citizens of France. But taxation in Ireland is mighty high, let me tell you, and in recent years has gone even higher.

The Irish government does its best to tax almost everything in sight. Employees pay three types of taxes: PAYE (Pay As You Earn, which is somewhat like the U.S. government's IRS Income Tax), PRSI (Pay Related Social Insurance, akin to U.S. Social Security), and USC (Universal Social Charge), a makey-uppy thing that the government brought in recently to rob more from us.

For most employees, PAYE starts out at twenty percent, jumping almost instantly to forty percent. PRSI is an additional four percent or so. Add another two to eleven percent in USC, depending on your income level. Then do your sums and the top-top rate for high income earners is: 56 percent.

By the way, your employer also has to pay an extra 11 percent or so in PRSI on top of employee contributions.

However, the government has also added a variety of indirect taxation — our so-called 'stealth' taxes. You see, during the 'good years' of the Celtic Tiger, the government managed to spend every euro it earned. It hired more public employees. It expanded services. It created more bureaucracy, and employed many more bureaucrats to run it. Total Irish government annual budgets increased from about 20 billion euro per annum in 2000 to over 60 billion euro per annum in 2008 (or so says an article in The Times Sunday newspaper). Unfortunately, the government was financing this spend from 'fair-weather' sources of revenue including taxes on home building, new car sales, and similar. Consequently, when the economy crashed here in 2008, so too did consumer sales (including the aforementioned housing and car sales), and government revenues spectacularly declined. The result? The Irish government continued to spend above its total annual tax take, and the IMF — our financial godfathers — didn't like it very much. Consequently, Irish citizens saw new taxes hit them, which still eats hard into disposable income,

For instance, a few years ago the government passed new property taxes. Until then, we didn't pay property taxes because we paid so many other taxes. But now every homeowner in the country must pay the tax based on a personally assessed valuation. This year I will pay □314 for the privilege of living in my home. Doesn't sound like much, I know. But you wait — what are the odds that a few years from now that small amount will have grown by a factor of 3, 4, or five? Our government has always liked taxes.

The government also introduced the Pension Levy. Now this one really gets up my nose. On the one hand: the government wants all of us to save for retirement because they don't want us to depend on the Exchequer when we reach old age. On the other hand: this tax levies any personal private pension fund .75 percent on its entire balance. So, in fact, it's a small disincentive to keep plonking your cash into a pension fund. The levy was supposed to have been withdrawn in 2016. It hasn't. Imagine that?

While we're all going to have to pay, and keep paying, for past government over-spending and general ineptitude, the Irish do get something for their high taxes.

For the dubious pleasure of paying high levels of taxation, workers receive modest unemployment assistance should times get tough plus a childcare allowance (based on the number of children that you have in your family) each month even when working. (Note: watch this space. The childcare allowance, which can add up to a few hundred euro a month depending on the number of children that a family has, and which helps many to keep the wolf from the door, has been under attack for some time. Many are fearful that this universal hand-out will be withdrawn altogether, which will put many families below the poverty line. The misery of COVID has brought a halt to any discussion about ending this payment. But wait for it — when the good times come again, so too will this particular war.)

When we all reach 66, we also receive a miserly government pension. It's very different to Social Security in the U.S. There, retired folks receive monthly payments based on the contributions they've put in over the years. Here, it's a flat payment meaning that no matter what we put in, we all get the same. When I hit 66, in only ten months' time, I will receive ☐248.30 per week. Which isn't so bad. But — and get this — retired people also receive a bus pass that allows us to travel on any public transport for free. Older people love this last perk: it's an inexpensive method of traveling the country on the government's dime.

But getting back to taxes: the government also rips off Irish consumers with any number of other 'stealth' taxes. We have a sales tax here with the inept title of 'Value Added Tax' or VAT. How it adds value is beyond me. Almost everything that a person purchases in this country automatically attracts a tax of twenty-one percent. So if you buy a can of Coke for one euro, the government will receive twenty-one percent of the purchase price.

VAT is applied to almost anything that you can imagine: shoes, men's suit coats, Christmas decorations, toilet paper, babies' nappies, bottled water, alcohol...you get the idea. To my knowledge the only items that are exempt from VAT are certain food items, postage (we already pay high enough postage rates anyway) and, thanks be to God, books.

But the government's take doesn't end there. If you buy a television, as a for instance, not only do you pay VAT on the purchase price but you are also obliged to purchase a wonderful little document called a Television Licence.

What, you might ask, is a Television Licence? This wonderful piece of paper, required by all of us who possess a television (or a radio, computer, or anything else that streams entertainment), is a great example of the type of creativity the government employs to rip off the Irish taxpayer. While it is called a licence, it is actually a tax on those invisible signals that fly through the misty skies all by themselves, and if you own a TV and don't buy a Television Licence you can be prosecuted and handed a stiff fine of ☐1,000. And, just to make things a little more serious, you can also end up in jail (no joke! Many already have.)

You are legally obligated to buy such a licence each and every year if you have a television (or any other instrument that uses an external signal to gulp entertainment) at your place of residence or at the job, and whether it is in working order or not. Technically, you are also obliged to buy a licence for each and every television and television receiver that you own. But most Irish draw the line at purchasing more than one hellaciously expensive licence and do their best to avoid paying for more.

As of this writing the licence fee is ☐160 per year, but don't worry, it's bound to go up.

What makes this fee even more galling is the fact that much of the funds collected in this manner go directly to that wonderful local publicly funded television station, Radio Telefis Eireann (RTE). With these moneys RTE is supposed to finance the production of well-crafted and entertaining programming. Unfortunately, and for years, RTE has been the butt of constant jokes. Until recently, RTE was renowned throughout the country for producing some of the worst television drama in Europe. Such mind-numbing programmes as *Fair City* (a soap in which both scripts and actors seem to have a perpetual case of rigor-mortis) and the delightful game show *Winning Streak* (an absolutely inane programme premised on the stunning idea that people behave credibly if they see an opportunity to win money) causes one to wonder why the production company receives anything at all in that any six-year-old could surely come up with more interesting premises.

However, more recent efforts have resulted in TV drama that is by far more compelling. A hospital drama – The Clinic – has received good reviews for its well-crafted storytelling. Another RTE hit, Love / Hate, a gritty crime drama, has rocketed in popularity due to the talented acting of its cast, the tense construction of its stories, and the engaging world within which it has been set. And to be fair, RTE does produce good (though sometimes biased) news programming, some great documentaries, and the occasional batch of wildly entertaining sports coverage.

The TV Licence is enough to drive a person to drink and rather makes you wonder about the effectiveness of publicly-funded organisations, doesn't it?

But if you suspect that the TV Licence surely must be the end of my list of nutty taxation, it isn't and not by a long shot. If you choose to move to Ireland take note that the Irish government has found an infinite number of other ways of removing the hard-earned money from your wallet.

Take cars, for instance. Not only do we pay twenty one percent VAT on automobile purchases but we also pay another tax (called VRT or Vehicle Registration Tax) that the government created simply to generate additional revenue. Now, Irish citizens pay more than almost anyone else in Europe for the benefits of an automobile. If we could do it, we'd all use mass transit. However, getting from A to B can be virtually impossible due to historic under-funding of both railways and the public bus service.

Or how about gasoline? Called petrol over here, Irish car owners are crucified every time we pull into the petrol station for a fill of juice. The Irish pay much well over twice what the folks in the United States pay for a gallon of gasoline. Why such a difference? You guessed it — taxes.

Combined with extortionate automobile insurance premiums (taxed yet again by the government), in addition to a yearly Car Motor Tax (think renewing your vehicle tags. In Florida, a private car costs $32.50 per annum. Here, our annual fee can cost anywhere from a couple of hundred euro to over one thousand euro per annum depending on the type of car you purchase), driving an auto in Ireland is exorbitantly expensive.

You could, of course, purchase a bike or take the train or bus if you want to travel from Dublin, say, to Cork. Or you could possibly purchase that donkey and cart but most of us put up with the expense of a car for the simple reason that we need the damned things.

How about cigarettes and alcohol? Do you drink or smoke? Then be prepared to pay for it. We have some of the highest taxes in the EU on these items. Currently we pay 14 euro per packet of cigarettes, which means that if you smoke you might consider breaking the habit when coming to Ireland. Mind you, the government has banned smoking from almost all public places, so quitting in Ireland is now easier than you might think.

Or what about the price of drink? Ireland, after all, is supposed to be a nation of drinkers and you'd think that the price of a pint would be kept within reasonable reach. Unfortunately, that's just not so. The price of a pint of the best has soared in recent years: a Pint of Plain (the local euphemism for a pint of Guinness) can now exceed four euro for the pleasure, and in some Dublin establishments can cost more than six euro. That said, alcohol prices have actually remained fairly stable recently in that drinkers were already raising hell at the high cost, and while drinking here is much less expensive than in Finland or Switzerland, a night out at the pub can still significantly dent your budget.

Or take house purchase taxes. When purchasing a house (assuming that you can afford to undertake that expense, anymore) Irish nationals (and anyone else for that matter) must pay the government a Stamp Duty. Unless you're a first-time buyer (in which case you're exempt from this scurrilous tax) this ruinous fee runs from 1 percent on homes less than ☐1 million, and 2 percent on those homes above that million mark and must be paid at the time of closing. I have to admit that it's much less than it used to be. The government lowered the Stamp Duty charge in an attempt to lubricate the housing market. But budgeting for the purchase of an Irish house? Then you still have to add a few thousand euro to your closing cost line items. Closing costs in Ireland are insane when compared to other countries. For instance: a friend of mine recently purchased a house in Florida. Closing costs, which including a few hundred bucks in government taxes, came in at approximately two thousand U.S. dollars. Now compare that to Ireland: another friend of mine bought a house here two years ago. It was a nice-ish house, and he bought it for about two-hundred and forty thousand euro at depressed prices (about $317,000 at current exchange rates, and fortunately for him, near the bottom of the market). His closing costs, including stamp duties and solicitor's fees, came in at over four thousand euro.

How about Credit Cards? The government has enacted a tax on these of thirty euro per annum per credit card for the pleasure of saying 'Charge it!' This is yet another example of how the Irish bureaucracy magically materialises more cash for the public coffers.

Do you have the resources to save money? Well, any interest you earn is subject to a 41 percent Deposit Interest Retention Tax (DIRT, and the government acronym is certainly appropriate), which goes straight into government coffers. Do you have a pension plan? The government recently enacted a levy of .6 percent on the market value of assets held by anyone with a private pension plan. In short, they are taxing today what people hope to retire on tomorrow.

Of course, we wouldn't mind the high taxes if we were getting value for money from the government. The citizens of many European countries pay high taxes but they receive plenty for it: great medical care, unparalleled unemployment assistance when things go wrong, exceptional public transport...the list goes on and on.

In Ireland, however, and though we pay through the nose, we also wonder what we're receiving in return. Irish taxpayers are a cynical lot, and having for years read about government waste and ineptitude in the newspapers, we really wonder if all of our hard-earned tax moneys are simply being flushed down some far-off government toilet. Until recently there was some good news: Irish taxation levels had actually fallen as the government started to pay down its substantial debt to international banking institutions, thereby decreasing its significant public borrowings. However, with the ending of the Celtic Tiger, the situation has reversed: the government borrowed billions from the Troika to finance even day-to-day expenditure. To that, we can now add the substantial borrowings needed to fight COVID. This, of course, will put pressure on the Irish government to raise taxes yet again. Speculation is running rife in the news media about not *if* the government will raise taxes, but by *how much*. Ouch, is all I can say.

There is a bit of good-ish news, however. Prices in Ireland, as mentioned above, are coming down (taxes excluded), just like almost everywhere. In fact, today's consumer price index lies in negative territory. Everything from a trip to McDonald's to a dress in an upmarket retailer such as Brown Thomas seems to be attracting a Special Offer price tag in order to encourage consumer spending. So...we're all doing what we can to look on the bright side.

I would, however, be remiss if I did not provide the following warning: Ireland can be expensive. If you land a job — even a good job — life can be something of a struggle. You may not be able to save as much as you're used to saving. Consequently, you must spend more time budgeting and planning personal finances and will need to take a closer look at such important future inevitabilities as the cost of your offspring's college fees and your own imminent retirement, and you must plan accordingly.

But having moved to Ireland, you can always forget about it all by taking a walk in the Irish countryside and breathing that clean Irish air. It's the one thing that the government has yet to figure out how to tax. And please God they never do.

Mind you, I'm sure they're working on it.

Still confused on how to move to, and work, in Ireland? Then may I present:

A Short-hand Guide to the Right to Work and Live in Ireland

(The following article appeared in a 2016 Post for http://survivingireland.blogspot.com. It's still current and I thought you'd find it useful.)

The backlash from Trump's recent win was anticipated. Yet I'm astounded at the tidal wave of queries I've received about working and living in Ireland from American's who are more than a little perturbed by the election's outcome.

Due to simple demand, I've put together a list of rules and websites that should answer a couple of often-asked questions: As an American, can I get a job in Ireland and live there? If so, how do I go about that process?

Before moving to these answers, I would encourage any would-be immigrant to pause for a moment, take a deep breath, and reflect on what such a move might entail. Having lived in this country for 34 years now, I will be the first to tell you that an immigrant's life is hard work. Though the Irish speak English, don't think for a minute that the culture will be the same as what you experience in Peoria Illinois, Walnut Creek California, or Boston Massachusetts. This is a fascinating country of contradictions: a wonderful people who can still be deeply misunderstood by outsiders simply because you're not Irish and have not grown up here. Depending on where you live, you might feel the place insular and foreign. Loneliness due to separation from friends and family is common. Making a living here can be difficult even with a good job because taxes are high and the cost of living even higher.

But I make no bones about it: despite the difficulties I'm happy with my life here. With that out of the way, let's move on to the rules for getting a job and residency in this fine country. As I've alluded, over the past two days I have seen a spike on this Blog of Americans wishing to move to – and work in – Ireland. For that reason I found it prudent to post this guide. However, first a warning: this is only a guide. Make sure you do your own research for accuracy because employment and residency legislation can change instantly. A good place to start for general information is: http://www.citizensinformation.ie/en/moving_country/moving_to_ireland/working_in_ireland/coming_to_work_in_ireland.html

The Rules

In general, visitors to Ireland are allowed to stay in this country for 90 days. During that time they are not allowed to work. To live and work here for a longer period, there are a number of rules and requirements:

- For non-EU citizens: Ireland is a member of the European Union. Citizens of EU member states are legally entitled to work and live in Ireland. Non-EU nationals do not have this right and must instead jump through many hoops.

·   If you are a foreign, non-EU student and studying in Ireland on an approved course: you may take up casual work without an employment permit, but only a maximum of 20 hours per week.

·   Working holiday agreements: Ireland has reciprocal agreements with a number of other countries including the United States, allowing non-EU nationals to stay in Ireland for longer than 90 days and work here. To do so you must apply for a Working Holiday Authorization. For more information go to https://www.dfa.ie/travel/visas/working-holiday-visas/

·   If you have Irish ancestry: Ireland has a 'grandfather' law. That is, if you can prove that your parents or grandparents were Irish you have the right to Irish citizenship. With citizenship comes the right to live and work in Ireland and anywhere in the EU. For more information go to http://www.citizensinformation.ie/en/moving_country/irish_citizenship/

·   Employment permits: Ireland has 9 types of employment permits. Some allow non-EU nationals to work and live in Ireland: General Employment Permits are usually considered for occupations with an annual remuneration of □30,000 or more. Critical Skills Employment Permits are available in a number of categories. To apply, the prospective employee must have a job offer. Upon receiving a permit your family will usually be eligible to join you. For more information go to http://www.citizensinformation.ie/en/employment/migrant_workers/employment_permits/green_card_permits.html.

·   Obtaining Irish citizenship through marriage: foreign nationals who are married to Irish citizens can apply for naturalization. For more information go to http://www.citizensinformation.ie/en/moving_country/irish_citizenship/becoming_an_irish_citizen_through_marriage.html

- Obtaining residency through civil partnership: if you can prove you are in a long-term relationship with an Irish citizen, you are legally allowed to apply for long-term residency.

- Retired and desiring to reside in Ireland: you may be granted permission to reside in Ireland for the longer-term if you can prove that you have: an annual income equal to €50,000 per annum and; savings equal to the cost of buying a home in Ireland and; comprehensive private Irish-based medical insurance. If you can prove that you will not become a burden to the state you can apply for longer-termed residency. For more information go to http://www.inis.gov.ie/en/INIS/Pages/non-eea-permission.

Gaining long-term permission to live and work in Ireland if you are not an EU national is tough work but not impossible. If you haven't been to Ireland make sure you visit first. Check out the place. See if you think you can fit in and survive in Ireland as I have. If your answer is yes, if you are determined and focused, you could well end up living the Irish dream just as I have. I wish you so much luck.

Guideline Four: Can't Get a Job? Then Do it Yourself

Castletownbere, County Cork   November 2016

'This country is a land of entrepreneurs. Because we are now part of the European Union with immediate access to three hundred million consumers; because ownership is part of the Irish nature; because we look for a challenge; because we desire to control our own destinies... for all those reasons, new business starts in this country are always vibrant. Though working for yourself is challenging and requires a great deal of commitment, there is nothing on this earth quite as satisfying.'

Noel Forde

Irish Entrepreneur

As outlined above, gaining citizenship, the right to work, and finding a job in this country is a little tricky. Unlike America, Ireland does not have a 'Green Card' lottery system that has allowed so many of its citizens (and the rest of the world) to settle legally in the United States. Rather, the Irish government is protecting its economy by making residency and citizenship more and more difficult to be had by would-be immigrants. Add a Rock n Roll economy to the mix and you might feel a bit uncertain.

However, there is another road to Irish residency; a method that is not talked about very often and which remains something of a secret. This option presents a personal journey that requires a little more work and risk than most, but that can also be exceptionally fun, financially rewarding, and personally satisfying.

And it's this: setting up your own business in Ireland.

If you can create jobs in Ireland — if you can contribute to the Irish economy — the Irish government will almost bend over backwards to make certain you'll stay here. And because of current recessionary pressures, the Irish government will always encourage inward investment — and entrepreneurial risk takers.

The Coming of Irish Entrepreneurship

Ireland has become a country of the self-employed, each hoping to reach their personal financial dreams and sense of self-worth. I should mention that it wasn't always this way. Since the advent of the independent Irish government and our constitution in the 1920's, and due in great part to this country's history of servitude that resulted from a continual stream of invasion and foreign intervention, many Irish people have historically been interested only in job security.

You would be too if your personal dream consisted of only surviving until the next day, hoping to avoid being tossed off your land by a difficult landlord.

For many years, up until the past forty years or so in fact, Irish parents hoped that their sons and daughters would join the ranks of the Irish civil service or other safe havens such as State owned banks and insurance companies. There, they knew that their progeny would be protected from the harsh difficulties of life. Back in the days of my parents-in-law, obtaining 'a pension-able job' became a catch-phrase symbolising success and achievement.

The problem with such a culture is that it reinforced a risk-free business environment. Most people would not take the personal risk of starting their own business for fear that they would soon be unemployed. While working for a government department, or an Irish bank such as Bank of Ireland or Allied Irish Bank, or within a semi-state company such as the P&T (Post and Telegraph, the semi-state body that years ago was responsible for both the post and telephone systems), Aer Lingus, or the ESB (Electricity Supply Board, another semi-state that made certain that Ireland produced and delivered enough electricity to serve its own needs) brought a guaranteed paycheque and retirement income, that aspiration to work for a large and risk-less organisation also fostered an unnerving sense of isolation within those organisations. This inevitably resulted in a national business philosophy that led to decay and poor business performance.

Such a business culture can have dire consequences.

When I moved here in 1982, Ireland had firmly established itself as one of the worst performing economies in Europe. Interest rates stood at over fifteen percent. Almost twenty percent of the work force was unemployed. The telephone system didn't work. The rest of Ireland's infrastructure – including the road networks, schools, and health systems – lay rotting in the Irish rain like so many blighted potatoes.

The government knew that it needed to do something. But what?

It took over thirty years to do it but the Irish government – and the people who live here – managed to turn around business attitudes and the cultural fortresses that rewarded safety. In doing so, they established a new environment that rewards not only growing businesses, but also the dynamic entrepreneurs that risk all to establish those organisations.

A few of the fundamental actions that resulted in this new climate include the following:

In the 1970's, the IDA (Ireland's Industrial Development Authority) was established with a remit to attract foreign investment. Its personnel took to the roads, visiting the United States, Japan, Germany and other industrialised nations with a view to motivating larger global companies to locate part of their operations in Ireland.

Bord Fáilte (now Fáilte Ireland), the Irish government's tourism body, was also given some teeth. It began to advertise the joys of visiting Ireland to the peoples of the world. The Irish have always known that their country offered something special. It was now the task of Bord Fáilte to promote this country, thereby attracting foreign dollars, Deutsche Marks, Pounds Sterling, Kroner, Yen, and other hard currencies into Ireland. Within a few years of the start of their efforts, tourism began to make a real contribution to the local economy.

Next, the government took a hard look at its tax system. Initially, it lowered taxes on corporate profits generated by manufacturing companies to 10 percent (more recently, it has raised them to 12.5 percent — still some of the lowest in the EU and is fighting hard to retain that low tax, despite opposition from other EU countries). It also made it easier for foreign companies to re-gentrify profits back to company headquarters located abroad.

Ireland also began the process of taking an active part in European business affairs. As an island nation located somewhere west of London, the movers and shakers of this country had always recognised that few Europeans ever thought of Ireland when considering possible suppliers. Ireland had been one of the original members of the EEC (the European Economic Community) that had been established back in the 1970's. Ireland's government knew that it was imperative to become a participant in any new economic structure that fostered ties with continental Europe and England. They would do anything they could to establish Ireland as a real part of a new emerging Europe.

For many years, Ireland laid the foundations that many hoped would bring a new sense of direction and fiscal well-being to this country. Then, over the course of perhaps ten years, and due as much to old-fashioned good luck as to anything else, Ireland's fortunes finally turned.

I remember a couple of the high points. At the time, no one could have really guessed what was heading toward us like a freight train burgeoning with Celtic gold. But looking back, it now all makes perfectly good sense.

In the late 1980's and early 1990's, Ireland suddenly became interesting to much of the world. Ireland's soccer team became a real force in the 1990 World Cup play-offs. While Ireland went crazy (literally) at the superb performance of its team, the soccer-watching citizens of the globe (and there are millions of them) became aware of this country through worldwide television broadcasts. In that Ireland had never been known for the outstanding performance of its sports teams, Europe and much of the rest of the world began to wonder just who these Irish people were.

Also, rock bands such as U2 and outstanding musicians and modern-traditional groups such as Enya and Clannad took the world by storm. As these artists journeyed around the globe, musicians like Bono communicated their vision of a New Ireland. While Ireland had always been known for its poets and writers, those past endeavours were now amplified with a distinctly modern twist. Ireland's enigmatic music touched millions with a contemporary beat and language that soon gave notice to the rest of the world that Ireland was part of the 'now'.

Other artistic endeavours also caused the world press to sit up and wonder. *Riverdance*, that wonderful dance musical and celebration of Irish culture, caused a ripple of pleasure throughout the world as it began touring to places as far-flung as New York, Sydney and China. Since its initial opening in February, 1995, this delightful theatrical event has visited over 450 venues globally, and has been seen by over 25 million people, making it one of the most successful dance productions in the world. This dance-fest also helped the world to focus on a new vision of Ireland.

As these small victories began to sweep across the world, new Irish talent gained column inches in the world press. This ripple effect began to swell, and for the first time in years people from London to Peoria, Beijing to Antwerp, and Berlin to Sydney began to sit up and ask themselves a question: who are these Irish?

Simultaneously, staff within the IDA, Bord Fáilte, and other Irish investment and public relations organisations turned up the pressure. In boardrooms throughout the world, practical managers of great global business institutions let themselves be won over by the famous Irish charm, the country's accessible location, the intelligence of its citizenry, and of course the substantial tax breaks.

Then, like a story from ancient Irish mythology, and as if the great warrior Cucullain himself had risen from the dead in order to lead the Irish to victory, an amazing storm gathered and for the first time in a millennia, everything came together. It was 1995. Ireland's Celtic Tiger was born.

Companies that had been attracted here by the IDA started to invest even more money. IBM, Intel, EMC, Microsoft, Dell, Hewlett Packard — pick almost any well-known blue chip corporation — started building manufacturing, research & development, and service organisations here. They started hiring. Unemployment fell from 15 percent, to 10 percent, to virtually nil. These multi-national organisations began sourcing more parts, more services, more of everything from local Irish suppliers. And at this writing, those forces are still at work. In recent years, eBay, PayPal, and Yahoo have all decided to locate European business headquarters here. More companies are on the way.

Local Irish business people — those long-suffering folks who had made do with very little for so many years — bolted out of the starting gates like run-away colts. Existing Irish businesses began to expand. Irish entrepreneurs began to gain confidence. And that confidence spread like wildfire to anyone who thought they might have a plan to make some money on their own.

Until the fires of the Celtic Tiger had been lit, Ireland had always been a country of civil servants, shopkeepers, and farmers. But from 1995 onward, it seemed like the entire country wanted to start a business. And so it was that a new culture, a culture of Irish entrepreneurship, was born.

Many countries in Europe put up fences to thwart the entrepreneur. In England, Germany and France (to name a few) managers of small businesses spend hours filling in forms and complying with strict employment rules all the while attempting to keep their businesses afloat. If you are a European with an entrepreneurial bent and are considering a move to Ireland, you will be pleasantly surprised by this country's support of small business. While Irish managers have to put up with assorted red tape and tax compliance issues, we have it relatively easy compared to our European counterparts. And coupled with dramatically lower business taxes, European business people view Ireland as a seeming Nirvana.

If you are from the United States you will feel right at home. The U.S. has always been a country that has fostered the entrepreneur. From Benjamin Franklin to Edison to Bill Gates, people from my native country have always dreamed of working for themselves. To Americans, building a business from scratch can seem like second nature. Until the Celtic Tiger, opportunities for establishing a business located in Ireland were limited. But now, Americans, Europeans, and anyone else coming here with a sense of purpose can mine gold from the hills of this new island of opportunity.

By combining your entrepreneurial heritage with a country that now supports the entrepreneur, you too can not only move to Ireland but also stay and prosper like so many others.

Ireland as a Centre for Business

Only thirty years ago or so, most people thinking of setting up his or her own business in Ireland had little choice because the economy was limited. Those wanting to try for financial independence might establish a small shop in a local village, buy a pub, open a Bed & Breakfast for the tourist trade, or otherwise try to ferret out a meagre living to stave off starvation and personal destitution. Yes, a few started businesses and grew rich even in the lean years. But those folks — mostly males, I might add — are few and far between.

It isn't that way anymore. Ireland can now support almost any idea that a person might have, as long as that idea is reasonable and tailored to some notion of reality, particularly in light of today's challenging economy.

But if you're considering setting up a business here it is best to remember the realities of this country:

Population

The population of the entire island of Ireland, including Northern Ireland, is about seven million souls, or so says the most recent government census. That's less than the population of Los Angeles. Unless you plan to export a product or service abroad (a highly commendable occupation, by the way, and looked upon favourably by a variety of Irish funding agencies), you'd do best to remember that you'll have to pull a living from what is a very small local populace.

In the United States, the United Kingdom, Continental Europe, and many other places, and because of the demographics of these regions, a good idea can make a person wealthy even if that idea is tailored only to the population of the contiguous U.S., the households of England, or the wine drinkers of France. In Ireland, it is a different matter. While real wealth can be had here, a business strategy that targets only the island of Ireland significantly limits your opportunities.

However, be aware — very aware — that Ireland is a member, and sits within shouting distance, of one of the world's largest and wealthiest economic entities: the European Union. Since its establishment, this economic powerhouse has grown rapidly. The current list of Member States consists of:

Austria, Belgium, Bulgaria, Croatia, Cyprus, Czechia, Denmark, Estonia, Finland, France, Germany, Greece, Hungary, Ireland, Italy, Latvia, Lithuania, Luxembourg, Malta, Netherlands, Poland, Portugal, Romania, Slovakia, Slovenia, Spain and Sweden. And more including Albania, Montenegro, Serbia, North Macedonia and Turkey are on the road to EU membership.

The current Member States use a common currency — the euro — for all transactions. With twenty-seven countries comprising a veritable engine of commerce all using the one currency, this economic strategy can only increase common trade among peoples. As time moves on — and assuming disaster doesn't strike — and as Member States come to additional agreements, the European Union will have removed all trade barriers, harmonized most taxation, provided its diverse population with a common citizenship, and will have otherwise created one of the world's greatest economies.

The results of this economic union between nations have already been staggering, despite the current fragile economy throughout Europe. Ireland, as just one example, has been the beneficiary of billions of euro worth of grants that has contributed to the development of its economic infrastructure, which helped the country to ignite the flames of the Celtic Tiger and get us through the Great Recession. Those same benefits are also significantly contributing to the economies of Spain, Greece, Poland, and the rest of the EU. Their citizens are reaping the rewards by becoming wealthier, thereby gaining greater disposable income and economic freedom. As time passes, these hundreds of millions of consumers will demand even more products and services, opening the door for even more businesses.

The European Union represents tremendous opportunities. And Ireland — sitting at its periphery — is a natural bridge between the vast potential of a combined European economy and the United States. American and European entrepreneurs thinking of relocating to Ireland might consider the opportunities that lie both to the East and West of this small island nation.

Infrastructure

Since my early days here, and the inability to acquire such basics as a telephone without sacrificing my first-born child for the pleasure, Ireland's infrastructure has seen improvements that are mind-blowing. While this country still has a way to go, living here is no longer akin to settling in the deepest wilds of the Amazon. Instead, it's rather like living anywhere in the United States or central Europe except the culture is, of course, different, the people talk with a different accent, and the back roads are still loaded with potholes (though even that bumpy characteristic is also slowly improving).

But Americans, Europeans, and other nationalities will no longer be shocked by the absence of life's little pleasures. Instead, I suspect that you will be pleasantly surprised by the situation — unless, of course, you were hoping to find a land steeped only in ancient ruins in which case you might be disappointed.

A quick run-down on the improvements to this country:

Telecommunications and the Internet — on the whole, Ireland now has one of the best pro-business telecom infrastructures in Europe. Broadband, while not yet available everywhere in the country, can be tapped in all major cities, and major population centres. Rural Ireland continues to see an increase in high-speed connectivity, supported by continuing government investment. The country's telecommunications infrastructure, having rapidly improved, can now support almost any business that requires extensive telecom and high-speed web access.

Prices do remain stubbornly high compared to my parents' telephone and broadband bill. But get this: it can now cost less per minute (only pennies) to telephone the United States from Ireland than it is to make a similar call from my old stomping grounds to this country. In a few short years, Ireland has put together one of the best telecommunications systems in Europe. Not only is it about time, but it is also a real pleasure.

Mind you, I do occasionally miss the opportunity of listening in on someone's conversation when the telephone lines managed to get crossed, as they did in the old days.

Roads - new highways and by-ways have been built everywhere. While you must recognise that Ireland is playing catch-up on a history of near-poverty, and though many Irish residents continue to be frustrated by potholed horrors that continue to plague some areas, on the whole the National Roads Authority is making great efforts to improve intra-Ireland transport. For instance, in the past ten to fifteen years, Ireland's Road Authority has spent literally billions of euro on new roadways throughout the country, including miles and miles of dual carriageway and motorways. They are also working with local County Councils to repave many of the country roads and within the next few years hope that Ireland's history of jaw-breaking potholes will be a thing of the past.

International Access - the Irish government, as well as local and international transport companies, continue to improve access to and from this country. International airports — with access to Europe, the United States, and other global destinations — include Dublin, Shannon (in County Clare) and Cork. Other local airports (Galway, Knock — which does have some international flights — Kerry, Waterford and Donegal) serve local needs and provide feeder airline service to main airport hubs, with some feeding directly to a variety of U.K. and Continental destinations.

Ferry services from Cork, Rosslare and Dublin provide direct sea transport to the U.K. and Continental Europe. The road network supports truck transport from any part of the country to these ports in order to facilitate export requirements.

In short, Ireland is no longer a European backwater. Due to its improved transportation network and telecommunications infrastructure, companies from as far a-field as the United States, Japan, Australia, Germany, France, the rest of Europe — and the world — are finding it increasingly easier, and less expensive, to locate to this country.

Taxation — past governments have substantially lowered taxation on business. Most businesses now attract only 12.5 percent tax on corporate profits. While personal taxation remains stubbornly high compared to the United States, many businesses are locating here due to these incredibly low levels of corporation profits tax. If you establish a business here, you'll attract a similarly low level of tax. The goal, then, is to figure out how to keep those profits in your pocket.

Grants & Assistance — Ireland has established a number of government agencies whose remit is to support the growth and viability of indigenous Irish businesses. These agencies include the IDA and Enterprise Ireland. A contact list is provided in the Reference section at the back of this book.

The point of all this is that, after many years of centralised mayhem, Ireland has at last become a country whose remit former U.S. President Calvin Coolidge would have admired: the business of Ireland really does seem to be business.

Now we'll start to look at how you can use this economic reality to help make your dream of living in Ireland come true.

Opportunities for the Entrepreneur

You should know that in 1987, I took the plunge and decided to become a real honest-to-God Irish entrepreneur. I am decidedly *not* a born businessperson. I suspect that the entrepreneurial gene was decidedly absent from my makeup. In fact, the thought of setting up on my own scared me silly.

Back in 1987, however, I had little choice. At that time the country was in a downward economic spiral and the chances of a quick recovery were highly unlikely. Back then, and having finally left my lowly paid position as a weighbridge salesman, I landed a job with a division of the Hyster Forklift Company, a subsidiary of the U.S. multi-national. The subsidiary was based just north of Dublin and I'd had the good fortune to find work there as a marketing type, albeit for a salary that was still barely adequate to keep our household afloat.

Once ensconced in my job, however, and having had the time to look around, I decided that things didn't look too good for the company. Not by half. The Hyster operation was funding itself almost wholly from Irish grants. Its mission to develop a series of automated guided vehicles was coming off the rails and its booked sales were not meeting targets nor contributing to overheads. I quickly became aware that the company was never going to survive.

I knew that if I didn't do something about it there was a good possibility that I was going to end up back on the dole queue. Of course, I thought about getting another job. But upon looking around it transpired that few were hiring. Those that were had no cause to hire an American. They had their own families and friends to think about.

Consequently, and facing impending unemployment head-on, I decided to take a careful – though frightening – look at establishing my own business.

When I first considered setting up a business in this country, and because I was not a shopkeeper, farmer, or civil servant, I thought that the only industries that might be open to me were one of those wee little cottage companies that dot the west coast of this country like so many clumps of multi-coloured heather. You know the ones: pottery making, knitting, painting, tourist bric-a-brac. Being an American, I automatically thought that the only real opportunities were going to be found serving the tourist market.

Needless to say, I was not a potter, knitter, or painter and immediately bemoaned my fate. I thought that I would never, ever be able to develop my own business. I was wrong.

In my case, I established a marketing communications agency. Looking back on it, the entire experience was — at first anyway — absolutely terrifying. I took on a partner (a fellow American as it turned out) and we beat a path to every large blue-chip organisation in the country, attempting to sell a not-yet-quite-developed expertise in direct mail and similar direct response advertising techniques.

For a while, and despite my foreboding, things went well. Initially, we established ourselves as a joint venture with a major Dublin-based advertising agency. Having purchased a certain credibility, we grew quickly. In 1989 we bought out the joint venture partner's shareholding and traded independently. We moved into larger premises. We took on more staff. We increased our capabilities.

In 1990, however, George Bush Senior decided to bomb Iraq. Within days, our source of revenue from blue chip clients — revenue that had taken years to develop — had dried up. I watched as those years of toil imploded. The company went into liquidation in early 1991.

In 1992, I tried again. This time I took a less ambitious approach. I set up completely on my own. I sold a variety of marketing capabilities again, but this time I sold them to a wider range of companies — smaller organisations, the occasional blue chip, anything to get by.

This time things have gone well. Over thirty years later the company is still in business. For many years, I employed only a handful of other people to serve a large portfolio of great clients. We all worked our socks off, but because I kept my company and its overhead structure quite small, and we always managed to make a profit. The combination of low overheads and careful planning seems to have worked in this country, and to the benefit of my family and fellow employees. While I am now semi-retired and work all on my own, the advice I pass along to any would-be Irish entrepreneur, and based on so many years as an Expat Irish entrepreneur is:

Ireland is small. So, keep your overheads small. If you do, you'll have a reasonable chance of succeeding.

But my other point is this: I never thought of myself as an entrepreneur. Though I went to business school as a graduate student I always thought that my career path would consist of remaining an employee, attached to someone else's burning star.

Once again, I was wrong. And if I can make it here in my own business, I like to think that any global citizen with a strong sense of commitment and personal motivation can make it, too.

As you consider your options keep in mind that the Irish economy was growing fast and will likely do so again. As of early March 2020, economists anticipated a rocketing 3.4%+ growth rate in GDP, one of the fastest in the EU and double what many other countries in Europe enjoyed. Though COVID has brought us all to our knees, those same economists are predicting continuing growth when this emergency passes. The rising tide of Ireland's economy should again provide opportunity to those willing to work hard and take risks.

As to where those opportunities might lie, see below:

Ecommerce

Ireland is at the forefront of technological development. While you're not about to start manufacturing Silicon Chips, you could look at something more practical. One area of burgeoning growth is Ecommerce. So, if you have an idea for an online retail website, and within a market segment that could survive with the Irish market as its core, then you may be onto a winner. Right now, Irish people are looking for bargains. Traditional 'bricks and mortar' companies are slashing prices (and many are going out of business) — and are hamstrung at least in part by high overheads including rents, staff and similar. Too, online purchases are blossoming during the virus, and that consumer behaviour is unlikely to change when things tick back to normal. If you have an Ecommerce idea that can operate with reduced overheads, while providing the Irish consumer with a good deal, you could do more than survive — you could prosper.

And if you have an idea that can use Ecommerce tools to tap international markets, while also selling Irish manufactured goods, you'll also be able to avail of considerable Irish government grant support.

Innovative Technologies

As mentioned above, the Irish government is also supporting technology initiatives that can lead to increased productivity, efficiency — and increases in Irish employment. So, for instance, if you have an idea for a 'cloud' computing process — an accounting software solution using cloud technology, for instance, or a consumer healthcare app — you might be in a position to avail of considerable support. Hundreds of new tech companies are springing up throughout the country, even in the teeth of the current economic storm, and many are prospering. Due to these efforts, and the success of attracting multinationals such as Google, Yahoo, PayPal, Facebook and so many more, Ireland has become a centre of technology excellence.

If you need proof, you need look no further than the success of Ireland's Web Summit. This technology event, only launched a few years ago, has become one of the most successful events of its kind in the world. Recent speakers included Elon Musk (think Tesla, SpaceX, and PayPal), Drew Houston (Dropbox), Jay Bregman (Hailo), Tim Armstrong (AOL), Nelson Griggs (NASDAQ), and over three-hundred more. Technology entrepreneurs, as well as established companies, are setting up shop here because as one Web Summit attendee stated, "Ireland is where innovative technology is happening." And while the Summit is no longer being held in Ireland, at least for a few years, the sentiments above still apply.

Are you looking for stories of Irish technological entrepreneurial success? Then perhaps look no further than Stripe. Co-founded by two Irish brothers, the market valuation of Stripe is now estimated to be somewhere between $70–100 billion. Competing directly with PayPal, and founded in 2010, Stripe is rapidly becoming one of the largest and most successful online transaction applications in the world. Now that's a story of entrepreneurial success. And if they can do it — why not you?

Tourism

Do you have an idea that would encourage tourists to part with their hard-earned cash by visiting Ireland? If so, have a good think. Currently, the global recession due to COVID has gutted tourism in Ireland. This is a disaster for the country because tourism remains one of Ireland's most important industries and has historically contributed a great deal of employment. But there's good news, too: for the last five years, Ireland's tourist industry has grown exponentially. Moreover, most experts think it will again when COVID is vanquished. Give things a year or so, but this country will again be awash with travellers from all over the world who choose to spend their time, and money, in Ireland.

I'll give you a small example of little things you can do to have a go in the tourism sector. In 2010, fed up with the craziness of Dublin and its motorised suburbs, I moved to southwest County Cork. There, in the wee village of Eyeries — a lovely spot nestled along the shores of Beara Peninsula — I happened to purchase a house with a large yard overlooking beautiful Coulagh Bay. A year or so after I moved in, there was a knock on the front door. A drenched-looking Irishman shoving a pushbike begged me to let him camp in my back garden. He explained that having planned on setting up his tent along the windy seashore, the day was simply too miserable to camp in such an exposed location. He looked as inconsolable as a drowning puppy, so of course I agreed. Ten minutes later, I looked out the back window at a tent thrusting skyward as my intrepid visitor grinned back at me from beneath his mobile accommodation.

Later in the day, the skies cleared and I made both of us dinner on the outdoor grill. As we chomped away on a burger, he asked me why I didn't do this all the time?

Me (not understanding): "Do what?"

Him: "Why, let people camp in your back garden, of course. There's nowhere else to go around here except the shore. And for many, it's too uncomfortable. It doesn't even have a loo."

Me: "But who would want to camp in my back garden? No one camps in back gardens."

Him (grinning): "I camp in back gardens all the time, and in different countries all over the world. It's great fun and I meet people from everywhere."

Me: "But managing it would be a pain in the arse, wouldn't it? I'd be spending all my time looking after guests."

Him: "Not on your life. It's tent camping, fer God's sake. What's to manage?"

Me (leaning back in my chair): "All right. Go on. If you were me, what would you do and how would you do it?"

So, for the price of a hamburger he spent the next hour telling me exactly what I should do: what to offer, what not to offer, and for how much. I thought about it for a week, then asked a local signwriter to create something special for me. His creation still hangs at the front of my house, proudly proclaiming: Solas Mor Tent Camping.

Since then, we've had visitors from all over the world camp in our back garden. We don't charge very much, nor do we have a great many people camp in any given season. For those reasons, you'd never be able to survive financially on what we earn every year. That said, we have met many astonishingly stupendous people who get here either by walking along the nearby Beara Way, cycling in, or, yes, actually driving here. In short, we stay open not for the money but for the people. Right now, of course, we're closed due to the pandemic and we must admit that we miss our visitors very much.

If we had a larger place, perhaps we could produce enough income to survive. I'm not sure. But my point is this: many parts of Ireland are witness to a steady stream of tourists. If you have an idea that might let you put your finger into that financial river, then by all means you should consider it.

Home Construction

Due to today's demographics — the fact that the majority of Irish citizens are younger, setting up families, and otherwise beginning that wonderful struggle called Living — the country has a pent-up demand for single family dwellings. That demand is growing even during the pandemic. Even now, during these months of COVID, local contractors are serving a thriving market for new housing. If you're a carpenter, plumber, electrician, contractor, framer, sales agent, or otherwise have skills in this area, and if you can quickly learn what it takes to meet the specific requirements of the home construction market in Ireland, you could get rich by setting up a home construction company here. Keep your eyes glued to reports on the economy, as well as bank liquidity. While lockdowns have prevented many would-be home purchasers from finalising plans due to short-term unemployment, there is no doubt that there is a fortune to be made in home construction. Of interest to would-be North American entrepreneurs in this segment is the fact that Irish tastes in homes are changing. For years and years, Irish houses were constructed of poured concrete and breezeblocks. Only recently has this market started looking at wooden framed houses – construction techniques that were adopted by U.S. builders years ago.

Wood construction techniques, and that includes standard framed houses, A-Frame homes, and Log Cabin type construction, are now all the rage. If you have experience in this area you could be onto a winner.

Additional Construction Related Industries

While we're examining homes, let's talk about those segments that support that primary industry, as well as Home Improvement.

If you have skills in anything from landscape architecture and design to outdoor deck construction; interior design to carpet and tile supply and fitting, you may well prosper here as restrictions lift and the economy rebounds. Because of recent changes in Irish consumer tastes, more and more people are transforming their homes into palaces that many Americans or Europeans would immediately appreciate.

Under floor heating, outdoor decking, in-built spas, redesigned and landscaped yards (called 'gardens' this side of the Pond), conservatories, complete extensions, redesigned and redecorated interiors, comprehensive home refurbishments, and all of the supporting elements that these products and services require will again be in demand.

Irish people want nicer homes. If you have the skills and experience that can help meet these demands, and when the economy again grows, you can consider this entire industry as ripe with opportunity. I'll give you two quick examples of people who have succeeded in this area albeit in the boom years, both in the tile trade:

A neighbour of mine emigrated from Italy. Having worked in the Italian home tile industry for years, he set out to establish an Irish company for himself.

He started importing tiles directly from his home country. His products are absolutely beautiful (I know — I retiled the kitchen of a past home using his products) and he quickly built a company and a good living completely on word of mouth.

The second tale is a quick one involving a Tiler, also from Italy. A friend of the tile importer above, this man — who can only speak a few words of English — and his wife are now subcontracted to lay all of the aforementioned Italian tile. His name is Roberto; her name is Maria. They are a delightful couple who work very hard and who laid the tile in my kitchen. They worked their butts off and laid that exceptional tile in a way that was absolutely beautiful.

I was so pleased that I started recommending the couple to the neighbours. These two hard working immigrants harvested a stream of continuing work just from our neighbourhood.

The above examples illustrate two points: first, if you have a skill that can be tied into the housing industry, you could be onto a winner as the Irish economy again recovers. Second, if you know someone in Ireland that is already supplying this area, and if you have a skill that can support that existing business, you'll be in a much better position to quickly mine this opportunity when the time is right.

Computer Support

Like everywhere, Ireland has become a country driven by the computer. Every company and individual now seems to have at least one PC or laptop, and sometimes two, three, four or more.

And where you find computers, you'll also find computer problems that create opportunities for those in the know.

Within the broader computer support industry, IT security possibly presents the greatest opportunity. I have a close friend who works in this area, and he built a wonderfully profitable IT security business on the back of those idiots who are generating Spam, porn, computer viruses and the like.

If you have the knowledge that can help reduce — or eliminate — the above-mentioned curses to Irish and international computer users, you should be able to quickly develop a profitable enterprise.

Additionally, Irish companies continue to invest heavily in new computer hardware and software including everything from comprehensive LAN systems to cloud architecture, to simple firewalls. While you will undoubtedly want to avoid those areas that are already over-supplied, and which attract low margins (computer hardware, for instance), you will certainly do well by developing services that support newer technologies. Computer consultants who understand Cloud applications, LAN, WiFi, firewall technology and software, data backup, and similar technologies are cleaning up.

Of perhaps even more interest is the fact that many small entrepreneurs are developing software products ripe for international export. *The Business Post* (Ireland's favourite newspaper for the smaller to mid-sized entrepreneur; you can find them at www.businesspost.ie) is consistently filled with articles about those individuals who had an idea to mine the opportunities inherent in the computer industry, and have subsequently made a fortune.

Irish entrepreneurs are now selling their computer-based expertise to countries throughout the world.

Health Care

Nurses & Doctors: first, if you're a qualified nurse or doctor and want to come to Ireland, know that you should have little difficulty in getting a job because skills in this area are in high demand. The COVID horror has resulted in even more demand because the Irish Government put out a cry for help to the global community. Irish healthcare workers from all over the world responded to the call and many have moved back to Ireland to assist during this emergency. But even after the virus is vanquished, Ireland will still require many healthcare practitioners.

If interested, you will, of course, need to examine certification requirements (your existing license may not be valid in this country), but Ireland is still in frantic need for people with these skills.

Alternative Medicines: the Irish have embraced alternative medicines with great enthusiasm. So much so that there now exist huge opportunities for entrepreneurs. Consider Ki Massage, Reiki Healing techniques, Native American sweathouses — anything that offers a spiritual alternative to traditional medicinal techniques.

Additionally, a number of Irish companies have established a whole range of manufacturing capabilities, supplying a spectrum of vitamins, essential oils, whole grain foodstuffs, low fat and no fat food substitutes, and similar healthy consumer goods, to meet the demands generated by Irish and international consumers.

Many of these companies are now exporting their products to Europe. Europeans love Irish food and alternative medicine exports simply because Ireland has always positioned itself as a land of clean air and clean living. Irish exports within this area are usually greeted with open wallets.

The Food Industry

If alternative medicines are not your bag, consider the wide variety of opportunities available in the food industry.

As mentioned above, many perceive Ireland as a country that fosters purity and all that goes with it. Consumers throughout the world continue to believe that Ireland's pure waters, rich soil, and relatively clean air help this country to create some of the best food products anywhere.

Though some of those beliefs are now suspect (the danger of pollution often goes hand-in-hand with economic growth), that thinking is for the most part still correct.

Entrepreneurs who have had the vision to develop new and useful food products have gone on to make fortunes. New businesses serving niche product categories including spring water, chocolate, cheese, yoghurt and other dairy products; mustard, whiskey and spirits, natural beer, wine (yes, some entrepreneurs have managed to grow grapes in this northern country), biscuits and crackers, and many other foodstuffs have prospered.

Speaking of beer — while Ireland was late to this particular niche market, Craft Beers of all sorts are making significant inroads against traditionally popular brands. Bord Bia (an organisation tasked with promoting Ireland's burgeoning food and drinks industry) notes that in 2012, Ireland had only 15 breweries. Today, it reports over 70, with the range of beers on offer growing at a record clip. Beer isn't the only drinks sector that is seeing a surge of entrepreneurial focus. Whiskey, gin, and similar offerings are seeing growth. As an example, in Castletownbere, County Cork (right down the road from my little village of Eyeries), a local couple established the Beara Distillery. Having created a unique Gin, their products are now being exported in to Germany and much of Europe. Do you have a desire to be a master distiller or brewmaster? Now might be a good time to try your hand.

The fishing industry also continues to be ripe with opportunity. While European fishing quotas have resulted in fewer fish being swept from the sea (giving them a chance to reproduce and thereby guaranteeing a fishing industry for Ireland's progeny) value-added products focusing on fish and shellfish continue to play an important part in Ireland's economy. An entrepreneur who has a good idea that results in new pre-packed fish dishes delivered to Irish and European grocery stores could very well find him or herself rewarded with precious pearls.

Do you have a penchant for creating new recipes? Can you think of something unique to offer the rest of the world? If so, you may not only find that you can make a fortune, but also make your dream of living in Ireland come true as well.

Franchise Opportunities

Franchises have been great wealth creators within Ireland. Of interest is the fact that many well-known franchise opportunities are available on these shores. But a number of famous franchises have not yet made it to Ireland and may be interested in coming here – which could offer you an incredible opportunity.

Fast Food: McDonald's and Burger King, two American stalwarts, have already surged into the Irish market as the result of changing Irish tastes. McDonald's in particular is seeing quick growth in this country and are on the lookout for new franchise operators. While you may not want to take part in a Mac's franchise, feeling that it represents U.S. global opportunism, it is a fact that this company is helping Irish franchise operators to grow wealthy. Too, the company purchases one heck-of-a-lot of Irish beef, as well as additional Irish product, and employs an army of Irish people.

Other Irish-originated franchise opportunities within the Fast Food segment are also available including Sabrurritos, Dickey's Barbecue Pit, Romayo's Diner, Pizzabaker, and SuperMac's (a home-grown competitor to McDonald's). All are seeking to expand through franchise agreements.

Coffee Bars

Many people often think that the Irish drink nothing but tea and Guinness. While the Irish penchant for a pint is still true, the Irish have managed to change their tastes regarding non-alcoholic beverages. Though the Guinness Book of Records maintains that Ireland is still the top tea drinker in the world, the Irish are also a nation of firm coffee drinkers. Recent research indicates that the Irish drink about as much coffee as they do tea — a change in consumer behaviour that would have seemed unthinkable only a few years ago.

Because of this shift in demand, most cities and larger towns now have their share of coffee bars — and a few individuals are getting rich by establishing chains that supply espresso, cappuccino and the like. As with fast food, coffee companies such as Insomnia and Esquires are offering franchise opportunities. But many people make a living by avoiding the franchise route and setting up from scratch.

If you believe that you have the talent to serve a meaner cappuccino, then perhaps this is the route for you.

Call Centre Support

You've undoubtedly read the news that many U.S. and European companies are exporting service support jobs to lower cost economies, particularly India. This, of course, is quite true. What you may not know is that for many years a number of international companies have established similar call centre and back-office support operations in Ireland.

Things have changed, of course, and this trend isn't as popular as it was only a few years ago. This is due to the simple fact that Ireland is no longer a low-cost economy. Skilled people here demand wages that are equal to — and often more expensive — than their U.S. or European counterparts.

However, due to a number of factors including the significant improvement in Irish telecommunications infrastructure, the fact that all Irish people speak excellent English, the fact that many Irish have fluency in French, German, and other European languages, the additional fact that those same people often have experienced an exceptional standard of education, the mere five-hour time difference between Dublin and New York City, and the proximity to the European continent, this area still offers opportunity.

Obviously, and due to the wage situation here, call centres that are price sensitive will not be economically viable in Ireland. However, centres that support higher priced goods and services (such as those supporting the computer or insurance industries) and that can support a higher overhead structure continue to attract interest.

Software Development

Ireland has become a Mecca for anyone with a penchant in this area. Having become a Silicon Valley for Western Europe, Ireland now possesses people, skill sets and infrastructure that promotes software development across a wide spectrum: everything from games for handheld devices including cell phones and PDA's to the latest in payroll and security software.

The Irish government is continuing to throw money at this strategic growth area. New developments in the Liberties area of Dublin, including a fully-fledged R&D facility supported by centralised high-bandwidth broadband telecommunications capabilities, are now attracting both start-up and operating companies. A variety of grants are also available to support this growing commercial sector.

International Export Opportunities

Ireland continues to export more than it imports, and that remains true even in these COVID times. For instance, recent statistics state that Ireland is the largest exporter of software in the world — and that includes the United States.

Exports continue to be critical to the growth of the Irish economy and they are now the engines for continuing economic success. While industries that serve only the Irish market can be eligible for government support, those processes and products that have export potential are more likely to receive grant support from Irish government agencies such as Ireland's Enterprise Board.

Today, Ireland's economy exports a wide variety of products — and skills — to many other nations throughout Europe, North America, China, Africa, and beyond. Exports include (but are not limited to): software, pharmaceuticals, live and slaughtered cattle, value-added food products, mushrooms, potatoes, furniture, fish and value-added fish product, consultancy services serving the duty-free area (Irish business people developed the duty-free concept and continue to service that area), electric power plant design and development, construction consulting, aero-space engineering expertise, pottery, crystal, and alcoholic beverages including liquor and beer.

If you have a business model that incorporates an export capability, the Irish government may support that concept with valuable grants and loans.

Financial Services

In the late 1970's, then-Taoiseach Charles Haughey (Ireland's Prime Minister) began to develop a compelling financial services model that he believed would turn Ireland into an international financial powerhouse. Though it took a few years to reach fruition, his dream has been turned into reality with the development of the Ireland's International Financial Services Centre (IFSC).

Located in Dublin on the north side of the River Liffey, this centre offers a variety of tax breaks to international financial services companies (and other qualifying companies) including: Corporation tax at 12.5 percent on trading profits, a 10-year exemption from municipal taxes, double rent allowances for leased property, 100 percent depreciation allowances for commercial buildings, plant and machinery, and no withholding taxes on dividends or interest. Since its inception, the IFSC has been attracting large-scale blue-chip companies and more modest financial services operations including fund administration, banking, insurance, re-insurance, aircraft leasing stock trading, and money management companies, like a magnet. Currently, over 38,000 people are employed with IFSC companies.

This influx of these active organisations has resulted in a number of opportunities for the individual and entrepreneur.

IFSC-based companies are sweeping up people with financial services backgrounds and can't seem to get enough of them. If you have experience in financial services, you may qualify to receive a work permit.

Entrepreneurs are also profiting by setting up support operations that feed into these large-scale financial services companies. Everything from software support to customer relationship marketing expertise is required by these operations.

On Being an Artist

While in office, Charles Haughey also decided to support those participating in the arts with an incredible tax incentive known as the Artist Exemption. With a stroke of his pen, he changed the law to state that income derived by artists from certain sources including creative writing and painting would not be subject to personal taxation.

Since then, Ireland has proven to be a tax haven for writers, painters, and other qualifying artists and their income. Since this law was passed, any number of people plying their skills in the arts has made Ireland their home.

If you derive your income from the arts, you may qualify. Getting an Artist Exemption can be somewhat difficult, but once you have one —band unless the powers that be overturn the law —you will have it for life.

The exemption rate has fallen recently. But artists qualifying for the exemption can still earn ☐50,000 per annum before paying any tax at all, except for relevant PRSI and another few percentage points in USC.

Contact the Irish Revenue Commission (www.revenue.ie) for more information.

Other Opportunities

If you have a skill or a dream and you think it might work in Ireland, then by all means consider it. Though I've mentioned tourism in the above list of possible opportunities, I'll dive in a bit deeper because the prospects could be of interest.

Possible additional opportunities within this sector include: the establishment of commercial websites that both promote Ireland and tourism niche areas; the purchase of local Bed & Breakfast operations or pubs; the establishment of local tourism companies whose mission it is to attract visitors from particular geographic areas in North America, Europe, or other countries to visit Ireland; and the development of small-scale cottage industries to produce local product for the tourist market.

I've met many immigrants who have settled in this country and who really are spinning both pottery —vand their personal dreams and fortunes — at wooden wheels while getting the most out of their lives.

The point of it all is this: if you really want to try working for yourself, Ireland offers the opportunity to do just that. You may not get rich in the process, but you'll enjoy the journey.

Some Advice on Doing Business in Ireland

Before moving on, a quick piece of advice — and it's this: the Irish, like any other nationality, love good service. Whatever you do, make certain that you under-promise and over-deliver.

When I first came here, service in almost any Irish business operation was pretty abysmal. From manufacturing to retail, companies just didn't seem to give a damn about making sure that their customers were happy. The reasons for this were simple: first, the dismal island economy of 1982 fostered a business environment of non-existent competition. If you became fed up with the local electrical appliance shop, for instance, you had little option of going elsewhere simply because there wasn't anywhere else to go. But as importantly, and at that point, the Irish didn't know how to complain very effectively which meant that Irish businesses had no real reason to get off their butts to make life easier for their Irish consumers.

Things have changed. Because of the vibrancy of Ireland's growing economy since the Celtic Tiger years, hundreds and hundreds of new businesses have set up shop and the winds of healthy competition now blow strongly through Ireland. With the coming of new choices, the Irish realise that they now have some real options and can vote with their feet if they don't like what they are receiving. And though they still have a little bit to learn, Irish consumers are becoming both street-wise and knowledgeable. If they don't get good service, if they think they've been ripped-off or otherwise offended, they'll let you know pretty damned quick.

Most companies within the country have responded well to this demand. Let's face it, this new attitude of the Irish meant that unless businesses got their acts together, their consumers would go elsewhere.

That said, and in my experience, companies still under-perform in ensuring that their existing customers remain happy. In short, and though things have improved, many Irish companies don't yet truly embrace a philosophy that includes exceptional customer service.

And this leaves a niche wide open. If you are determined to set up in this country, start from the very beginning by over-servicing your customers. Tell people the truth, make good service a part of your strategy, be on time when delivering a product or going to a meeting (the Irish are prone to being late and appreciate timeliness), come in at a fair price, make your terms known, and be certain that your customers understand those terms and stick to them. Having made everyone happy, make sure that you get referrals. Word of mouth goes a long way in this country.

If you make certain that everyone is happy, you'll quickly achieve that level of success that you're hoping for. And the Irish will love you for it.

Your Right to Remain in this Country

As stated above, and unless you are already an EU citizen or can prove ancestral Irish blood, North Americans and citizens from other parts of the world can find it difficult to obtain a Visa and permits to live and work here.

However, if you create jobs in this country it's an entirely different matter. In that the Irish government is always promoting job creation, they will look most favourably upon your decision to develop a business that serves the employment and tax creation needs of the country.

Recently, I talked to an individual within an international office of the IDA regarding 'illegal' immigrants who set up a business within Ireland but who had not yet received an appropriate Visa from the Irish government. The IDA official, while circumspect, made it known that government officials would view favourably those individuals who were creating jobs and generating tax revenue for government coffers.

Those individuals who choose to invest in this country will, for a while anyway, be living in something of a phantom zone in that they will not have any true legal status. For months, they may have to flit back and forth from Ireland to their home nation, while managing their new businesses on the fly. But should these new entrepreneurs continue to create jobs and pay taxes they will eventually be welcomed by the Irish government as legal residents. After a few more years, these individuals will also have the opportunity to apply for citizenship, should they so desire.

The point is clear: if you are willing to set up a business in Ireland, your dream of permanently moving here is within your grasp.

Guideline Five:
How I Bought Myself a Little Corner of the Irish Dream

San Francisco, California

December 12, 1982

My dear son,

I am writing this in the closet, the paper lit only by a candle, because your father has vowed never to talk to you again and this is the only way that I can pen a message to you so as not to upset him.

As your mother, I must say that I am truly in despair. Did I do something terrible to you when you were a child to have caused such misery that you must now seek revenge? When Ronald (a lovely man) wrote to your father and told him that you had actually purchased a house over there, and were less likely than ever to return home, I thought that Daddy was going to have a heart attack. How you could ever leave our spacious suburban house for the cold of Ireland is simply beyond me.

I enclose twenty dollars. Buy yourself a knit scarf, will you please?

Your loving Mother

Having found a job by hook or by crook, your next step toward fulfilling your Irish dream will probably revolve around the purchase of your own Irish sanctuary. At least that's what I did.

Buying a house in another country can be an exciting, though often fraught, journey of discovery and self-preservation. As perhaps the largest purchase a person will ever make, buying a home is a reflection of self and family, an expression of upbringing and personal ambition. Moreover, the type of house purchased seems to be determined by a number of factors: lifestyle and self-image; family size and age; hobbies and interests; financial wherewithal and investment awareness; and perhaps as importantly, the dreams and aspirations that we all live for.

For years, the roaring Celtic Tiger economy pushed house prices into the stratosphere. Except for a brief respite during the Great Recession, those prices continue to climb. Many of us thought that the current COVID scenario which is wrecking much of Ireland's economy might provide a bit of respite. In fact, many economists forecast a price decline of 12 precent in 2020. But for better or for worse, this has not been the case. House prices continue to soar.

Upward price pressure is due in large part to a shortage of supply. New construction never caught up with demand following the Recession. Now under lockdown due to the virus, most construction activity is verboten. Simultaneously, and a surprise to most people, home buying has actually increased. It's a typical Adam Smith scenario: when high demand meets constrained supply, prices will rocket.

While the greater Dublin area is experiencing a bit of a breather, many rural areas (historically known for relatively low housing prices and smaller annual price inflation) are undergoing rapid price increases. Remote working would seem to be at least partly responsible for this pressure. Many people no longer have to make a daily commute to the office. Instead, they are working from home. This new flexibility, a surprising outcome of the pandemic, means that many now have a greater choice on where to call home. No longer forced to looking for housing near their place of work, some are choosing rural Ireland. The consequence of this new surge in demand is an inevitable rise in rural house prices.

But whatever the surge in prices, people are still buying. And if you come here, you could, too. More than any other purchase, home-ownership is an emotionally charged experience. We can all become frighteningly carried away by our own imaginations. Our sense of reality can be confused by dulcet imaginings that only a movie director might construct. We might see ourselves living in an Irish Georgian mansion complete with waiter, cook, gardener, and assorted staff to take care of our every need. The reality, however, can often be in stark contrast to the cobweb of wishes that we develop on any dark and lonely evening, while pondering our ambitions over a short glass of whiskey. While we desire the luxury of genteel living, we may discover that our bank balance can only fund a hovel.

When I came to Ireland back in the early '80s and considered purchasing a home here, I too let my imagination run wild. Ruminating over a bottle of cheap plonk in the cold, dingy house that we had rented — the only place we could afford — I imagined that my family would be quickly ensconced in rural surroundings like that of an Irish fable. As with John Wayne in *The Quiet Man*, I too would own a thatch cottage surrounded by acres of wooded property, a quiet brook singing to us as it trickled tranquilly over moss-covered stone, and a local pub located within an easy walk through verdant green fields.

Needless to say, I found that my dreams were quickly shattered. Irish housing prices and much of the administrative routine of making a purchase has changed since 1982, but perhaps the following might indicate the processes that my young family — and this ignorant American — went through as we sought our Irish dream home.

I should explain that since arriving in this country, I have lived until recently in what used to be the small sleepy town of Navan. Located in the middle of County Meath and situated approximately thirty miles north of Dublin, it is no longer a sleepy town because the recent economic booms have turned it into a traffic-clogged nightmare. But back then it was quiet enough.

My wife's parents also live here, or did until they both unfortunately passed-away. Because Bernadette was born here, had friends here, and felt a part of the place, she didn't want to live anywhere else. Upon our arrival she had made the irrevocable decision that there was only one place to live in Ireland and that was in Navan.

'Couldn't we live in Dublin?' I had croaked upon realising that I was to live in what then was a backwater of a town for what would probably be the rest of my life. 'Dublin has universities. It has wonderful theatres. It has life, for God's sake.'

'Dublin smells,' she had replied. 'Besides, Navan is a wonderful place to live.'

Possibly. I was about to find out. And I did. I was to also discover that my initial assumption about the town was the correct one: back in 1982, Navan really was an Irish backwater. My second assumption was not quite correct, but close to it: I lived in Navan for almost 30 years until I decided that I just had to move (which I did — to the magical seaside village of Eyeries in County Cork. But more on that later.)

When I had first immigrated to Ireland, Navan had one major employer: Tara Mines. This zinc mine, the largest mine of its type in Europe, apparently had enough zinc reserves to keep the world going for a million years or so. Back in 1982 the entire town depended on it.

Navan at that point looked like something out of a World War II black and white documentary. It held ten thousand people living in small damp houses that resembled the working set of a Depression Era movie. It had a few schools, three churches (two Catholic and one Church of Ireland Church just to keep the few Protestants happy), a main street full of run-down shops, a couple of fish and chip joints managed by Italian immigrants who constantly complained about the weather and who continually chattered about the brilliant prospects of the Italian football team, one Chinese restaurant that produced fairly reasonable food, two cinemas both of which smelled of mould and were in need of immediate demolition, a brand new shopping centre that to my eye looked already to require refurbishment, and well over thirty pubs.

On weekends the pubs were mobbed as the local miners tried to forget what they did for a living. The locals would all pile in on a dreary, wind-swept Friday evening, then engage in a pub crawl throughout the rest of the weekend. A pub crawl, while it might sound obscure, is self-explanatory: drink in one establishment until you get bored then move on to the next public house just to see if the conversation there was more interesting. Navan had over thirty pubs so a conversationalist had plenty of choice. By the time your money ran out, you would find yourself crawling on hands and knees to your final destination, undoubtedly passing out and puking in the street before getting there.

If you were lucky, a friend or passing Navanite would find you and call the local constabulary who would kindly escort you safely home. Hence the origins of the phrase. I have survived a pub-crawl or two in my lifetime and I can vouch for it as a time-honoured profession.

During the working week, of course, the pubs were as quiet as churches because everyone had already spent their pay packet and couldn't afford a pint of Guinness despite the fact that it sold for a mere sixty pence in old money — about a buck a pint. Come Monday morning, everyone would descend into the zinc mines or otherwise go to their places of employment in order to work their posteriors off so that they could start the process all over again.

Navan was an eye-opener to me. The streets were full of potholes that could take the fillings out of your mouth. The paths ('sidewalks' to North Americans) were broken and filled with weeds, and street lighting was almost non-existent. The telephone system wasn't even a system. It was, I suspected, a work in progress that would not be finished for another twenty years.

When I first came here, and though as previously mentioned it has improved immeasurably since then, I discovered that acquiring a telephone was akin to obtaining the status of royalty. Not only would I have to pay five hundred pounds (close to seven hundred bucks at the time, the equivalent to a full month's wage for yours truly) for installation but I also discovered that having paid this ruinous fee it would take almost six months to have said telephone installed. Once installed, the damned thing rarely worked. If it did, you were almost certain to be cut off in mid-sentence or had the dubious pleasure of overhearing Mrs Kelly, a woman on the far side of town, talking about her sister in a most unfortunate turn of phrase. On those rare occasions when you did get through you commenced to pay some of the most outrageously expensive call charges on the face of the globe.

Needless to say, the newly immigrated Richards' clan did without a telephone for well over a year. This was a terrible surprise to a middle-classed American used to running down to the Phone Company, paying his twenty-five bucks, and then hauling a brand new touch-tone into his apartment whereupon he would plug it into an obscure fixture in the wall to be instantly connected to the rest of the world.

In 1982 Ireland, that wasn't going to happen.

Back then Navan was fairly typical of the rest of the country. The town is much like the Peoria, Illinois, of the nation in that if it's true in Navan it's probably true in the rest of the Irish Republic. Navan was poor. I wouldn't say destitute — no, not that bad. But it was difficult enough. Almost twenty percent of the town — and the country within which it nestled — was unemployed. A productive day out was standing for a couple of hours in the rain outside the unemployment office, waiting for the weekly dole. The entire country was suffering from one of the worst recessions in living memory and no one seemed to know what to do about it: except the government, of course, and all that they did was raise taxes and declare that we'd just have to put up with it all.

Few people owned cars. Fewer had a garage in which to put them. Most people made their way around the town on foot, which felt wrong somehow but which, over the years, I began to appreciate. Back in America, and if I wanted to buy some donuts, I'd hop into my Chevy, turn the key, and drive the four blocks to Johnny's Donuts where the smiling Vietnamese lady would plop twelve waistline-expanding items into a large box. In Ireland, I didn't have a car because I couldn't afford it. I couldn't go to Johnny's or anything like it because donuts weren't, except in rare instances, available. The Irish did have absolutely yummy cream cakes that we used to purchase on special occasions such as when my parents came over on a misbegotten visit but that was about it. If we wanted them, we'd walk the half-mile into town and get them. My feet hardened into steel bricks but I can say that I felt much better for it all the same.

When we first ventured to this side of the Pond, I had determined that we would rent a fine house in a fine estate then take our time to look for that dream home that I longed for. Unfortunately, few rentals were available back then and those houses that were for rent seemed to be owned by landlords that cared little for the health of their tenants.

Our fully-furnished semi-detached rental house was damp, mouldy, came with central heating that we couldn't afford to run, was accessorised with wood-framed windows that had been attacked by wood rot so much so that they were in danger of falling out, and whose floors were covered by mouldering orange and green carpeting that looked as if it had been around since the days of Saint Patrick.

Because of the dismal state of our rental house, and firmly believing that the health and lives of our entire family depended on quickly relocating anywhere else, my wife and I determined to purchase a home as quickly as we could.

With little fanfare, we started the process.

We looked and looked. Being of low financial means, we found that our choice was limited because of the scant money that we had in our pocket. When I eventually found a job here, our choices were limited even further by the fact that, due to my obscenely low wages, I simply could not afford a large mortgage.

Looking back on it, I realize that what we should have done was to have borrowed up to the hilt and to hell with the consequences. For instance, we viewed a lovely two-storey farmer's cottage complete with outbuildings built on a couple of acres of land and located at the top of a gloriously windswept hill. It held sweeping views of the Boyne Valley and at the time could be had for a mere thirty-two thousand Irish pounds (about forty thousand U.S. dollars). Today, that same property is valued at over ten times as much.

However, back then and like most, we simply didn't have the money. So, we had to make do. Irish property — then and now — offered a short spectrum of house types:

Bungalows — are defined as stand-alone homes, usually one-storey, usually built on a larger plot of land (often on a quarter acre or more), and most often located in the country.

Estate, or Detached, Homes — usually defined as a typical 'neighbourhood' in the United States, are either one or two-storey stand-alone homes, usually available in only one model type, and all residing in a single area, usually built by a single contractor.

Semi-Detached Homes — often known as a townhouse in the U.S., Semi-D's as they are affectionately called over here are two houses built together, having one common wall. Often an entire estate (neighbourhood) will be composed of nothing but Semi-D's, all of the same model type. Semi-detached homes, the most popular type of house in Ireland due to their affordability, are often comprised of three or four bedrooms, a living room-cum-dining room, kitchen, one or two bathrooms, and often a one car garage. Square footage is usually limited to approximately 1500 square feet or less.

Terraced Homes — kind of, sort of, 'condominiums' (depending on your location in the U.S.), this house type has gone out of fashion in Ireland and few are currently being constructed. Terraced homes are built in a continuous line of anywhere between four and ten dwellings. Each has two common walls (except for the two end houses, of course, which only have one common wall), which means that you share the wall structure with your adjoining neighbours. Terraced houses come in one and two storey versions and are usually quite small, perhaps only a thousand square feet or less, comprised of two or three bedrooms, a kitchen, a bathroom, and a living area. Many terraced houses were built in the early 20th Century as public, or Council, homes. These houses were owned by the various County Councils (county government agencies) and were provided to local tenants at exceptionally low rental rates.

Over the years, most council houses have been purchased by their tenants and can now be sold on a 'freehold' basis by the owner to any purchaser who might be interested.

Manor Houses, Castles, and Unique Homes — Ireland also has its fair share of gracious homes set in locations that are right out of a textbook on faeries and folklore. Castles dating from the 13th Century, complete with thick stone walls and populated by assorted ghosts, sometimes become available on the Irish property market.

Manor Houses (also known as Great Houses) were built at the time of early English rule by Anglo feudal lords who were rewarded for their energetic subjugation of the Irish with substantial land grants. These beautiful homes, often using Georgian architecture, not only feature elegant window fascia and wonderfully plastered ceilings but also often come complete with sweeping staircases and unique internal features.

Typically, they rest on large plots of land, much of which has been developed into elegant gardens.

Additionally, Ireland has its fair share of unique homes that have been designed by professional architects to the original owner's requirements and specifications. These occasionally come on the market and can attract great interest by not only the local population but also those erstwhile potential immigrants from the United States, Germany, Italy, England, and the rest of the world.

But getting back to the search for our Irish Dream Home:

Having made the decision to purchase a house, we visited the local realtor, known as an 'Auctioneer' or 'Estate Agent' in this part of the world. Having determined our limited means, he proceeded to inform us that our meagre budget would only allow us to consider the purchase of a Terraced Home. As it happened, he had only one on his books.

In that we were desperate we immediately began the process of purchasing.

It's been so long since I've lived in the U.S. that I forget the machinations of home purchase there. I do, however, remember it to be a frustrating process. It's no less frustrating in Ireland and seems to take months to complete.

The owner of the Terraced House was asking seventeen thousand Irish pounds for his turn of the century, somewhat dilapidated, two-bedroom, one toilet house. We bid sixteen-five. He wouldn't take it. We bid sixteen, seven-fifty. He remained firm. We finally offered him the asking price and he accepted.

We provided our Auctioneer with a cheque for the required ten percent deposit and then the fun began.

First, we had to hire a lawyer (known as a solicitor in this part of the world). Our solicitor contacted the owner's solicitor. Various papers went back and forth and forth and back. Initially, the title for the property could not be found. It turned out to be lying in the dusty cabinets of the County Council and it transpired that the house had never been properly registered as a private home, but still resided on the council books as a public Council house. It took weeks — and money — to have the home re-registered.

We also applied to a local bank for a mortgage. At the time, interest rates were a mere seventeen percent per annum and the suspicious bank manager looked askance at providing a sixteen thousand pound mortgage to a young maverick such as me who in all probability would never be in a financial position to maintain his mortgage repayments. However, with pleading smiles and a few warm words from my wife (the fact that she had been raised in the town undoubtedly influenced his decision), the bank manager finally agreed to lend us the money.

Now in possession of mortgage approval, we knew that the rest of the purchase process could proceed. In my ignorance, I firmly believed that such a process would be quick. I was to be proven wrong in my thinking. For a further three months the solicitor that we engaged to look after the closing of this transaction swapped a variety of mysterious paperwork with the seller's solicitor, activity that seemed to have little to do with the purchase of the house but which could have been more concerned with pumping up the price of the solicitor's fees. My young family, still living in the damp rat hole of a rental home, became desperate.

Finally, when it appeared that we would all die of hypothermia, our solicitor contacted us. 'Congratulations. You can pick up the key,' he stated. My wife shrieked in exaltation.

In Ireland picking up a key to a new home is cause for wild celebration. Greeting card companies sell 'Congratulations on Your New Home!' cards for just such occasions. My wife was crazed with excitement and we withdrew to the local pub for a well-deserved drink.

Having received the key, we immediately took occupancy. And that's when the trouble really started. The previous owner, contrary to contract, had exorcised the house of anything that was not nailed down — and even some items that were. Every light bulb in the house had been taken. The curtains were gone. The mirror — which had been screwed to the bathroom wall — had been removed. Even the toilet roll holder had mysteriously disappeared.

We experienced the coupe de grace when discovering that an entire fitted closet had been completely dismantled and removed leaving a large untidy hole in the carpet where it had previously resided. Angered by this theft, we immediately contacted our Auctioneer who informed us that pursuit of our newly purchased accoutrements would be in vain. Such 'theft' was common in the early 1980's for a simple reason: many people could not afford replacements and took such luxuries with them to their next place of residence.

I had learned a hard lesson, one that I remember to this day. Since our first home purchase we have moved four times. When signing contracts, we now insist that all items being sold with the house are line-itemed in the contract. Even small items such as toilet roll holders.

And so it was that we moved into our 'new' seventy-year-old Terraced Home. It was only then that I truly discovered how different living in Ireland would be for me, and how much of a gap I would have to bridge between the culture of my birth and the culture in which I now chose to live.

Back in the early 1980's, many Irish people still heated their houses with coal fires. Some homes were heated with natural gas or 'modern' central heating, and many others were lucky enough to have solid fuel central heating, meaning that the main fire in the house heated a central water cylinder that then transported said heated water into a variety of clanking radiators. In mid-winter these managed to keep the room temperature of this type of centrally heated house warm and toasty.

Our terraced home didn't come with such luxuries and certainly was not in possession of central heating. Consequently, and come wintertime, we simply froze. Often, I would get up on a winter's morning and scrape the ice away from the bedroom window in order to see what the day might be like. This was much different to my boyhood days in wintry Chicago when all I would have to do was turn up the thermostat and the king-sized forced air heater would kick out enough warmth to make me believe that I was in Hawaii. In Ireland my wife or I would get up early, clean the fireplace of its bucket full of ash from the previous day's heating, and pile as much coal as we could within, then huddle over it, praying for a quick dispensation of much needed warmth. We were not alone, of course, because a large minority of the Irish population had to do the same thing. No wonder many of us had such high incidence of asthma, chest infection, and the general feeling that we were going to die come the winter.

While we possessed a refrigerator, it wasn't capable of making ice (not that anyone without central heating would ever want ice). Our toilet facilities, such as they were, resided down a short hallway on the ground floor. Neither the hallway nor the bathroom were insulated which meant that in the winter we all literally froze our ass's off when making the call to nature.

Accessing hot water was an experience in patience. We could make hot water in any one of three ways. The first was the back-boiler: the stamp-sized coal fireplace — our only source of heat — came complete with this so-called 'back-boiler', a system that supposedly turned cold water into hot. This gizmo, which was hidden behind a large plate of steel immediately behind the fireplace, contained assorted pipes filled with water. Upon lighting the fire, the steel plate came into contact with the flames. The steel heated the pipes that in turn heated the water. The water rose through the series of pipes and was finally disgorged into an abysmally small copper tank that was hidden somewhere deep within the kitchen.

The problem was that to make hot water in this fashion we had to keep the fire going twenty-four hours a day. At six pounds in Irish money — about eight euro — for a bag of coal, a large sum of cash in those days, this prospect was not very likely. Too, the copper tank seemed to contain only enough hot water for approximately one half of one bath. Taking a lukewarm bath in the middle of an Irish February is not my idea of fun. Try it sometime. You'll come out wondering at the strange bluish colour of your extremities.

We did, by the way, have a 'shower'. We did not, of course, have a separate shower cubicle the likes of which my parents had in the United States and which I borrowed as a teenager in order to soak myself for half a day, then to come out looking like a steamed prune. The shower in our terraced house in Navan was a simple rubber tube that we could connect with some difficulty to the spout in the bath. A ridiculous spray unit was glued to the other end of the tube. The tube wasn't long enough to allow us to stand up, so instead we had to sit down in the bath.

In winter, and should I desire to put myself through torture, I would sit in the ice-cold tub at which point my buttocks would become firmly attached requiring immediate rescue by my wife. In that the house had the water pressure of a squirt gun, the resultant dribble from the ineptly engineered spray unit might result in the application of mere ounces of water, not enough to engender even the slightest excitement from a bar of soap.

For this reason, I rarely took a shower.

But back to the hot water: The second option was to turn on what was euphemistically called 'The Geezer'. This was an absolutely ancient, ugly as hell contraption that was bolted onto the wall just above the bath. It ran on electricity. This 'Geezer' was comprised of a copper tank filled with water. Electricity, which at the time seemed to cost more per kilowatt-hour than plane fare to Hong Kong, was applied at which point the water would heat up and the knowing bather would then open a stubborn tap, spilling the hot contents into the bath. Here, the problem was possible electrocution. Consequently, I avoided use of The Geezer whenever possible.

The third option was the jug kettle. When all else failed we boiled up one small kettle after another, transported these in shifts from kitchen to bathroom, and poured the contents into the bath. In that our kettle only held one litre of water it took quite a few kettles and much boiling to fill the tub. Of course, by the time we had completed this mission the bathwater had again turned lukewarm so we were as well to light the fire and wait for the back-boiler to rattle, hiss, and otherwise make us aware that hot water was on its way. The jug kettle option, however, also allowed me to make a cup of tea for my good wife at the same time, so wasn't a bad option depending on the state of our relationship.

The outcome of all of this was that we managed to get quite dirty for a few months, until I had acquired enough cash through incredibly hard toil to upgrade the hot water facilities. In the meantime, our baby got her bath in the kitchen sink. But we all survived, nonetheless.

As to the house itself, and as partially described above, it was an old two-bedroom council house made prettier by a carpet of small white flowers which I soon discovered to be a variety of local weed that poked through the unkempt front garden. I now remember that upon first seeing the house I really did think that it looked quite 'quaint', a reaction that should have set off all sorts of internal alarm bells, but which at the time only made me feel cosy. It sat in the middle of a row of such houses and was built completely of poured concrete. The walls were at least twelve inches thick. While it was never going to fall down, putting up a picture or moving an electrical socket meant heavy excavation work and a heightening of blood pressure as I drilled through the heavy concrete walls, choking on early twentieth century cement dust that did its best to cover anything — including the baby — in a shroud of white.

The rooms were so small that had I tried swinging the proverbial cat I would have caused immediate decapitation. This version of reality did not, of course, match the dreams that I had during my ruminations over a pint at the local. Instead, we lived in a turn of the century dwelling that felt like some sort of industrial site and that allowed us to have a bath only when we could get the hot water to work. In short, I despised the place.

But I must stress that those feelings of squalor have long since left me. It took me years to understand why I reacted to that house as I did, but the answer was simple. I was a spoiled American who had grown used to the 'finer' things in life. Despite my best efforts not to, I was being dragged kicking and screaming through the process of adjusting to a new culture, and a new way of living and looking at things.

Back in 1982, and while there were wealthy people around who possessed all of the accoutrements of being wealthy, we didn't have much and neither did many of the people whom we knew. But in hindsight, I marvel at a simple realisation: none of these people — people who I considered 'poor' along with myself — missed anything simply because no one had anything either. Instead, they worked day-to-day and managed to get by. And not only that, but they were happy and content with their lot.

For instance, my mother-in-law lived in a similar house to our own just down the road for most of her seventy-five years. In that structure, which could have easily fitted into my parents' backyard, she and her husband made a loving home and Kathleen raised eight children including my wife, Bernie. Bernie's memories of living there are not of hardship but rather of great fun and a warmth of living that is sometimes difficult to find in modern Ireland, or come to think of it, almost anywhere else anymore.

Now, I look back on those early days with a certain fondness and I'm glad that I went through the experience. If I had stayed in America, I'm not certain that I would ever have been as broke, and the experience has allowed me to value what I have today. And looking back I now see what I couldn't see at the time: we never had to lock our front door because crime was almost non-existent. We relied on our neighbours in times of difficulty much as they relied on us. We shared what little we had with each other because that was the way of things. In short, we had become a part of the local 'tribe', and tribe members take care of each other.

I had trouble living in our cold little home simply because I was used to instant hot water, nuclear-powered central heating, rooms big enough to house entire villages, and a bathroom that wouldn't cause personal injury every time I went to dispose of yesterday's lunch.

Over the past forty years, however, things in Ireland have changed dramatically, some for the better, some for the worse.

Navan can now be a quite pleasant place to live, thank you very much. With the coming prosperity of the country, the town has managed to benefit substantially. What with the expansion of Dublin, over twenty thousand people have moved into the place, turning Navan on its head and creating some amazing opportunities. The shopping centre has been expanded and refurbished in order to accommodate the swelling crowds. Older shops have been repainted and entire new retail sections of Navan have been built, selling everything from apples to exercise equipment.

Townspeople no longer have to rely on one Chinese restaurant. Now, they have a choice of anything from Thai food to the best Italian fare. Streets have been torn up and resurfaced; broken footpaths replaced by lovely brick walks that glisten prettily in the soft rains.

The River Boyne, which flows through the town and which had heretofore been thought of as nothing more than an amenity for local fishermen, has been upgraded with lovely walkways along its historic banks. Prior to my move to Eyeries, many are the days that I spent whiling away my time by walking beneath the beautiful archways created by oak trees and yew, the sun-dappled river talking to me in hushed conversation.

And though I eventually moved away from it, even my old terraced house has seen the benefit of new windows and a coat of paint.

When I first arrived in Navan, and for a number of years, it is true to say that I absolutely hated living here. The gap between cultures — between how I was raised and what I was used to, and what I found here and how I had to adapt — proved incredibly difficult. Hell, when I first moved to Ireland I couldn't even buy peanut butter.

But things have changed. The country has moved on. No longer are immigrants from the States, Europe or elsewhere confronted by an ancient economy that can bring thoughts of suicide to a confused and dangerously homesick mind. The phones work, and the system is now one of the best in the world. Houses are heated properly. Everyone has a car, sometimes two, sometimes three. Most of us can afford to take expensive holidays. In short, Ireland is no longer a poverty-stricken nation. And though it is not America or mainland Europe and takes some getting used to, it offers many of the amenities that the U.S. doesn't seem to have anymore, such as a joy of living and a recognition of personal relationships that seems, sadly enough, to have grown unpopular back home. That, and a whole lot more.

But Navan, as with the rest of the country, has lost something in the transition. Though its streets are clean, they are clogged with the traffic of a successful economy. Today, people keep their doors locked because they are concerned about vandals and theft. While neighbours still look after each other, no one has as much time to chat or get to know each other simply because everyone is working so very hard. And though my now-grown children all live in modern homes with modern plumbing and all of the hot water they could ever need, when I go back to Navan and see our old terraced house, it brings to mind the realisation that I not only survived — despite my American-ness — but have also managed to prosper in this country.

For years I thought of grabbing my family and escaping from Ireland back to the land of my birth. But just as the country has changed, so too have I. I've now discovered that I'm glad that I stayed. I survived the challenge. Now, I realise that I've earned the right to stay here — perhaps for a lifetime.

As the years have passed, I have gradually come to regard Ireland as my home.

Guideline Six:
How to Buy a Piece of Irish Heaven for Yourself

Chicago, Illinois

August 14, 1983

Dear Tom,

I am astonished that you have taken the trouble to write in order to give me advice you know I could not possibly follow. You know very well that I would never be interested in living in Ireland, no matter how beautiful it is or how affordable the housing.

I think that there is the distinct possibility that you have been kidnapped by a cult and have become brainwashed into their nefarious ways. It could well be that you require the help of a psychiatrist.

Do please struggle against their methods! You are too well loved to become a lost soul in that land of bogs and constant rain. For me, the American Dream is sacrosanct. I will never succumb to a land hallmarked by tales of non-existent Leprechauns.

I continue to care for you but I would never willingly move to Ireland. Thank you anyway for the invitation.

Ronald

Location, location, location. Isn't that what the property gurus always tell you? It's no different in Ireland. The question, of course, is what kind of location you'd prefer and what price you'd like to pay.

From the top of the market in late 2007 / early 2008 when housing prices had become unaffordable to anyone except property magnates, prices fell like a brick during the Great Recession. During this period house prices had dropped by more than 50 percent, on average. In Dublin, a three-bedroom apartment in the city centre that used to cost upward of half a million euro could be had for half the price. Sometimes even less.

And then...Ireland's economy recovered. And with it, a surge in housing prices.

As already described, the cost for homes across the country has risen sharply. That said, if you keep your eyes open and are flexible, you could still find a home that satisfies. So, if you choose, like I did, to nay-say the nay-sayers and come here in pursuit of your own small corner of the Irish dream, you have a great deal to consider. For instance, where-oh-where in this wonderful country would you prefer to make your home? Every location in Ireland — as with many other nations or geographies — has something different to offer.

Are you interested in living in a City Centre? You can choose from the vibrancy of any of Ireland's major cities and towns. Dublin, Waterford, Cork, Galway, Wexford, Athlone, Belfast...each has something different and unique to give to the erstwhile seeker-after-Ireland.

Like the rest of Ireland, all major cities and towns have benefited from a significant facelift. Dublin, for instance, has undergone substantial redevelopment over the past forty years. When I first arrived on these shores, many of the beautiful Georgian houses that hallmarked the city centre were in danger of falling down from lack of maintenance, and the River Liffey was blighted by an assortment of rotting tenements and ancient warehouses that lined its famous banks.

But significant investment by the European Union and the Irish government, the vibrancy of the local economy, together with an upsurge in incomes, has provided the country with an unprecedented level of prosperity. The infrastructure of Dublin has benefited from this. Starting in the mid-1990's, the city has been hallmarked by dozens of construction cranes dotting the cityscape. Many of the nineteenth century Georgian homes have been gutted and completely refurbished while maintaining their lofty ceilings and unique external fascia's. Entire Georgian office blocks running along the River Liffey were completely redeveloped.

New apartment blocks were constructed: an entire community of shops, pubs, arts centres, offices and flats, running along the south side of the Liffey, was recreated in the Temple Bar area. To the north of the River, and in addition to the development of the International Financial Services Centre, the area has been bolstered by the construction of river front walkways, small shops and cafes, new bridges that have been thrown across the River, and any number of street-side apartments.

On O'Connell Street, at the heart of Dublin, we even have a relatively new piece of architecture to argue over. The Spire — a piece of exquisite aluminium — now thrusts into the skies above the city like a New Age toothpick. It replaces Nelson's Pillar, a throwback to English colonialism and a past tribute to the famous English Admiral. Erected in 1808, three years after the naval commander's death, it was finally blown up on March 8, 1966 by IRA sympathisers who believed that a memorial to the victor of the Battle of Trafalgar was entirely inappropriate rising, as it did, to its lofty height above the Irish Republic's bustling capital. For years, the Irish argued over a suitable replacement. Finally, and after much to-ing and fro-ing, the powers that be finally decided on The Spire. Though this contemporary structure was expensive and many argued that the money could have been better spent on a new hospital wing or decreasing the price of petrol, I think that it's pretty and certainly illustrates the potential of this proud country and the future that it is energetically pursuing.

Taking a stroll through Dublin is a unique experience. The Abbey Theatre, the Gate Theatre, shopping along Grafton Street, a visit to local cafes for afternoon tea and scones – all are within walking distance. To live in Dublin is to share some of the experiences of the life of James Joyce. And though Dublin is now a modern place complete with modern architecture, the city planners have managed to retain the old fascia and the sense of charm and history that had until recently been lost beneath the grime of an economically troubled period.

Of course, the onslaught of COVID has left its negative mark. A number of well-regarded retail outlets are facing permanent closure. Bewley's Café on Grafton Street, an historic and celebrated landmark, has swayed on the pendulum of solvency for many months. As I write this, the country is still enduring Level 5 restrictions, meaning that the vast majority of businesses are closed until those restrictions lift. We worry, however, that these vibrant parts of our community will not have the financial wherewithal to endure the continuing downturn. Many may not survive.

However, I regress. Ireland will reopen, of that there is not doubt. And when that happens, you too may want to move here. So, if you're not interested in the Big Smoke of Dublin, where else might you consider?

Smaller cities throughout the country have also benefited from a significant polish during the exceptional years of economic boom. Pick a city and you will inevitably find your own special mix of old-world charm and modern infrastructure.

Wexford with its narrow streets and pleasant harbour, Waterford and its quick access to overseas ferries and the rest of Europe, Cork and its pleasing shopping streets and intimate pubs, and the surging city of Galway, one of Ireland's smallest cities and oldest, which is renowned for its world-class University, seafood, singsong and Irish craic. All of these locations may prove of interest.

If city life doesn't appeal to you, look to rural living. Ireland's Midlands (find Portlaoise or Athlone on the map and you're looking at the Midlands) offer a quieter life mostly devoid of larger city crowds, smog and stress. In their search for a location, most people never think to even look to the Midlands. But much of it is pretty. A millennia ago, the countryside was levelled by the glacial flows of the Ice Age. These icy protuberances were not only responsible for destroying a countryside full of leafy Irish oak forests (which have since become bogs and which, until recently the Irish harvested as peat to burn as winter fuel) but also levelled everything else in their path. What remains — mostly, anyway — is as flat as a pancake. But through the Midlands courses the River Shannon and along its waterway reside both some wonderful towns and beautiful lakes.

If seaside locations appeal, take your time about selecting a desired place of beauty. Ireland's coastline — from west to east, north to south — undergoes a tremendous change of character within even the shortest of distances. The East coast along the Irish Sea offers plenty of sandy beaches and a reasonably temperate climate. Go south to County Cork (where I now call home) and you'll find pleasant seaside inlets and somewhat warmer days.

As you move up the Southwest coast past County Kerry and toward Limerick and Galway, the coastline becomes tougher and more unforgiving. High cliffs catch the surging ocean, tossing sea spray skyward, while north of Galway — up in County Donegal — rest some of the best beaches and purest waters anywhere, rivalling the world's better known locations for their un-surpassing beauty.

If you fancy sea life, the West coast also offers some spectacular aquatic encounters due to the close proximity of the Gulf Stream. Dolphins, porpoise, whales, basking sharks, and some of the best diving in Europe are available up and down the West and Southwest coasts of Ireland. If you can brave the cold of the Atlantic, you'll be in for a unique diving experience that you'll not soon forget.

Or drive north from Dublin and venture into Counties Cavan and Monaghan. Here, the countryside undulates in a series of hills and valleys, and small lakes and ponds dot the place. Property prices in these counties are still somewhat reasonable, and a prospective purchaser would be remiss if they did not at least investigate the area. For instance, semi-detached four-bedroom houses are selling for well under two hundred thousand euro (less than two hundred and seventy thousand U.S. dollars at today's exchange rate) in Moynehall, County Cavan: a good bargain compared to the prices that one now finds in Dublin, a drive of only two hours south of that pristine region.

If you want to click n' flit over the country to suss out housing prices, may I suggest www.daft.ie. It's a useful property website.

My suggestion? Visit the country and stay awhile before choosing a location. For Heaven's sake, don't do what I did and make a location decision without the benefit of seeing what was available in the rest of the country. For such a small island, Ireland has an incredible choice on offer. Take in its beauty before making up your mind.

Choosing the Right Estate Agent

Ireland has any number of real estate agencies. A few of the biggest include Gunnes, Douglas Newman Good, Hamilton Osborne King, and Sherry Fitzgerald. These are national agencies, but many medium-sized to larger towns and all cities will also have their own local auctioneers.

My gut assessment is that the smaller and more intimate the agency, the better their knowledge of the local area and what is on offer. While the local agents may not have a national scope, their attitude seems to be friendlier and one that is determined to satisfy all parties, both the buyer and the seller. They will go to almost any length to close a deal that is satisfactory to everyone.

National estate agents, on the other hand and by their very nature, offer a network of offices throughout the country that can provide a one-stop-shop facility to those of you interested in searching out properties both near and far.

If you have a reasonable idea of the location that you're interested in, try a local auctioneer. If, on the other hand, you don't yet have a good knowledge of the country, then try the national agents.

In most cases, the agents that I've worked with have been both highly professional and honest. But I've heard the war stories of agents who, having spotted the rich accent of a prospective American or European buyer, rub their hands in greed. As with any financial undertaking, my suggestion is that you not only interview a prospective estate agent but also try to get your hands on references.

Unlike the United States and many parts of the rest of the world, and no matter whom you choose, you will soon find that Irish estate agents are not the most motivated folks in the world. In the U.S., it seemed that a real estate agent would drop everything at the first phone call to ferry a prospect from one end of his or her territory to another in the hope of closing a deal.

Here, things operate on a much different timescale. Having made contact with the estate agent of your choice, expect things to happen at what can sometimes seem a snail's pace. The estate agent will inevitably have to book a viewing with a seller, and that viewing might be days away. If you're in a rush make it clear that you need adequate attention, and that you wish to see more than one property a day. Also, give the estate agent adequate time to organise multiple viewings for the same day.

New Construction

Until recently, Ireland enjoyed a surge in new construction in what seemed to be almost every corner of the country. Entire new towns, new communities, and new estates have popped up like mushrooms in a damp field. For years, Ireland's property market gained momentum, hotting up until prices became absolutely unaffordable. What seemed to be the entire Irish populace champed at the bit for a place on the surging property market. For that reason, they would buy almost anything. They would form long queues outside of the latest property opening, hoping to buy before others had beaten them to it. They would buy off-plan, without even one house of a new construction built. They would bid up asking prices by five, ten, fifteen, twenty percent, and more in hopes of getting on the property ladder.

But then the bubble burst. For a few years, the shoe was on the other foot, and buyers held the power. Many newly constructed estates (Ireland's so-called 'Ghost Estates' of which there are hundreds) still lie half-empty. Research indicates that the average price of a house had fallen by at least fifty percent since early 2008. Until recently, Irish — and foreign — prospective home purchasers were being presented not only with affordable housing, but also with an amazing choice from which to select.

However, as I've mentioned, the pendulum has swung once again. As of this writing, and due to a continuing shortage in supply, homes near larger urban areas have once again become unaffordable to many. Search more rural areas, however, and some can still scratch together enough change to make a down-payment.

As Ireland reopens for business, building contractors catering for all financial markets will once again gear up, building everything from city centre one bedroom apartments, to estates filled with ubiquitous semi-detached housing, to more salubrious estates featuring houses with large living areas, broadband wiring, multiple bedrooms with en suites (which are separate bathrooms attached to the bedrooms, e.g. a Master Bath), under floor heating, huge outdoor gardens, and often coming completely furnished down to the tiniest inessentials. Most construction here is composed of the concrete breezeblock type, but non-traditional methods including wooden frames and log cabin kits are also making an appearance.

Heating and insulation methods are critical in this land of cold and damp and many builders have bettered their specifications with uPVC double- and triple-pane windows, hi-spec insulation, and in-floor heating methods. Heating types vary throughout the country: all new houses incorporate central heating as standard. Depending on the home's location, energy sources can include oil heating, natural gas, or solid fuel (coal fired). Note that due to recent carbon-neutral objectives, most new housing no longer incorporates open fireplaces. Solar heating is also making large inroads, however, this option can be somewhat expensive if installing yourself, rather than buying as part of a new build.

Natural gas is by far the least expensive and most trouble-free of all heating options. It certainly beats cleaning out the soot from a central fire every day. Unfortunately, natural gas is not available in many parts of the country, which is an appalling state of affairs especially considering that any number of international oil companies have found incredible reserves of this resource off the coasts of Ireland. However, the government — through its semi-State company Bord Gais — is currently doing what it can to bring this economic fuel to the rest of the country.

Ask your estate agent about availability of natural gas in your area.

Renting

If you move to Ireland, you may of course consider renting first. This is exactly what I did back in 1982. Of course, back then (and as described above) this was a challenging prospect. First, the lack of housing stock meant that very few rentals were on the market which also meant that our choices were limited. Having little choice, we moved into a damp, horrid semi-detached house in the outskirts of Navan. The structure was poorly built. Everything was so damp that it felt like we lived in a Rain Forest. In fact, my eldest daughter came down with pneumonia while we lived there, which I directly attribute to the lousy living conditions present in that awful little home. The furnishings, including carpets and curtains, were also absolutely poxy. We moved as soon as I could afford to.

Today in early 2021, I have good news and bad news about property rental. First the good news: house construction today is first class. Except for the few bad apples on the market (hallmarked by lousy maintenance, lousy finishing and lousy insulation - keep your eyes open), most homes are dry, warm, and well-appointed. As I say, that's the good news.

The bad news? Rental prices are at all-time highs particularly in the Dublin area. However, there's a bit of additional good news: on aggregate, rental prices are dropping or so reports property website Daft.ie.

Despite the mild fall, rental prices are still ruinously expensive. Why you might ask? It's a combination of things. First, the last recession resulted in the decimation of any new builds. Simply put: houses weren't being constructed anymore. So, the supply of new housing stock was limited. At the same time, demand grew. More people live in Ireland and they require more homes. More people are unable to get mortgages so they require rentals. More people are either broke or bankrupt or have been forced from their existing homes due to the last recession, and today's pandemic. All of these factors have put upward pressure on rents.

What's very sad is: higher rental prices aren't only being faced by the economically solvent who can afford to pay — even if it means paying through the nose. The unemployed and those on Social Welfare are also being subjected to higher rents. And that has led to a single very disturbing fact: Ireland, and Dublin in particular, has more homeless people than ever before. Until housing stocks increase, or unless the Irish government does something about the situation, the crisis of homelessness will continue in this country. For the poor there is some good news: the Irish government has put a freeze on rental rates and, during the pandemic, has outlawed evictions. This new legislation could of course open another Pandora's Box: investment in new rental stock could dry up as investors turn to other opportunities hallmarked by higher returns. However, and at least for now, tenants have some sort of certainty regarding the rates being charged, if only for the foreseeable future.

The bottom line is this: if you're thinking of renting in Ireland, be prepared to pay a steep price for the privilege.

And A Final Word About Prices

As mentioned above, I have good news about house prices in this country. When I first came here in 1982 Ireland was an incredibly inexpensive place in which to buy a home. Housing was cheap by American and European standards and even though I struggled to buy a house here, my circumstances were due to the fact that I arrived in this country almost penniless. Back then, an immigrant with a bit of cash in his or her wallet could buy a modest two-bedroom dwelling for less than twenty thousand U.S. dollars. An abandoned cottage could be had for less than fifteen thousand.

I even heard tell of a fifteenth century castle going for less than the price of a suburban tract home in the San Francisco Bay area.

Unfortunately, all of that changed as the economy grew. As a little background, let me explain what triggered higher home prices:

Ireland is no longer a banana republic. As a member of the European Union this country has prospered at an incredible rate. On a per capita basis and despite the recent recessions, Ireland continues to be one of the richest countries in the EU. It is also one of the most expensive places to live in Europe.

Ireland also possesses one of the youngest populations in the world. And all of those young people seem to want to get a leg-up on the property ladder.

Combine these factors with the current shortage in supply of new housing and every economist will point out one inevitable consequence: housing was bound to get more expensive. And it has.

I've already mentioned my experience of purchasing a property here in 1982. Let me tell you another story that illustrates the accelerated increase — then decrease — in property values in Ireland since that time.

In 1992 my wife and I made another purchase, this time moving to a modest four-bedroom semi-detached home located yet again in Navan. At the time, the town was still considered to be a part of the hinterland despite its location only thirty miles up the road from Dublin. In that year, we bought our house for a mere forty-three thousand Irish pounds, or approximately sixty thousand U.S. dollars.

Then a funny thing happened. The global economy started to grow like mad, propelled by the advent of new technologies. Starting in 1995, things in Ireland (including prices) went crazy. All of a sudden everyone was talking about stock options rather than the lowly state of their financial affairs.

The country grew rich. With money in their pockets — an exciting new experience for many — people rushed out and bought things: BMW's, new computers, designer make up and clothing, luxury watches, Jacuzzi's, mobile telephones...everyone seemed determined to make up for a history of poverty with the sudden urge to buy. And as I watched, what heretofore had been a country on the last rung of the economic ladder quickly turned into one of the most prosperous countries in the world.

For the next five years, until the Internet bubble floated into history, the Irish Gross National Product grew at double-digit figures. Ireland seemed to set record after record: it exported more computer software than any other country in the world. Its unemployment — approaching a disastrous twenty percent when I first ventured to this wonderful part of the world — fell at an unprecedented rate to virtually nil in 2002. The country flexed its entrepreneurial skills and more new companies were set up over that period of time than at any other time in its history.

Awash with cash, awash with demand, awash with a new (and perhaps disjointed) perception of themselves, Ireland's citizens bought and bought and bought. And one of their most sought-after purchases was a new house. Consequently, the housing market — also fuelled by cheap mortgages — took off like a rocket-powered aircraft attempting to set a new altitude record.

Sitting in our little semi-detached home in Navan, my wife and I watched with ever-growing astonishment as the economy bubbled and brewed and began to hiss like a teakettle. Navan quickly became a bedroom community as Dublin people attempted to find themselves a little corner of the Irish dream and exited the city in search for more affordable accommodation. Our neighbours began selling up, making profits that were unheard of even a few years before.

And in 1999 we decided to cash in.

We put our modest house on the market. We received an initial offer of one hundred and ten thousand Irish pounds. We couldn't believe it. Our estate agent, an intelligent woman and wise to the new market conditions, told us to wait. Two other bidders entered the fray. The price moved to one fifteen. Then one-twenty. Finally, on one bright April day, when my conscience could take no more, we asked the two bidders who remained engaged in a battle that I feared might lead to their financial ruination to submit a sealed envelope with their final offers.

The winning bid? *One hundred and twenty-five thousand and one pounds.* Almost three times what we had paid for it a mere seven years earlier. I remind you that the new owner paid this plush amount — and considered it a bargain — for a house of only thirteen hundred square feet, four small bedrooms, and one bathroom. The amount paid then was equivalent to approximately one hundred and fifty thousand U.S. dollars. For the same amount, and at that time, I could have purchased a twenty-five hundred square foot home in Tampa with a swimming pool. Amazing.

It was the best investment that we ever made. And it was all due to timing.

For the next few years, Ireland's population became transfixed with the price of property. Even though the world economy had cooled following 9/11, Ireland's property market was, and continues to be, ever on the increase. And even now, in the midst of a pandemic, Ireland's home prices continue to rise.

My worry is that we'll never learn. The Great Recession in Ireland was made worse here by the inflationary impact of our housing price bubble. Up until 2008 or so, Irish people climbing on the property ladder thought they could do no wrong as they bought homes at prices that could not possibly reflect sustainable economics. Then, of course, we had the crash. Many people went bankrupt and lost their homes. Some have still not recovered, well over ten years following the country's economic recovery. Now, in 2021, I fear we're again entering a bubble property market, despite negative economics brought on by COVID.

As an example: a few months ago, my only son Jonathan, wanting to get a foot on the Dublin property ladder, took a good look. He had a fistful of money to hand for a down payment. He has a good job and therefore qualifies for a mortgage. But he could only scratch his head in disbelief when looking for a home to call his own.

"Dad," my son said to me during his search, "it's absolutely nuts out there. Yesterday morning, I put a bid on a 2-bed apartment. The seller was looking for 170k, so I offered him 180k hoping to snag it. But by the end of that day, the price had gone up past 210k. I simply cannot afford to buy a home in the Dublin area. At least not now."

This is a sad state of affairs for people working in and around Dublin city. However, take heart! As mentioned elsewhere, there are still good deals to be had all over the country — just as long as you avoid Dublin.

But I do have other good news which is this: it's my belief that an investment in Irish property is still one of the best longer-termed investments that you'll ever make. Consider this: when my wife and I sold our semi-detached four-bedroom home in 1999, we purchased a brand new twenty-two hundred square foot house — with three centrally heated bathrooms, thank God — right up the street. At the time, we paid one hundred and seventy-two thousand Irish pounds for it, which equates (in new euro currency) to two hundred and eighteen thousand euro, or at the time, over two hundred and seventy thousand U.S. dollar.

At the top of the market — in early 2008 or so — my friendly auctioneer reliably told me that my house carried a value of over four hundred and twenty thousand euro. In that we'd lived at the new house for almost seven years that worked out to an appreciation of over twenty-eight thousand euro each and every year of our ownership. It wasn't to last, of course. The Great Recession took care of that. However, assuming that you're careful with your timing, and due to (and I'll say it again) low supply and more people looking to purchase, you stand a good chance of doing quite well.

Investing in the Irish property market has historically carried much less risk than the stock market, bonds, or other financial instruments except, of course, for the minor hiccup. Unless you manage to buy at the very top of the market, and assuming you keep the property for a reasonable period of time, your initial investment could see a reasonable return. And investing in Irish property must certainly provide a better return than the miserable one percent interest rate or less available on any savings you might have in a bank account.

The other piece of good news is the fact that even greater bargains — comparably speaking, of course — still exist in Ireland if you're willing to stay away from city centres. The inland counties of Cavan, Monahan and Leitrim continue to offer exceptional value for even larger homes. For instance, in the town of Ballyjamesduff, County Cavan (a 1.5 to 2 hr trip from Dublin and notable due to being mentioned by songwriter Percy French in *Come Back Paddy Reilly*), a modern 4-bedroom detached two-storey home is on the market for ☐115,000.

If you're willing to look around, you can still find reasonably priced properties close to seaside and country amenities. On the Ardagh Causeway in County Kerry, a derelict cottage on .69 of an acre and located just off the Coast Road south of Ballyduff, is on offer for sixty nine thousand euro. And I suspect that the owner would consider any reasonable price.

Here, in Eyeries, County Cork, a 3-bed newly built semi-detached with sea-views is going for just shy of ☐180,000.

While the days of picking up a run-down cottage in need of refurbishment for only a wink and a nod and the price of a Pint might be long dead, Irish property prices are still affordable, if you're willing to locate to more rural areas.

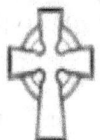

Guideline Seven: Ireland is Expensive. Or Is It?

Chicago, Illinois

January 15, 1984

Dear Tom,

I am concerned that you have not written to me since my last communication. However, your Mother assures me that you are safe.

I thought that you would appreciate the fact that we have just finished an absolutely wonderful, obnoxiously materialistic Christmas season. Robert came home from Peru and we forgave him by giving him his own brand-new Firebird complete with eight track player and some tapes by groups of strangely named birds.

Helen received her own multi-functional vacuum cleaner and I let Santa treat me somewhat extravagantly to a complete wine cellar filled with assorted bins of Cabernet Sauvignon.

But enough of us. How was your Christmas? I do hope that you are enjoying your newfound poverty. I suspect that you have been surprised at your lack of employable skills in a country renowned only for its unemployment. I am also shocked that you have managed to survive for as long as you have in that country. I suspect that you miss the comforts of America.

Do come home at once!

Yours,

Ronald

When I received Ronald's positively infuriating letter, I remember wanting to tear it up and throw it into the smouldering coal fire. Instead, I folded it neatly thinking that I'd keep it to remind myself of my days of poverty. Then, determined to make myself more miserable, I emptied my pockets and discovered that I had exactly seventy-two pence on me and realised that this fortune would have to do until the next payday. In the meantime, we were going to have to eat. A neat trick back then, because in those days of the early 1980's Ireland was expensive.

In fact, it can seem to be as expensive now as it was in 1982 if not more so. If you're planning on immigrating to Ireland, I strongly recommend that the first thing you do is run out and rob Fort Knox before boarding the airplane. Even if you are crazy enough to imagine yourself living here as a New Age Hippie, hoping to squat in some field with only a tent over your head, do remember please that even the simple things in Irish life can set you back plenty.

Back in 1982, my own personal circumstances — and those of most of the country — were tough enough. My first job here was working as a salesman for an industrial weighing company, travelling the width and breadth of Ireland trying to sell worthless bits of metal to farmers' cooperatives and tight-fisted Irish business people at the princely take home pay of five hundred old Irish punts a month. Ireland didn't only seem expensive to me, it was.

I was not alone. The average industrial wage at that point was just over one hundred pounds a week. Each payday, everyone ran home to rip open their pay packets, spilled its contents onto the kitchen table, and prayed that somehow they'd manage to get through to the next week. At least that's what we did.

Out of our monthly earnings, my wife and I had to pay for:

Mortgage	£117 per month
Food	£100 per month

Coal	£ 30 per month
College Loan	£ 30 per month
Petrol	£100 per month
Car Insurance/Taxes	£ 50 per month
Electricity	£ 25 per month
Clothing	£ 20 per month
Miscellaneous	£ 20 per month
Total	£492 per month

This left us eight quid per month with which to do exactly as we pleased. With this extravagant sum, and back in the early 80's, we could either: purchase approximately fourteen pints of Guinness, go to the chipper four times, buy a few packs of cigarettes each, or otherwise go entirely mad with our vast fortune. We could, of course, have put this into our savings but I had entirely given up on the prospects of retiring any time before my one-hundredth birthday. Back home in the States, I had always tried to save ten percent of my salary. Having gone to the bank I would hold up my bankbook in satisfaction, hoping that those pennies would someday give birth to an outrageous fortune. In Ireland, however, and considering our circumstances, saving would have to wait and the entire concept of acquiring wealth, or even achieving an acceptable level of financial comfort, became only a fading dream.

We never considered extravagances like a foreign holiday or the purchase of a new car. That kind of thinking was considered reckless and ill conceived. Besides, what would we do with a new car? We couldn't have afforded the insurance.

Many other people in the country lived like this as well. Very few of us owned cars and almost no one went out for a four-course meal in a fancy restaurant or hotel except on those rare occasions such as weddings, Confirmations, or funerals.

On those special moments everyone threw caution to the wind, borrowed a tidy sum from the local credit union, feasted as if there was no tomorrow, and woke up petrified the next day knowing, as they did, that they had signed a slip of paper promising that they would pay back the debt for the rest of the year at a staggering five pounds per week. Unfortunately, those were pounds that few of us could afford.

When I first stepped off the plane, with very little cash available to ward off starvation, I hadn't thought about such trivialities as being able to afford to eat every day. The thought never even occurred to me. Based on what I had seen in The Quiet Man, and those rousing scenes of large plates of boiled potatoes being thrown at equally large farmhands, I assumed that the country was awash in good fortune and I imagined that life in Ireland would be at least affordable if not luxurious.

I was wrong.

The first shock that I received was my purchase of a fourteen-inch colour television set. When Bernie and I lived in America we had bought a similar set but because the U.S. operates on 120 volts while the rest of the world seems to run on 240 volts, the damned thing wouldn't work in Ireland. It's also a fact that television signals are transmitted and received differently in Ireland (PAL in Europe, NTSC in the United States), and therefore our U.S. television would only show snow if we had brought it along. So, we gave it to my sister and knew that we would have to buy a new one once we had successfully planted our feet in our new home.

I had bought the U.S. set in a high-quality shop near East Meadow, New York, for exactly $249.99, on sale because it was an old model, but a good make despite that fact.

A few months later, and having moved into our Irish terraced council house previously mentioned, I knew that the next step to permanent residence in the country was the purchase of our own television. I walked down the pathways, looking like a drunk as I tried to avoid the broken bits of concrete, and into town. There, I entered Navan's only electrical appliance shop, a rundown establishment that looked as if it had barely survived British occupation, with optimism in my heart.

I, the sophisticated American, was going to take the Irish retail establishment by storm and strike a bargain.

The salesman on the shop floor, surrounded by broken televisions, telephones, old radios, and the other flotsam of his trade, looked up from his cashbook and tried to engage me with his best 'I'm a fellow you can trust' look as I approached.

'Good morning, my friend. And it's a wonderful day, isn't it, if the rain would stay off,'" the old fart said, and I knew he was trying to soften me up because I had just walked through a virtual downpour and he was only making small talk. Pleasantries aside, he quickly got down to business. 'And what can I do to help you? A radio perhaps to listen to the Irish football?'

'I'd like to buy a TV,' I stated firmly.

'Now would that be a used TV or a new TV?' he asked. 'Black and white or colour? With or without one of the new remote control units?'

A used television? For me? Not on your life. I thought about it for maybe two seconds and decided to go the whole hog. 'New, colour ...,' then, thinking of the lowly state of our savings account, '...but maybe leave out the remote.'

'Well, you've won the Irish Sweeps, haven't you? And isn't that marvellous!' He gazed at me as if he'd found a recently butchered fatted calf, then reached up toward a tangled mass of dusty catalogues on a shelf above his head, pulled out a book that looked as if it had never been touched, and plopped it on the counter in front of me.

Eagerly, sensing a large profit, he thumbed through its pages. He found what he was looking for and turned the page toward me. A fairly standard television stared back. It looked ordinary enough. It was black. It had a screen. It had little push-button gadgets and rabbit ear aerials for those of us that didn't have cable.

Cable in Ireland was non-existent in those days, so the rabbit ears were just fine.

'Now this will do the job for you,' he said. 'Yours for only four hundred and thirty-nine pounds, fifty pence, and quite a bargain at that.'

Four hundred and thirty-nine pounds! For a fourteen-inch colour television without remote, one almost the same as the one I had bought less than a year ago for a couple hundred bucks? This was an outrage!

I swallowed hard. 'You're certain about that? I just emigrated here from the States. Twelve months ago I bought exactly the same thing for a just over two hundred dollars. That's only one hundred and fifty pounds or so.' I poked the photo in front of me. 'And now you're telling me that this thing is going to cost me six hundred and sixty dollars?'

'That, as they say, is the price of living in Ireland.' He smiled sweetly, probably knowing that I was going to have to buy it from him or spend the rest of my days staring at a blank wall. 'Well, you could always do the H.P. You pay a fiver a week for five years and it's yours. That's what most people do.'

Back in the old days of the 1980's, many Irish citizens purchased larger capital investments — such as a twelve inch television — on the HP. Higher Purchase was, I have since learned, a despicable financing arrangement backed by most retailers that cost the poor Irish consumer over double the already outrageously inflated price of the product in question. Retailers became rich on such gimmicks while their fellow townspeople simply became poorer. I was determined to avoid H.P at all costs. I calculated quickly. At a fiver a week for five years, purchasing this un-ornate television with no remote control so that I could watch the latest episode of Dallas was going to set me back thirteen hundred quid. Back home and for the same price I could have bought an entire entertainment system complete with Dolby surround-sound, with the Beatles greatest hits thrown in for the hell of it.

No thank you.

'Why the hell is it so damned expensive?' I demanded to know. Surely this guy was trying to rip off an innocent American. I wanted to know why.

'It's the VAT, you see. The government has us there, now don't they?' he stated, thereby blaming the Irish government for everything. In some ways he was, of course, correct. As previously mentioned, the Irish government, as well as most governments in Europe, tax everything that moves and most of the stuff that doesn't. Unlike U.S. state tax, where the five or seven or eleven percent tax is added onto the product price as a separate line item, VAT is always included in the price so that the poor consumer must mentally calculate this outrageous rip-off.

The Irish government also taxes everything else that you can possibly think of and at preposterously burdensome levels: some food items, drink, petrol, houses, land, animals, cars, cigarettes, alcohol, restaurant meals, plastic bags, hay, flowers, aircraft landings, new construction, old construction, and tickets to the next Riverdance concert. Over seventy percent of every gallon of petrol goes to tax. Almost half of any new car purchase ends up in government coffers.

The average working stiff actually ends up with just under fifty percent of his or her income to buy things with. The rest goes to the government.

In the case of the television, I was paying the Irish government an astonishing £74.45 for the honour of making the purchase. Every now and then some jarhead U.S. Congressman suggests the idea of VAT. Not too long ago, for instance, I noticed in a Tampa, Florida newspaper a small article that quoted a number of U.S. officials, including the Chairman of the Federal Reserve, saying that they firmly believed that a new consumption tax would be a good thing for America. If they haven't told you, and I doubt that they have, a consumption tax is the same thing as VAT. These idiot politicians and bureaucrats believe — and rightly so — that this tax would be akin to printing money and would finance all sorts of new government salaries, perks, and other useless line items. I shudder to think about it. My advice to the American taxpayer: any member of Congress who so much as utters the word 'VAT' (or 'consumption tax' for that matter) should be voted out of office as quickly as humanly possible. VAT has to be one of the most unfair, outrageous, and inflationary taxes around.

But back to the TV: the shop proprietor gazed at me with his perfectly innocent eyes and said: 'Well, you could always buy a used one.'

Needless to say, I swallowed my dignity and wrote an Irish cheque on my new, and almost-empty, bank account. Then, for my trouble and because I couldn't afford a car, I had to carry the damned thing all the way home. However, it's fair to say that for four hundred, thirty-nine pounds, fifty pence it did after all turn out to be good value. After all of these years the bloody thing still works.

But there's good news about prices in Ireland. As mentioned elsewhere, things have changed in Ireland. Increased competition, increased production efficiencies, and increased consumer demand have all helped to put downward pressure on the prices for many Irish goods. This started with the advent of the Celtic Tiger, and as the recession took hold in late '08 and early '09, prices continue to plummet. Lo and behold, many prices continue to fall.

Today, you can buy a brand new 14-inch colour television with remote control for as little as one hundred euro! Not that anyone buys 14-inch televisions anymore. Anything smaller than a 32-inch flat screen would be considered an insult. Other electrical items have also declined dramatically in price. Everything from electric kettles to hairdryers, washing machines to electric toothbrushes, digital cameras to Personal Computers cost much less than they did in the first days of my Irish residency. While we often still pay more than most U.S. and European consumers for comparable electrical goods, I often discover that Irish prices for brown and white goods approach those of many other retailers, even when purchased in the Wal-Marts of this world.

Other consumer items have also fallen in real terms: air travel, for instance, has dropped substantially due to increased competition. An example: in 1982 a round-trip flight to London (only just over an hour by air from Dublin) could be had for the staggering sum of well over two hundred Irish pounds (approximately two hundred and fifty euro). That same flight can now cost as little as a few euro cents — plus government taxes, of course — on Ryanair. Flights to the United States, Continental Europe, and many other parts of the world have also declined significantly due in most part to increasing competition among the world's airline carriers. For instance, I recently flew to Berlin. The cost for a round-trip? Just over one hundred euro.

Package holidays (two weeks to Spain, Greece, France, or Portugal for instance) have also fallen dramatically. A place in the sun for two weeks for you and your family, staying in a lovely bolthole like the Algarve in Portugal, will only set you back just over a thousand euro, and that's all inclusive. Would you rather plan your own Continental holiday? Then do what many people do and avail of the substantial savings to be found on the World Wide Web. A few years back, I took my good wife to Sorrento in Italy. We had a fabulous stay in a hotel that was perched on a cliff, looking for all the world like some sort of monastic enclave, only with hot running water and food that couldn't be beat. The stunning views of Mount Vesuvius didn't hurt, either. I booked the entire holiday over the Internet. The total cost for four wonderful days? A few hundred euro.

Like most places in the world, communication costs in Ireland have also fallen substantially. I recently signed on for a VOIP-based telephone service (www.mytello.com). A phone call to the States from Ireland that could cost me about 50 pence a minute in 1982 now costs less than two cents a minute. So my charges now are often less expensive than a similar call made from the States to this country. The same is true for telephone calls to Continental Europe: calls to London, Berlin, Paris, Barcelona, and anywhere else I can think of are only a few euro cent a minute. That sure beats the torturous telephone prices that I experienced when I first came to this country. While it's true that we continue to call the country 'Rip Off Ireland', it is also true that due to increased competition and demand, prices on many items have actually fallen and often by substantial amounts.

But while some things have come down in price, other items here remain extortionately high when compared to the U.S., England, or mainland Europe. The cost of driving any type of car, the price of taking your love out for a good meal and a bottle of palatable wine, the ridiculous expense of purchasing simple treats such as a gas barbeque — all of these can set you back plenty when compared to many other countries. Unfortunately, Ireland continues to be an expensive place in which to set up shop. To fight back, you just have to keep your eyes open and search for those good deals.

What's So Expensive About It?

As of this writing, Ireland continues to be one of the most expensive EU countries in which to live, outdistancing even the Northern European nations in our drive to discover just how much the Irish wallet can take. Therefore, keep in mind: Ireland is an expensive place to live.

Taxes, as outlined above, continue to drive up prices. To balance its budgetary books, the government has also implemented a number of new direct and indirect taxes. For instance, a few years ago it launched property taxes which many Irish citizens, already strapped for cash, are finding simply penal.

But price increases for general goods and services are mostly responsible for the pain that we're all feeling, followed by a drastic cut in disposable income. Let me explain:

Over the past decade or so, and as the country grew richer, employees sought much needed wage increases and received them. Then local distributors and manufacturers, keenly aware of the mountain of disposable income floating through the economy, increased prices which meant that inflation increased and the working masses sought even greater wage hikes to keep up. Until recently Ireland had become a textbook case of a wage and price spiral. Prices increased, then wages went up, then prices bound ahead even further.

During the Great Recession, the wage and price spiral stopped in its tracks. Instead, those lucky enough to be still working saw disposable income drop considerably. Both private and public employees were forced to take significant wage cuts as private companies and public institutions (such as Ireland's health care organisations) struggled to rein in costs. Some employee segments including publicly-employed nursing staff, teachers, and administrators saw take home pay slashed by 20 percent if not more. And while certain general cost of living prices fell (food and clothing for instance), it became more and more difficult for the average Irish person to make ends meet.

As the economy recovered, some received wage hikes. Some didn't. But the cost of everything is again accelerating.

Today, discussing the cost of living — and how to put food on the table — has become more popular than talking about the prevarications of the weather. And Irish people have always had a great fondness for discussing the weather.

A typical discussion goes like this:

Neighbour: 'Did you hear? The government, damn their souls to hell, is going to put a tax on water.'

Me: 'What else is new? They've taxed everything else.'

Neighbour: 'But what are we going to do about it? I'm already paying through the nose for my house payment, the new property taxes, keeping the family in food, the kids in clothes, and have just about enough money left to keep the car in petrol. Mind, I hear petrol is going up by another 10 percent, so I could be running the kids to school on my push-bike.'

Me: 'Things could be worse. You could lose your job.'

Neighbour: 'Thanks so very much. Now I won't be able to sleep tonight.'

Just like any other culture, the Irish love to bitch and moan about the high cost of living here and how difficult it is to make ends meet. But they've earned the right. For years they've been the brunt of a constant stream of rip-offs. For instance: things became much more expensive a number of years ago due to the arrival of our new currency, the euro. The Irish, with much wringing of hands, traded in their old Irish pounds and pence for euro and cent, thinking that they were going to get ripped off in the process. And you know what? They were right.

It seemed that just about every retailer in this country took advantage of the currency confusion to increase prices. In many cases, and depending on the product, prices soared skyward by over twenty percent.

But we weren't the only country to suffer from price increases. Our neighbours in the so-called 'Euro Zone' did too. France, Germany, Italy, Spain... all of their citizens complained about the magical increases in the cost of everything from cheese to candy bars as they swapped local currencies for the new common one.

All that I can say is that we're only going to get one currency change in our lifetime, so retailers won't have the opportunity of again pulling the wool over our eyes. But while prices have grown higher, and though we bitch and moan, is Ireland really so expensive? Even in these COVID times?

Yes, some things really are expensive, as has been outlined above. The cost of housing and almost anything having to do with running a car seems laughably overpriced, even today. Taxation, both direct and indirect, significantly adds to the burden. But other things seem fairly equal to what you might be paying in the United States, Europe, and many other places around the globe. And some aspects of the Irish way of living remain absolute bargains.

Food: when comparing food prices here with those in the United States or the Continent I'm fairly confident that many prices are on just about an even footing. Yes, some things here are more expensive, particularly if they have to be imported. Much of Ireland's fruit and vegetables (everything from apples to oranges to potatoes — that's right, potatoes) are now imported. The small Irish population and shipping costs mean that we pay much more than others do for these items. And frankly, the quality might not be up to scratch. Today, in 2021 and due to Brexit, we also worry that new red tape and assorted bureaucratic BS will push some of those prices up even further.

That said, increased competition among food retailers has also helped to keep prices down. Lidl and Aldi, both German food retailers, launched here a number of years ago. Today, they have hundreds of stores scattered around the county offering absolute bargains on everything from biscuits to bread to dishwashing soap.

This new competition motivated existing companies (think Tesco, Dunnes Stores, and SuperValu —vthe major grocery chains here) to take notice. In reaction, these juggernauts slashed prices on many goods to maintain market share. Competition within this sector has therefore helped the Irish consumer to keep bread on the table.

Too, Irish manufacturers do not often offer 'value' packs of products like those that are available Stateside. This means that most consumers here —despite comparatively larger family sizes — pay over the odds for many consumables including baked beans, peanut butter (yes, they finally distribute peanut butter in Ireland), frozen garden peas, and other products.

But to be fair, Ireland does have its deals. The Great Recession forced suppliers to reassess pricing in order to motivate consumers to spend. Some of those deals are now still here, despite a growing economy: two for one offers, 30 percent-off promotions, and a variety of so-called 'loyalty' promotional programmes are here to stay. And other retail avenues are available that help the Irish to get more from their hard-earned money.

Open-air markets are available in most towns and larger villages. Prices for many food items, including fresh and canned foods, are lower there. Value for money is also available in bakeries. Though the price for a loaf of bread might seem more expensive than elsewhere, the taste and nutrition of the product can't be beat. Like anywhere else, you get what you pay for and you have to shop around. So, while it might cost a little more here to keep food on the table, it isn't much more.

Clothing: it's true that if you're looking for designer wear, you'll still pay through the nose. But if you're looking to simply keep yourself warm — and don't mind purchasing what everyone else does — you'll find Ireland something of a bargain. Major Irish department stores such as Dunnes Stores, M&S, and Penney's offer just about everything for everybody: kids clothes to adult, underwear to suits, it's on offer.

Local retail shops can also be a source for bargains. That said, boutiques can be rather pricey but are still a great source for the latest in fashion. And the current economic climate means that more sales are on than ever before. Men's speciality shops can be a source for great bargains in suits. I buy all of my suits here (not that I have many) and often save substantial sums when compared to the U.S. That said, an Irish friend of mine, recently returned from visits to both Europe and the States, raved about the bargains to be had in the U.S. for men's clothes when compared to Ireland. So it pays to shop around.

If you're looking for clothing bargains in Ireland, try the local drapers. A 'draper' does not seem to have a U.S. equivalent, though a typical country store back home comes close. Drapers sell just about anything that can be made of cloth: from curtains to towels to clothing. And it's great fun to sort through mountains of material in search of that special bargain.

However, you might want to hear what my wife and daughters have to say on the matter. Clothing is a way of life for them and they constantly bitch about the comparable prices of buying 'glad rags' in Ireland.

Their counsel is this: when it comes to ladies' undergarments, jeans, blouses, towels, and bed linen, the U.S. and Continental Europe win hands down on both quality and price. Every time we venture back to the States, the women in my life make a beeline to the closest strip mall in search of new supplies. If you're planning on venturing this way, perhaps visit your local shopping mall to stock up. For instance, I was planning a trip to Tampa recently and decided that, prior to departure, I'd buy myself a new pair of jeans. I priced Wranglers at our local men's shop and discovered that they wanted over fifty euro for a pair — approximately sixty-five dollars. I decided to wait and it's a good thing I did. Upon arriving back in the U.S. I visited my father's local Wal-Mart. I bought the same Wrangler jeans for a measly fourteen bucks.

That's quite a savings. Still, I don't think that we're being completely ripped-off here when it comes to clothing. Look around. You'll find good clothing at competitive prices.

Furniture: Ireland is renowned for its furniture. In fact, for ages I lived in the furniture capital of the country. As it turns out, Navan has more furniture stores per square mile than any other town in the land. You'll find the fashion in furniture to be quite different than back home not only in basic design but also in the selection of fabrics on offer. If you're into Early American you'd better bring it with you because Ireland doesn't make it. Ireland does, however, now import extensively from Europe. So, if you're from the Continent you'll find designs that are quite familiar, but at inflated prices.

Quality, like everywhere else in the world, has declined over the years, but Irish furniture company owners still take pride in their work. Spend a reasonable sum on your furniture and it will last you for years.

Electrical Equipment: as alluded to above, the cost of electrical goods in this country has tumbled in recent years and the selection has increased along with everyone else's. You can buy just about anything you can think of for reasonable prices. It's true that in some cases you might pay over the odds for the most recent technology but competition and the law of survival of the fittest quickly plays in to the hands of the consumer.

Everything from TV's to washing machines, stereo systems to freezers can now be had for no more than what you'd pay in the U.S and Europe. But be prepared to be startled at differences in design. Refrigerators, for instance, are much smaller than in the U.S. and rarely come with external ice machines (recently, however, U.S.-sized refrigerators have become available to Irish consumers but at prices much more than in the States). Garbage disposals are almost non-existent (I had to look everywhere for mine and I suspect that we're one of the few homes in the country capable of grinding its leftovers into oblivion).

Washing machines are also smaller than their U.S. equivalent and are invariably front-loaders, and the same can be said for dryers. My wife constantly bugged me to purchase a U.S.-built pair of machines for her weekly washing. It seems that some smart guy in Dublin started importing them, and has also reworked the motor to handle the difference in electrical current. This has only given my wife another excuse to attack me for more cash. But while it is true that the larger size would make her daily chores more efficient, the cost of the U.S. imports are astronomical. Too, they're so big compared to Irish machines that I'd have to rebuild the utility room. Which, of course, I eventually did and she now enjoys a set of Whirpools to manage daily washing.

As previously mentioned, Ireland operates on 240 volts so if you're coming from the States be aware that bringing along your electrical equipment is usually not a good idea. That said, people in the construction industry often use U.S. manufactured power tools, coupling them to a transformer to make the voltage transition.

Immigrants from Continental Europe have much less to worry about in that their countries already operate on 240 volts. Be aware that the only difference is in the shape of Irish electrical plugs. These conform to U.K. standards so Europeans from other countries are advised to bring along a slew of plug converters or buy new ones here and refit their appliances.

Cars and Car Insurance: anything having to do with the trusty motorised buggy is expensive here. But you can save money in a couple of ways. First, don't buy a new car. A new car purchased in Ireland can cost over thirty to fifty percent more than the price of its U.S. or European equivalent. So, consider sticking to a good used car. Remember too that because of petrol prices, cars are smaller here, compared to the U.S., anyway. Forget the benefits of a six- or eight-cylinder engine. Most European cars come with four cylinders. But better technology, including the development of sixteen-valve engines, means that our little buggies can still pack a wallop. Hybrid and fully electric cars are also making inroads. Prices, however, are still very high (despite government grants) and the infrastructure to support them (such as a national grid of charging points) is still in its infancy.

Because of the prosperity here people had been buying new cars like wildfire which means that used car lots are awash with chunks of metal that hopeful salesmen would just as soon be rid of. Many of these vehicles are only a few years old and in good shape. Make a reasonable offer and you'll soon be on the road.

Second, consider importing your car from the U.S. or Europe. While an American car and many European vehicles are obviously left-hand drive — and we drive on the other side of the road over here — it will work just fine. Parts can be a problem, but most everything is available at a modest price from the United Kingdom and they will be delighted to deliver it to you using a 24-hour shipping facility. (At least it worked this way up until Brexit. What with new regulations and tariffs, we'll have to see what happens.)

Speaking of Brexit, up until only a few months ago, many Irish bought their used jalopies in the U.K. and shipped them in due to the low prices across the Irish Sea. This is likely to change significantly due to new tariff and import duties. My suspicion is that the Irish will now look to the Continent for similar deals. The jury is still out on this one.

Four other items while I'm on the subject of automobiles:

Insurance: automobile insurance premiums in Ireland are scandalous and the insurance companies are under constant scrutiny by government watchdogs for anti-competitive behaviour and price fixing. Teenage boys are the worst hit. A few years ago, I bought my then 23-year-old son a 1.1 litre Ford Fiesta. He asked for quotes from three auto insurance companies. The best quote he received was almost two thousand euro for one year of insurance. And that was simply for fire and theft.

Needless to say, I ended up shelling out for the insurance because my son simply couldn't afford the expense. If you're young, and even if you're skilled behind the wheel, be prepared to pay exorbitantly for the privilege of driving here.

Older folk can fare much better. For instance, I'm driving a pickup truck and paying just over seven hundred euro a year for full coverage. I think that's as competitive a price as I'd get anywhere.

But remember this one piece of advice: no matter what age you are, before you come to Ireland get a letter from your present insurance company stating that you've been driving for over five years without an accident.

Why, you may ask? It's this simple. Insurance companies here offer what they call a 'No Claims Bonus'. If you have a no claims bonus you will be eligible to receive up to 70 percent off the 'standard rate' of an insurance premium. As an example: over twelve years ago I did something stupid and had an accident. It was my fault and I lost my no claims bonus. My insurance bill prior to the accident was four hundred Irish euro. Following the accident it had more than tripled. It took me five years of accident-free driving to prove to the insurance company that I was once again a safe bet. Only then did my premium rates come down.

If you are a safe driver, you have to prove it. Bring that letter from your insurance company or broker along with you when you move here.

NCT Tests: if you own a car that is four years old or older you must prove to the government that it is road worthy. For that reason, you must take your car for an NCT test (National Car Test). If you don't take your car to be tested it can be suddenly impounded. But take heart. Your car isn't the only vehicle in Ireland that must be tested.

Rather, you and every other Irish person must take their car to a specially authorised garage that will give it the once over.

These tests are, if you pardon me, another way for the government to remove money from our ever-thinning wallets, but that's the law. The cost is only thirty euro or so but once every two years you must bring down the old jalopy for its check-up. The testers put it through its mechanical paces: checking lights, tyre quality, engine fitness, and otherwise making certain that your family auto isn't going to fall apart anytime soon. And if your buggy fails the test you must have the offending item fixed before your car will be declared roadworthy. If you do not have the item(s) repaired within a fixed period of time, and you continue to drive the offending vehicle, your modest buggy can be impounded.

Most cars are so well cared for at this point, and so new, that an NCT test seems to be a waste of time. However, make sure that you comply with this procedure. Otherwise, you're breaking the law.

Road Tax: like the U.S., Britain, and Europe, everyone owning a car in Ireland pays an annual tax on his or her auto. This so-called Road, or Motor, Tax is charged based on either the size of the car's engine, or if it's a newer car, the amount of emissions it produces. For older cars, the bigger the engine the more tax you'll pay. For newer cars, the more emissions it produces, the more Road Tax you'll be hit with.

Unlike most countries in Europe and almost all States in the U.S., however, you'll be in for a shock when you get the bill. Road Tax in Ireland is expensive, with the lowest rate (for a car powered by two squirrels and a rubber band) being almost two hundred euro per annum and thereafter climbing into the stratosphere. If you want to impress your friends and neighbours with a Humvee powered by a ten-litre engine you will not only find it uncomfortable to drive on our narrow roads but you'd also better be prepared to pay the tax for such luxury.

Driver's Licences: for the first three months or so of residency (or more if you're lucky and no one finds out) your U.S. licence will work just fine over here. Thereafter, you must get an Irish driver's licence. Like the U.S. you'll have to take both a written and practical examination. I suggest paying a few quid for lessons at a local driver's training school. They know what they're doing, can significantly increase your odds of passing the test, and won't panic when you suddenly go into a fugue-state, think that you're back in Philadelphia, and choose to drive your vehicle on the wrong side of the road.

Driver's examinations are the province of the local county council so contact your nearest for more information when you get into town. Do it soon because an avalanche of new would-be drivers has put incredible pressure on the time that it takes to schedule a test. A neighbour's son recently applied for his test and was told that he couldn't be scheduled in for another eight months.

Driver's licences are still a good deal, however, with a ten-year licence costing only fifty euro or so.

Do note: if you are a North American citizen moving to this country you will not be able to get automobile insurance until you earn your driver's licence. So, plan accordingly.

European drivers coming to Ireland from other European Communities will find that their existing EU driver's licences will do just fine in this country.

The Cost of Higher Education

While it is true that Ireland can be expensive (just ask anyone who has managed to survive here), there are many aspects to this country that are still incredible bargains. One of the great bargains to be had is the incredible value of education.

If you are a citizen of Ireland and happen to have one or two — or more — children, you'll find the financial planning for their higher education something of a doddle. While the Irish may complain about it, and though the present Minister for Education seems to be doing everything in his power to make it more expensive, Ireland is almost scandalously inexpensive when it comes to the cost of obtaining a diploma.

For instance, my three children have now graduated from college. All of them went to national universities. The cost per child? Approximately nine thousand euro — about twelve thousand US dollars — per child per year. And that included almost everything: from tuition to rooms to food to books. I paid for it all, of course. If the kids wanted a beer — which isn't included in that figure — they'd have to pay for it themselves.

Why so cheap, you may ask? In Ireland, all publicly funded colleges and universities have a set Student Service Charge — somewhat like a tuition fee — of only three thousand euro per annum or so (in 2021, I might add. Don't worry... it's bound to go up). Of course, you could send your kids to a private school where the costs can increase dramatically but the quality there isn't guaranteed. Better to keep them in public universities and colleges.

What's more, that standard inexpensive fee is applied to every public institute of higher learning: from the great halls of Trinity College right down to the smaller local institutes and regional technical schools. And the cost?

As I say, in the current academic year, the cost of the student fee will be three thousand euro per annum per student. That's not bad by any standard. Not for a first-class education.

Having moved here you can of course send your child back to the U.S. or Europe for their education if that's your preference. My daughter wanted to do that. Playing to my pride, she one day asked me if it would be possible for her to attend my old undergraduate

Alma Mater. Naturally, I was somewhat pleased with the fact that she wanted to follow in my footsteps so I agreed to look into the matter.

I phoned the Admissions Department.

'Hi,' I said. 'I'm a graduate from ought-six and my daughter is thinking of attending the old homestead.'

'That's wonderful,' the Registrar stated gleefully, undoubtedly thinking of the large sum that he would see for the benefit of winning over another sucker. 'When was she thinking of starting?'

'Next year.'

'Oh, then I'd better start filling in the application form for you. Admissions are just around the corner you know. Name, please?'

'Just a second,' I stated. 'Before we get into that can I ask how much this costs?'

'What?'

'You know. The tuition and what not.'

The line hissed with static, then he cleared his throat. 'Well actually it's a mere ...' His voice trailed off into a barely audible whisper.

'Would you repeat that?' I asked.

He said it again and I almost fell out of my chair. One year of tuition and full board was going to set me back over twenty-five thousand bucks. Which meant that I was going to spend a hundred grand before she finally graduated from college.

I quietly hung up the telephone. Over the years, of course, that cost has increased. Today, I hear that my old Alma Mater charges the guts of $65,000 per annum. I still can't get over it. Having convinced my daughter that the price was out of reach, she went on to a wonderful college in the Midlands of Ireland where she majored in business studies. She seemed quite happy. And at a price much less than what I'd have paid if I'd sent her to the States, I was happy too.

Similarly expensive fees can be charged in much of mainland Europe. And while the quality of education in the U.K. or on the Continent can be wonderful, I'm completely satisfied with the quality of schooling in Ireland.

Going to college or university here can be a wonderful journey. The quality of education is first rate, and while Irish colleges might not have the breadth of courses on offer compared to many U.S., U.K. or Continental institutions, students can still select from any number of courses: everything from engineering to computer science, law to medicine, fine arts to marine biology, business and accounting to sciences and math.

For years Ireland has been renowned for the quality of its school system, as well as its graduates. This country's higher education system constantly ranks highly against colleges located in both the U.S. and Europe. For that reason, American companies and their European counterparts have long recognised the high quality of students graduating from Irish institutions, viewing this potential workforce as a resource to be tapped. A wide range of blue chip companies continue to set up or expand existing operations here because they can snap up highly qualified IT personnel, engineers, marketers, accountants, scientists, and other skilled employees. And right now, there's a shortage to meet the demand, which provides young people with excellent future prospects.

Irish colleges and universities continue to represent some of the best value for money in this country. For that reason, if for no other, I elected to stay here.

But the university system isn't the only aspect of the Irish educational structure that brings a smile to my face. The quality of education in the lower levels of the system is fantastic, too. My kids have all benefited from an educational infrastructure and teachers that are devoted to the basics. Not only are my children now literate and numerate, but I also like to think that their Irish education has prepared them well for their futures, and whatever they want to make of them.

Do I Bring Everything or Do I Leave It All Behind?

When I came here, and as already mentioned, I was broke. Consequently, I could never have afforded to bring all of our household contents. But in the past few years a number of friends of mine who have considered immigrating have always asked me a standard question: should I bring everything with me when I come or should I leave it behind?

Forty years ago, I would have suggested that they bring everything over, even the kitchen sink. But things have changed and I've reversed my advice.

In my considered opinion only bring with you those personal effects that you absolutely must have and those items that you might need to get you through the first few months. Shipping anything else will be a waste of money.

Again, remember the difference in voltages. So, if you're from America leave behind your refrigerator and washer. Your hair dryer and vacuum. Your 100-inch television and expensive, custom-built hi-gain radio.

Rather than bring everything I suggest that you sell (or store) your furniture and get rid of the lawn mower. The weight to value ratio simply means that it makes little sense to ship it all over when you can purchase similar items here at prices that are not that much different from back home. Too, your imports might attract import duties, and those taxes should be avoided at all costs.

The only thing that you might consider bringing over is your car (which I've already discussed) and your pet turtle — assuming that you can get it through customs.

Speaking of pets: Ireland is rabies-free which means that the Irish aren't particularly keen on seeing immigrants of the four-footed variety. You'll soon learn that bringing in a pet to the State of Ireland requires your friendly Poodle to spend a minimum of six months in quarantine to ensure that he or she is clear of that most rabid of diseases. Consider carefully whether or not you want your feline or canine best friend to spend such a long period of time in prison prior to release.

But if Ireland is so expensive, why come here at all? Yes, on average Ireland really is more expensive than many places within the United States and Europe. Yes, it can now cost a comparable fortune to run a car and buy a house. But despite these facts thousands and thousands of people immigrate to this country every year.

Why, you may ask, do they do such a thing? For many reasons, of course. But one of the best is quite straightforward: they come because Ireland is so beautiful.

Guideline Eight:
Come for the Pleasure of it All

Tampa, Florida

January 5, 2001

Dear Son,

It's been almost twenty years now since you bravely started to march to your own drum. After so long, you undoubtedly have learned to cope with living in such a different society. Your mother and I simply hope that you are happy with such a long-term decision.

And though we've been at loggerheads for years, I do know that you've raised some great kids. Our grandchildren have obviously benefited from what is a wonderful country.

Continuing to Love You Despite Everything,

Dad/Grandpa

P.S. It's 90 degrees under sunny skies here as I enjoy my retirement in our brand new home that cost only a few thousand bucks even though it sits on the tenth tee of the golf course. I hope that you are enjoying the rain and expensive housing in your new country. If you should change your mind about living there, and are contemplating a return to what really is your rightful home, do give us a call. We miss you...

I was talking to the U.S. Embassy awhile back and was informed by them that as of 2016 — get this — over sixty thousand citizens of the United States call Ireland home. That's right. Sixty thousand. Of those, 10,519 are permanent residents. Add to that the thousands of immigrants that have come to these shores from countries in the European Union as well as Canada, Australia, Nigeria, the Balkan states, and farther a-field, and you quickly realise the Ireland must have something very special to offer.

Certainly, all of these people couldn't be wrong. So what's so wonderful about Ireland?

My Dad's take on the country is probably a good indication. Though he was positively horrified that I had moved here with his grandchildren, placing a mere ocean between us, and though he had stopped talking to me because of this, I eventually won him around.

I did it cleverly enough, I think. In 1984 I invited him to spend some time here with us. It took some doing (including the promise of never again asking him for money) but I eventually convinced both of my parents to come out for a visit. Dad, with much grumbling, bought the tickets and they came over.

I picked up my parents from the airport on a miserable summer's morning. As usual, it was raining. It was cold. The wind was blowing. Both of my parents were not impressed. 'What a lovely country!' my mother lied as she shivered beneath her thick overcoat. 'Bah!' my father said, obviously annoyed by the trouble of crossing thousands of miles and numerous time zones in an economy seat much too small for comfort.

Dad was in a bad mood. If he had his way, he would be spending a couple of weeks on a Hawaiian beach somewhere. But because I had begged him for months to at least try it here, he had instead agreed to bask in the cool, temperate, but rainy climate of Ireland, if only for a few days.

I drove the car up and saw him standing at the airport's Arrival's curb, his summer coat turned up against the miserable weather, his facial expression fixed in that particular way that suggested he was not having a good time.

I stopped the car and grabbed their bags.

'When does the sun shine?' he asked grumpily.

'It always rains here,' I explained. 'It rains even when it's supposed to be summer. It rains so much that often we don't recognise the sun when it eventually chooses to shine on us. We stand staring up at it, saying: "Look, Maggie! What's that yellow orb in the sky?" But you'll like it despite that fact. Honest. Just try to be open-minded.'

'Open minded my ass,' he mumbled as he squeezed himself into my tiny Ford Fiesta, a car a good five sizes too small for him. He became resigned to two weeks of misery.

But my wife and I had already talked about the visit and were determined to win both of them over. Rather than stay in Navan and increase Dad's displeasure by imprisoning him in the postage stamp-sized council house with no central heating, we hit on the incredibly wonderful idea of taking him to West Cork.

West Cork, which is a region in the west of County Cork as the name suggests, is a place unto its own. I had learned about the quirkiness of that region of the country during my first job. In search of potential sales for my weighbridge company, and having decided to visit some of the more hidden places of Ireland, I had managed to become incredibly lost.

In those early days, and without the benefit of a satellite navigation system, and even though I owned a good map, I could find myself lost almost anywhere in the country on even the driest, clearest of days. This was due, perhaps, to two reasons: first, and because of history, Ireland has literally thousands of miles of roadways snaking between her shores. The second reason is due to a decided lack of adequate road signage. The Irish seem to hate signs, particularly those that would effectively help a visitor to get from A to B. While I've never been able to prove it, I suspect that the Irish rather enjoy it when foreigners get lost in their land, driving from one end of the country to the other, always on the lookout for some sort of landmark, always hoping that they will eventually get to where they want to go. Perhaps this propensity goes back to the British occupation, as a sort of defensive measure. After all, if the enemy could go astray within the confusing labyrinth of Ireland's unmarked road system, there was a good chance that they would starve to death before finding any source of succour. And that would be one less John Bull to worry about.

Even to this day Ireland's smaller roads can lack an adequate navigation system. And in that many of the smaller back roads are lined by high hedges that prevent a driver from gaining a reasonable view of the surrounding countryside (often precluding the discovery of landmarks that might instantly help you to locate yourself), and because these road can look so very similar to each other, and due to the fact that the sun is often obscured by an overhang of grey cotton clouds thereby giving the driver no clue as to whether he or she is heading north, south, east or west, you could well think that you were driving south toward Cork when in fact you are actually heading north and back to Dublin.

The fact that many roads are not signed – or are signed poorly or obscurely – make journeys interesting in that a person might never quite be certain where they really are. For instance, I might be driving down a country road trying to get to Ballydehob. Map in hand, I'll come to a crossroads and ... no road signs. I'll strain my neck hoping to take note of signage buried behind a tree or stuck on the wrong side of a barn. Not a chance. With no signage I'll have no idea whether to turn right, left, go straight ahead, or perhaps turn around and go back in the direction from which I came. The decided lack of signage can promote heart palpitations, backache, dizziness, and general frustration. But one thing is for certain: a trip is always an adventure.

Things have improved a bit over the years, but frankly it's not that much better, at least not on the back roads. Trying to give directions to a person unfamiliar with the country is akin to sending people on a journey to the dark side of the Moon. With no reference points to help them, you can only point them down a road and hope for the best.

Don't expect a map to help, either. Once lost on the internal roads of Ireland it is quite possible that you might never be found again. When travelling, it's best to pack a survival kit suitable for excursions into the interiors of Antarctica as a safeguard against possible starvation and hypothermia.

It's a wonder that more foreign visitors haven't disappeared into the Irish road system without a trace.

While Ireland is now connected by an artery of high-speed and well-designed motorways, the rural parts of this country still rely on a network composed of thousands and thousands of miles of blacktopped narrow roads, potholed though they might be. Most of these roads don't seem to go anywhere and I've often wondered why they were built in the first place. With the dawn of the Celtic Tiger the National Roads Authority, the government agency responsible for road infrastructure development, embarked on a courageous campaign to improve the state of Irish roads. But the task that they faced was monumental. The entire population of this country still expects that in a few more years the NRA will fix a problem that took generations to create. While they have managed to make great progress over the past ten years or so — Ireland now truly has miles of modern Motorway, but I assure you these roadways will never rival the Highway systems of either America, Germany or England — they still have a great deal of work left to do.

Despite millions and millions of euro poured into road development and maintenance, we in Ireland continue to enjoy some of the worst roads in Europe. We've come to joke about the fact that the potholes in Ireland can often swallow entire cars, and the subsequent wear and tear on suspension systems, gear boxes, tyres, and the people who drive them has a great deal to do with the fact that a new car in this country rarely gets more than ten years of usable life.

It's no wonder that the Irish government instituted the NCT Test.

But back to my first trip to West Cork, prior to the visit of my parents. On that particular day in the early 1980s I had turned off onto a back road and within a very few minutes felt my stomach heave as I experienced the faint possibility that I was lost. I turned down another road, then another, trying to find my way back to the main thoroughfare, but to no avail. Finally, I pulled the car over — an ancient Ford Cortina Estate that had been assigned to me by my new employer — and studied my trusty map. Not that it was going to help. Because of the lack of signage, I had no idea what road I might now be parked on, which meant that I had not the faintest possibility of determining even an approximate location of where I was. And if I had no idea where I was, I hadn't the foggiest notion of how I might get to where I hoped to go.

I had been journeying to a small farm holding owned by a certain Mr Hanratty who would undoubtedly be displeased with my inept attempt to sell him an all-singing, all-dancing forty-foot-long weighbridge and who would undoubtedly throw me off of his land with much screaming and hollering. However, motivated as I was by impending destitution and the cries of a starving family, I had decided to throw caution to the wind and try to win the sale anyway.

But having become lost, it was now highly possible that Mr Hanratty would not have to put up with my poor sales strategy, and having become lost on the narrow back roads of West Cork I began to wonder if I would ever be found and instead die of starvation.

I finally got out of the car and stood in the middle of the road, shivering slightly in the misting rain, and looked down the spaghetti-thin line of pot-holed tarmac as it disappeared over the far horizon.

No car, no person, not a living thing could be seen. I looked in the other direction. Nothing. I was not only lost, but as happenstance would have it, I had become lost in an area seemingly devoid of any breathing human from whom I might possibly get directions.

Prayer crossed my mind.

And then as fate would have it, I saw in the distance a small dot make its way over the winding roadway. The dot slowly grew until I beheld a man on a bicycle. I flagged him down thinking that I had found salvation.

As I keep saying, things have changed in Ireland since those early days of my immigration. But the sight that I beheld back then was something straight out of an Irish tourist guidebook or an old illustration about this country's colourful past.

He was an older man, possibly in his mid-seventies. His face was lined and creased and held a few days growth of stubble on his cherry cheeks but despite his age he pumped at the rickety two-wheeler of his as if his life depended on it. His black torn trousers were tied up with a length of rope possibly used for hangings back in the days of the Old IRA. In his teeth he gripped the stump of a pipe and on his head he had perched a fading pork-pie cap that had obviously seen too many days of revelry. He rode an ancient Raleigh bike that had possibly been used during the Emergency, what the Irish government had in its wisdom chosen to call those terrible days of the Second World War.

What approached me was a vision out of the mid-nineteenth century and upon seeing the distressed stranger who was waving like a madman at the side of the road, the ghostly vision coasted to a stop in front of me and dismounted.

He doffed his cap, wiped his brow, then like the vast majority of the people of Ireland, he greeted me warmly as if he viewed it as his solemn duty to help a stranger in distress.

I was saved. I would find my destination in no time, convince Mr Hanratty of the significant benefits of weighbridges, close the deal, and be back to my wife with the good news of not only a substantial bonus but the possibility of an immediate raise. And then the old man opened his mouth and I knew that I was in trouble.

You see, many of the people in West Cork speak English like everyone else in Ireland. However, they speak it in such a way as to be absolutely unintelligible to almost anyone living outside of their area. It seems that you have to be born and raised there if you're going to gain an ear for their impossible, albeit wonderful local accent.

'Ah!' he croaked. 'And a whashimish do ye hassat in de beer rood?'

I nodded, possibly looking like a lunatic, as I attempted to understand him. 'It is a fine day, isn't it?' I said, thinking that like many here he had made his opening shot at conversation with his views on the weather. 'I'm afraid I'm lost. Could you help me?'

'Nossa problem, ye weefellayou weer. Assa bein goin afer, ahye?'

I needed an interpreter but none was to be found on that rainy summer day. I raised my voice, in that moronic manner that people have when talking to someone who speaks in foreign tongues, as if more vocal volume might help my plight. 'I'm looking for the Hanratty's? Do you know them? I think they live around here somewhere? It's a large farm?'

I had involuntarily sunk into the verbal repartee of treating the old man like an idiot savant. The old man, however, didn't seem to mind at all.

After much to-ing and fro-ing, and fumbling attempts at extracting the necessary information from language that I could understand only with great difficulty, here are the directions that I finally received:

'Well, lad. If it's the Hanratty's that you're looking for you've taken the wrong road.'

He sniffed, possibly thinking that I should have stayed in bed that morning or should have at least hired a guide to lead me through the savage back-lands of the Old Country. 'What you need to do is turn around and go back to Murphy's house at the bridge. Do you know where that is? Not the old man Murphy's, now, but his Young 'Un.

'Then you turn and go down to where the pub used to be before it was burned to the ground in the fire. You'll know it because of the new growth of fabulous vegetation that's hidden the foundation. Turn left there, travel along the road for a mile or two — or maybe a few more — and you'll find the Hanratty place on the right, behind the hill that overlooks the river that you can't quite see from the road.'

'Thank you, sir,' I replied, knowing that I had come no further in finding my way to the Hanratty's.

'And toyerself, and Godbegoodtoyou, so loofarna, now. Slàn!'

With that he climbed back on his bike and tranquilly peddled off into the distance, certain to share his conversation about the idiot Yank over his next pint with friends and family.

I chose to abandon the quest for the Hanratty's and eventually found my way back to Cork City where I instantly rang my wife, who as it turned out had become nervous at my failure to ring her on our brand new telephone, and told her that she could stand-down the search and rescue operation and that I had survived the back roads of Ireland.

The only person who never forgave me for getting lost was my boss who became annoyed that I had also lost the sale.

With any luck, you will be able to survive the back roads of Ireland too. Of course, you could simply hide in the bigger cities, there to be almost certain that you will never find yourself lost, but the adventures of discovering the secrets of back-of-beyonds Ireland will certainly prove too much for you to resist.

I certainly found it difficult to resist. Years later, in 2010, I moved permanently to the rugged wilderness of West Cork — the Beara Peninsula to be exact — and have enjoyed being lost in its tranquil embrace ever since.

The Captivation of Ireland

When we decided to plan my parent's trip, we instantly determined to take them to West Cork simply because it is so beautiful there. It had been over a year since my first misdirected adventure to that part of the country, and the old man's directions. With twelve months as an Expat under my belt I had decided that I could successfully navigate the roads of Ireland to just about anywhere they might lead me.

My mother was game for anything and had no objections to the adventure. My father was more doubtful but would do anything to get out of the teensy council house. Hence, we piled most of our luggage into our tiny Ford Fiesta car and the rest into the tiny Fiat car that my father had rented and determined to start our journey.

For what seemed like days my parents experienced the jolting nightmare of Ireland's potholes as we travelled through Dublin and thence to Cork City. We turned west there, and began the three-hour trip to the coastline.

When we arrived at our destination my father looked like he was ready to have a heart attack. Either that or kill me. He was incensed at the poor roadways, stressed by the lack of courtesy that Irish drivers then (and now) showed each other, and otherwise believed that he was lucky to be alive.

'I'm getting us the hell out of here before we all get killed!'

I had thought that our plans to win him over had completely backfired.

And then he walked into the cottage.

As it turned out we had planned our trip well. My wife and I, at what then had been a fairly considerable expense, had rented a holiday cottage in Skull, a tiny village located on the south-western edge of the County of Cork. We had not had the opportunity of seeing for ourselves what the cottage — or its local environs — had on offer. The Internet at that point was a mere concept in some mad scientist's mind. Instead, we could only believe what we had seen in the tourist brochure.

Fortunately for me, what the brochure had said in print turned out to be true in reality. And it saved the fracturing relationship with my father.

The cottage was, in fact, a brand new two-storey affair with all of the mod-cons at our fingertips. It held a large kitchen, a fully furnished and very comfortable living room, a wonderfully situated coal-burning fireplace, three large and airy bedrooms complete with adjoining bathrooms, and it had central heating.

My father was impressed.

He was even more impressed when he saw the view. It was spectacular. The cottage was situated above a bay with an absolutely incredible panorama of a sun-streaked ocean, followed in the evening by positively picturesque scenes as the sun set. He watched the view while my good wife and I made dinner: Irish bacon, fresh cabbage, spring potatoes, and an apple tart that was like heaven on earth.

My father was even more impressed.

With his belly full, we decided to take a little turn around the small village. 'How about a pint of Guinness at the local pub?' I suggested innocently.

'What's a Guinness?' Dad asked. He had lived a sheltered life. In short order, we made our way down to the local establishment.

It will take another book to adequately describe the warmth of welcome that the Irish have for the thousands of visitors that travel through their country every year. The Irish are unlike any other populace that I've ever had the good fortune to know. Except for dark, dismal places that one occasionally finds here and within which the local people treat a stranger like some sort of East Asian disease, the vast majority of Irish people greet even the strangest of strangers like a long lost relative.

My father, living as he has for most of his life in the vast, faceless spaces of American suburbia, was initially quite suspicious. 'Who are they and what do they want?' he asked sceptically upon receiving a warm welcome from Joe the Publican who plied his wares from behind the solid mahogany bar. 'If he thinks he's going to take me for a fool, I'll call the Marines on him.'

'He's Irish, Dad. Give him a break.'

Joe plopped a Pint of the Best down in front of my father. Dad viewed the dark brew even more sceptically. Not knowing any better, he picked it up immediately and prepared to quaff the drink like an insipid lager.

'For God's sake, man, let it settle!' Joe squealed. Dad, of course, thought that this was the height of rudeness. But when I told Joe that my father was an American tourist and didn't know any better, and then told Dad the secrets of a correct pint of Guinness, both looked at each other with a new respect and decided to give the other the benefit of the doubt.

If you haven't experienced a true pint of Guinness for yourself, you're in for a treat. Guinness is unlike any other beer in the world. There is a fine art to both the pouring and the drinking of a pint, and if you don't obey the rules be prepared to be treated with both scorn and derision by the rest of the drinking population.

What will first strike you is the fact that a barkeep will not simply slop some beer in, pouring your pint to the top of the glass. Rather, he'll pour two-thirds of a pint and put it to the side. Don't think that you're being short-changed, however, because that good publican is only giving his art time to settle.

Though you might be parched and salivating to beat the band you will have to contain your excitement and wait while a marvellous miracle takes place. Tiny bubbles work their way to the top of the pitch-black body of the drink forming a velvety surface that looks like golden snow. This vision of foaming excellence is enough to drive a devout Guinness drinker mad.

When the barkeep believes that enough time has passed, only then will he fill the glass to the top. But even then the drinker isn't yet done waiting. He or she must keep their anticipation at bay as the drink again settles. And then, only then, may he or she embark on their journey of liquid self-discovery.

My father, a bona fide Budweiser drinker, kept looking at his watch, the second hand marching by ever more slowly, as the Publican's beady stare prevented him from taking pint in hand and downing the drink. Finally, when the glass had settled in to a perfect black body topped by a "Bishop's Collar," what every bona fide Irish person entitles that good inch of rich, golden, velvety snow, only then did the Publican nod his approval. And my father drank.

His eyes went wide. His face glazed. His body settled into a position of absolute contentment.

'What is this stuff?' he asked me in amazement.

'It's a pint of Guinness,' I replied.

'I think I'll have another.' And he did.

If you've never had a pint of Guinness, or have only had the opportunity of drinking Guinness in bottles or in lands outside of Ireland, you've probably never had a real pint. True Guinness is poured, not bottled. It is brewed in St James Gate in Dublin and nowhere else. No other drink is quite the same.

My father drank quite a few pints that night. Each pint made him more relaxed, so much so that by the end of the night he was talking like a local to his fellow drinkers. A night out in an Irish pub, with a good pint in hand and willing Irish fellows nearby anxious to share a good joke, start a sing-song, or simply discuss the events of the day, are an unforgettable experience here. If you are lucky enough to enjoy the warm friendliness of an Irish country pub, it will be a golden memory that you will always remember.

It is an even more astonishing experience if you live here. Live here and your pub can quickly become an extension of your living room. You'll get to know the locals as well as — and sometimes better than — your family. Is it any wonder that wives spend so much of their lives walking from pub to pub in vain searches for long lost husbands?

When the clock approached midnight and Joe — from his station behind the bar — sounded the last call we half carried my father into the night. It was high summer and in these northern climes a magical twilight streaks the sky's dome with an ethereal soft light. When the sun finally does shine, the summers of Ireland are something golden, as if Old Sol is reluctant to leave the open hospitality of this famed land. Honestly, on a clear evening with twilight flickering in the western skies long after you would expect it to, it is as if one could reach up and touch the face of God Almighty Himself.

My father looked up in awe.

'Isn't this a wonderful part of the world?' he said almost reverently. Awkwardly, he patted me on the back. 'Maybe you were half-right in moving to Ireland.'

I wasn't half-right. I was completely right. Moving to Ireland was one of the best decisions that I have ever made in my life.

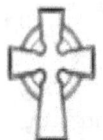

Guideline Nine: Deconstructing Your Nationalisms

Recently overheard in a local Irish hotel:

'I wish they'd bloody well shut their gobs and realise that we don't give a good damn about how much they have in their bank account.'

Anonymous Irish woman whispering to a friend about a conversation that she had with an American tourist

A number of years ago I was walking along a beach in County Louth, thirty-five miles or so north of Dublin, when an older fellow, his checked trousers and pale blue jacket announcing to the world that he was an American tourist, walked up to me and started chatting. Having detected my obvious Yankee twang, he began as so many American tourists always do when discovering that I live here and have done so for some time.

Him: 'You're an American. You're on vacation, I take it?'

Me: 'No, sir. I live here.'

Him (incredulously): 'You're kidding? How did you manage to do that?'

Me: 'Well, you know, I climbed on an airplane and came over.'

Him: 'How long have you been here?'

Me: 'Just over twenty years now.'

He eyed me suspiciously, as if I had just declared my allegiance to the Communist Party or some such thing. Then he took out a large handkerchief, blew his nose, and sniffed loudly.

Him: (sceptically): 'Seems a little unnatural, an American living abroad. (Blustering). You know I live in Levittown. That's in New York, on Long Island.'

Me. 'Yes, sir. I know.'

Him (his voice growing louder): 'I fought in Korea and got married and had three kids and worked my ass off and saved a fortune and I have over half a million bucks in my 401K and my house is paid off and I love my country and George W is a great guy and if any of these cocky Irish people even thinks to criticise the American military's right to enter the Gulf and chase down Saddam, that no good son of a bitch, I'm gonna haul off and slug them right in the nose.'

I suspect that I looked somewhat shocked at this sudden series of personal revelations but the retired soldier never blinked an eye. Instead, he stuck out a hand and assumed the role of American Mr Nice Guy, his transition as smooth and as practiced as my Aunt Wilda's homemade split pea soup. 'Well, I'd better get back. The tourist bus is leaving in five minutes. You have a nice day now.'

As he marched back along the beach all I could do was sigh.

Americans are renowned throughout the world for their honesty, loyalty, energy, determination, forthrightness, but also — dare I say it — their ability to be a pain in the ass. I'm not saying that every American wears their heart, political persuasion, and total financial net worth on their sleeve the way this guy did but I'll tell you one thing: sometimes my fellow countrymen and women can be downright embarrassing. Usually this is due to one particularly annoying trait: many of my country people don't know when to keep their mouths shut.

I'm generalising when I say it, and of course not every American behaves this way, but I've found that many Red, White and Blue tourists work hard to give the American-bashers plenty of ammunition that allows them to beat the hell out of American values.

In my experience, there are enough Americans on vacation who make it their business to blow off unwanted and inhospitable steam and otherwise seem determined to give the world a bad impression of America that I can begin to understand why Americans abroad have developed the image of bullies among those nations whom they choose to visit.

Worse, these folks will also explain in detail what they don't like about the place that they're visiting and compare that country's downfalls in detail with the privileged lives that they enjoy back Stateside. For instance, I might be enjoying a cup of coffee in a local hostelry, Jury's Inn in Dublin, for example. A tourist bus will pull up and what seems like the entire population of Lowell, Massachusetts will pour off the transport and make their way up to the bar (not that I have anything against Lowell, mind you. Many of my relatives still live in Lowell and I rather like the area).

Anyway, and upon seeing the assorted tourists trouncing like an out-of-control rugby ruck in my direction, I'll instantly cringe because I'll know what's coming. Anxious not to be associated with them, I'll sidle down toward the other end of the bar, watching in embarrassed silence as the Irish hotel employees, knowing that they are under threat of certain attack, work hard to keep these people satisfied.

First of all, the Americans will be loud. I don't mean just a little noisy. I mean *loud*. Their booming voices can often seem to pack enough decibels to break crockery on the far side of the bar. What is it about many Americans that they think they have to be heard on the other side of the Atlantic even when making simple conversation? Their entrance announced at top volume, I'll put my head in my hands and wait for the pantomime show to start. Often, the pageant will pan out something like this:

An American woman, her thick gold jewellery and magnificent Rolex watch announcing to the world that she is Jane Millionaire, might order a scone. As her tiny treasure is quickly delivered to her, she might say, 'I wanted the scone with margarine, if that's all right with you' to the overworked barkeep as he makes his initial foray into the fray.

'That's fine, madam,' he will state, making a deft recovery. 'That will be an additional fifteen cent.'

'What?' she might reply, as horrified as if she had been asked to pay for the construction of the Panama Canal. 'Fifteen cent? But in America, we don't have to pay any extra for our margarine.'

'I'm sorry, madam,' the barkeep will say, already knowing what's coming. 'But that's the policy at the hotel.'

'Frank? Frank! Come over here.' Frank, her six-foot four-inch ex-linebacker, but now retired, husband will make his way through the crowd like an incoming battleship.

'What's wrong, honey?' he'll state, instantly assuming that the poor creature whining at his elbow has somehow been assaulted and could very well be dying of knife wounds or worse. 'Is somebody bothering you?'

'Frank, this guy wants me to pay fifteen-cent for this tiny little pack of margarine. That's ridiculous. Can't you do something about it?'

Frank, towering above everyone like a living Mount McKinley, will bend down and look the poor barkeep right in the eye and start talking: 'Do you know how much we've spent in your country? Do you realise that without the United States, Ireland would be nothing? Aren't you aware that if it weren't for America the world would be a much worse place to live? Don't you know how many Irish, those poor Mick's, have come to our country and made a fortune out of us? And now you want to charge my wife fifteen cent for the privilege of buying a puny packet of margarine? Are you out of your mind?'

At the other end of the bar, I bury my head further into a newspaper, doing my best to look like one of the natives, something at which I'm now fairly adept.

The barkeep will clear his throat, realise that he's dealing with a maniac, and do his best to make light of things. 'Now, sir, we do really appreciate the fact that you've found fit to grace this country with your presence. And we have long acknowledged that America is the land of liberty and we are forever beholding to you and yours. But I am only a simple employee and the policy of the hotel is not up to me. You wouldn't want me to lose my job, now, would you sir?'

And with that, the barkeep has managed to turn the tables. The American, now believing that he has the power to make this poor guy's life a misery of future unemployment, will gloriously surrender in a show of Yankee goodwill. He'll reach deep into his pocket and put down not only the requested fifteen cent, but often an entire twenty-cent coin to boot.

'Ah, shucks. We didn't mean to make any trouble. You just keep the change. Come on, Janie,' he'll say to his now teary-eyed wife, 'let's get out of here.' Having made an emotional mountain out of a packet of margarine, the guy will steer his wife toward the exit, and the poor Irish barkeep's impression that all Americans are crazy will only have been reinforced.

As I say, those Americans of an insensitive nature can be horrible.

It seems that many of my American co-patriots will bitch and moan about almost anything: they'll take exception to the weather (I'll let you in on a secret: it rains quite a bit in Ireland and don't expect otherwise. That's why the grass is always green); they'll complain about the prices (Ireland is expensive and just because you're bringing your hard-earned currency to the country doesn't mean that you're automatically entitled to a discount); they'll laugh at the road network (though it's improving, Ireland still has thousands of miles of potholed roads to make right, and it's going to take a little time to fill in the gaps).

Americans, of course, are not the only nationality to make their opinions about Ireland known to everyone. I've encountered French, German, English, Spanish, Poles, Russians, Nigerians and many other nationalities that seem to get some sort of bizarre thrill out of putting down this country, albeit in a manner that is peculiar to their own culture. It seems that citizens visiting — or moving — here from larger countries can take a while to get used to the place. In the meantime, they risk not only embarrassing themselves but also annoying the locals by comparing Ireland to their homeland.

People from much of North American, Europe, Australia, and similar nations are used to convenience: major stores on every street corner, prices that seem reasonable, transport systems that (usually) work, roads that are paved to be smoother than a baby's bum. And when the Irish reality ends up contrasting so vividly with visitors' mystical impressions of this land — well, it's bound to cause a little resentment. Many people will vent that resentment almost instantly. While they are entitled to do so, the manner in which those views are expressed often raises the hackles among the locals.

But I'll let you in on a little secret: most Irish people really don't give a damn about immigrants' and visitors' opinions of their country. And if you're thinking of living here, and unless you want to be treated with scepticism and derision, I'm suggesting that you tone down your act.

As a rule, the Irish are a forgiving lot. They are a peaceful, pleasant, usually welcoming people. But give them enough grief and though they'll take their time about it, they'll get their own back and in some very surprising ways. For instance, a Canadian who had been assigned to live here by his company spent his entire two years doing nothing but bitch about the place: how the food stunk, the fact that the prices were so outrageous, the state of the roads, and on and on and on. His Irish colleagues and neighbours smiled at him, saying nothing for the longest time, instead only doing their best to help him cope with the situation.

Then, toward the end of his stay and with his bitching growing in ever-increasing volumes, one of his neighbours walked up with an old suitcase and suggested to the visitor that he pack his bags, shut his mouth, and kindly leave at the first opportunity.

The Canadian put in for a transfer and was gone within weeks.

If you move here, and while it may seem obvious, you are immigrating into a foreign country. Things are *different* in Ireland. Many of the roads are not up to most U.S. or European standards. The food is different, as is the health system, the education system, business methods, the way that people interact, and the manner in which we all queue for a bus.

It's a different country; a different culture. And if you take some time to quietly listen to it and absorb it, you'll soon learn to appreciate it.

When I first came here in 1982 life in Ireland was tough. I was a spoiled, twenty-something middle-classed American, used to the conveniences and finer things in life that I thought could be found only in the States. Rather than getting over it and accepting what was to be experienced in this delightful country, I began to develop a many-layered coat of resentment. I took peevish pleasure in pointing out to my Irish friends and neighbours what Ireland lacked: at that time, in 1982, Ireland lacked so many things. It was an easy target for criticism.

My Irish neighbours could only shake their heads and hope that the spoiled American would go away.

Over the years I began to appreciate the fact that Ireland had something special to offer, something that I had not permitted myself to see in the first ten years of my residency here. Because of my inability to look over my personal horizons, I made life pretty miserable for myself and almost everyone else around me.

For instance, living in Navan, County Meath as I did, the River Boyne — one of Ireland's most pleasant waterways — was right at my doorstep. Though I took many walks along its peaceful banks my mind was full of what I was missing back in the United States. The waters sang to me in a magical voice but I never heard it: all I thought about was Italian food, inexpensive telephone systems that worked, and indoor plumbing that held a lifetime supply of hot water. And I'd work myself into a lather, bitching and moaning about how much better life was on the opposite side of the Atlantic.

The Irish, God bless them, only nodded in seeming sympathy. I suspect that they knew that I'd either get over my difficulties in accepting things the way they were — or I'd leave and they'd have one less complaining American to listen to. Not that they would have minded.

If you're reading this book, you are possibly a braver and more resolute person than I was when I moved to this country. You are probably prepared to look over a far horizon toward a new dream and a new life, knowing in your heart that things will be different. Unfortunately, when I came here, my mind was not prepared to accept the reality of something so completely foreign to the land of my birth.

As a potential immigrant, what therefore do you need to do to be happy in your new life among the Irish? One of the first things that you'll need to do is to deconstruct some of your Nationalisms. Whether you are German, Italian or French; American, Canadian or Australian; Polish, Russian or Lithuanian; Nigerian, Tanzanian, or Kenyan, you will have to leave behind many of the personal perceptions that you have been brought up with in order to finally embrace the Ireland of today.

Here are some tips from a guy who almost destroyed himself and everyone else around him during his early life as an immigrant:

Listen rather than talk. You might learn something.

When I first came to Ireland, and like many of my fellow Americans, I took particular pleasure of informing every one of my absurd belief that I had been specially blessed because I had been born and bred in the United States. And I took almost perverse pleasure in running down Ireland and comparing it to the always-golden country of my birth.

I'm not sure why many Americans take this view. It's a cultural thing, I'm sure. Perhaps it's due to the fact that we say the Pledge of Allegiance at school every morning — or at least we did when I was a kid. My opinion on the matter is this: from an early age, most Americans are taught that our way of life is sacred. After all, it's what the entire population of the rest of the world should aspire to, isn't it? For what other reason would America be a land of continuing immigration? Mexicans aren't risking life and limb by illegally swimming across the Rio Grande River for nothing, are they? America seems to many Americans to be the latter day Rome, something that anyone in their right mind aspires to, no matter if they have been born in China, Ireland, France or Botswana.

Of course, this cultural parochialism isn't limited to Americans. Many British love being British and some refuse to acknowledge that the old Empire is a thing of the past. Quite a few French that I've met believe that the sun rises and sets on their country. And any number of Australians wouldn't trade their huge nation for anywhere else in the world. While cultural patriotism is understandable, it can result in problems because a limited view of the world isn't practical for those of us who, for whatever reason, end up living in another country.

And if you happen to be the type who enjoys vocalising your cultural preferences at the top of your lungs, you'll find getting along in Ireland somewhat more difficult.

Therefore, the simple practice of listening, rather than trumpeting on and on about the privileges that might be found in your particular nation, can make life much easier for everyone, particularly the new immigrant. Listen and you'll soon discover the magic of this country for yourself: the warmth of her people and their love of life; the importance that they attach to family and friends; their willingness to lend a helping hand to those in need. And though many Irish lost a bit of this cultural charm during the boom years and the craziness that was the Celtic Tiger, these values are the essence of this country's people. Now that the boom years are behind us, you'll discover that most Irish are reverting to form: once again, they are realising that it is *people*, not stuff or a vault full of cash, that makes their lives special.

To smooth the way to a settled life here, just listen: listen to what the Irish (usually!) discuss: chatting amicably over a cup of tea, their sing-song voices might touch on the problems of the teenager down the street; or the fact that Mrs Flynn is in hospital and my, but she's always been in wonderful health to this point; or about the pending wedding of a friend's friend's daughter, and how well she'll look in the gown that she bought at Cleary's Department Store at an amazingly special price.

But insist on blathering on and on like an eejit and you'll soon find that your mind will be closed to the beauty of the country and its people. Keep talking and criticising and all you'll do is piss off the locals. After all, you're a visitor to a new country, aren't you? For that reason, you might let people know that you appreciate the privilege of living here.

Ireland isn't Disney World

Maybe I'm getting old and cantankerous. I'm not sure. But one thing I can't stand anymore are those folks who think they've earned some sort of privileged status and have decided they're entitled to almost anything. Time and time again over the years, I've run in to visitors who are just plain rude. And I'd be remiss if I didn't mention that those who insist on behaving like deranged peacocks are often American. As an example:

A few years ago, I received the shock of my life when someone decided my little Irish home was a tourist attraction. Here's what happened — and what I hope visitors to rural Ireland might not replicate.

As I've already noted, I now live in Eyeries, County Cork, something of an idyllic location perched in the very southwest corner of this country. Too, I'm blessed to live in a rather 'quaint', blue cottage-like home overlooking the sea. Like most homes it has...windows. You know: those things holding glass in a large frame that let in light and let you look out. Windows have another sometimes bemusing function, of course. They also let other people look in.

Living in Eyeries as I do, we get a stream of tourists visiting the area mostly during the peak summer months. Because my home is on the only Main Street in the village, all sorts of people walk past. And many are attracted to the front window because — well, they're curious, is all. You must understand, if you look into my front window from the Main Street you can see all the way through the house, all the way to the back room ... and right out the far window which happens to overlook Coulagh Bay and the Atlantic Ocean beyond. If the weather happens to be fabulous — a rare event in this part of the world — that little view is staggering. Which means, of course, that the front window operates rather like a magnet. People walking past will glance at the window. They'll get a glimpse of what's beyond. They'll stroll up to the glass. And they'll stand there, gawping at the view.

Now if you happen to live in this house like I do, you get somewhat used to living in a fish bowl. I'll be sitting on my living room couch. I'll look up — and there gawking in to my front room will be a half-dozen tourists. Honestly, it usually doesn't bother me. Usually. But there are occasions when it does.

Particularly, when a mad woman from Texas decides to pass by. You see, on that particular day, I was in the back room of the house and chanced to walk into the living room. I looked up — and there was yet another tourist gawping in to my home's front window. Only this one was acting somewhat brazenly. This one was holding a camera. She was pointing it into the interior of my home. I realised instantly that she intended to take a photo of the stunning view out the back window. Which was absolutely fine by me. I walked toward her with a grin on my face, intending to make her welcome and perhaps even offer to take her on to my back deck. The views there are unobstructed, naturally, and she would get a much better photograph. Anyway, as I approached her, I noticed one of her fingers pointing at me. Then it began to wave madly as if some sort of insane human metronome. For a minute I couldn't figure out what she was doing. Then I realised:

I was blocking her view. She was ordering me to get out of the way because I was spoiling her picture and her fun. Even though it was my home.

I wanted to kill her.

I am not proud to say it but I lost the plot. I stormed out the front door. There, the woman was still standing at my front window, camera in hand, ignoring anything else except her intention to get the best photograph in all of Ireland. I approached her like a missile trained on its final target.

Me (steaming mad): May I ask what you're doing?

Texas Nut (ignoring me): I'm trying to take a photo. Now if you don't mind, I'd like to concentrate.

Me (gobsmacked): I beg your pardon?

She (still not turning): Look, sweetie. Can you please be quiet for a minute? I'm almost through.

Me (starting to boil): Where are you from?

She (finally turning to me): What? Why do you ask?

Me (this time it is not a question): I want to know where you're from

She (realising something just might be wrong): Why I'm from Texas, honey.

Me: I'm from Chicago. Do you understand that this is my home? You wanted me to move because I was spoiling your pathetic little picture and... this is my home? You are possibly the rudest individual I have ever met in my life!

She (still not quite getting it): Rude? Why are you angry? Everyone from Ireland is so nice. Why aren't you nice?

Me (not believing the comment): Because I'm from Chicago. I'm nice when people treat me nice. Now get away from my house. Right now, before I unleash my nasty dog (I do own a dog but he's frightened of even small things like buzzing flies and wouldn't harm a soul).

The Mad Texas Woman gave me a look that suggested I was insane. Perhaps believing I was an escapee from a mental ward, she walked carefully around me, then legged it down the Main Street.

My point here is fairly simple: rural Ireland is not Disney World yet some people don't seem to grasp that fact. The Mad Woman from Texas certainly didn't which is why she didn't have the slightest idea why I was angry. Instead, and due I suspect to her sense of undeserved privilege, she believed (as a very tiny minority do) that all the quaint little village structures — the houses and shops and wee little pubs — have been magically fabricated just for their entertainment. These slobs think they have the right to do just about anything. They touch and grasp and stand on stuff and ignore signage printed in bold lettering: PRIVATE PROPERTY. KEEP OUT. These are the rude ones. They have no respect for almost anything and from a local standpoint, quickly out-stay their welcome. The village sighs a collective breath when they leave.

I don't want you to think Mad Americans are the only ones who can behave like this. I've run into Germans, French, Dutch, Italians, English ... rude people can be from anywhere.

For instance, two years ago I caught a German couple who decided to have a picnic in my back garden. I'd been away at a meeting and came home to find Hans and Gretta perched on my sun loungers eating sandwiches. When I suggested they were trespassing, they became offended. "Gretta, we won't come back," huffed Hans. And they marched out the side fence door.

The next week it was a bus load of French. Again, I'd been at a meeting. Again, I came home — this time to find 20 people snooping around my back garden. "Ah, don't you realise this is private property?" I asked the crowd. "I mean, the entire yard is fenced in. Isn't it obvious this is a home?"

My twenty French visitors shook their heads in unison, making them look like a troupe of Parisian Puppets on parade. "Private property? It cannot possibly be private property," they muttered with a particular nastiness, and of course, they knew that I knew they were lying. They did realise it was someone's home, not that it made any difference to them. They decided to invade my back garden, uninvited, for a better view. That's all there was to it.

Or on another occasion: it was about 8:30 in the morning. I'd just taken my shower and was standing butt naked in the kitchen getting a cup of coffee. The front door, which I forgot to lock, suddenly opened. A woman who never had the chance to put a name on her nationality walked into the room.

She: "Oh I say! That's a wonderful cup of coffee I smell."

Me (absolutely flummoxed): "Ah, yes."

She: "Could I buy one, do you think?"

Me (unbelieving): "Ah, no. Ma'am, do you always barge in to someone's home without knocking?"

She (the light suddenly dawning): "This isn't a cafe, is it?"

Then she noticed the state of my dress — or rather, undress — squealed, and fled. I've kept the door locked ever since.

If and when you visit rural Ireland I honestly think you'll love it. The people are warm and inviting and will make you feel at home. You'll experience some absolutely stunning views and you'll make some wonderful memories. All I ask is this: remember that what you're seeing and visiting — those quaint little buildings that could be a part of a Disney World Main Street location — were not built by Walt & Co. They are private homes and businesses. People — including parents and kids, dogs and cats, cows and sheep — live there. Please respect that, okay? And if you decide to take a picture through someone's front window, don't wag your finger at him to get out of the way so you can get an unobstructed shot.

If you do that, you may find you have annoyed an immigrant Yank.

Forget your net worth. No one else is going to give a fig about it.

America is still the richest nation in the world. Unfortunately, you would be surprised at just how many Americans desire to let the world know that they are significant stakeholders in that wealth. Of course, I've found that this characteristic isn't limited to Americans. I've run into people from many other nations, including Ireland, who truly believe that the worth of their persona is intimately tied to how much money they have in the bank.

Honestly, you'd be entirely too surprised — and perhaps ashamed — to know how many times I have been told by an erstwhile visitor to Ireland of the significant funds that they have in their bank accounts, trusts, common stocks, and underneath their mattresses.

It's positively sickening. And often humiliating. For instance, a few years ago and while on a quick trip to Galway City, my wife and I had what turned out to be the uncertain opportunity of dining in a well-known restaurant. That night the place was packed. The waitress, a lovely local lass, asked us if we would be willing to share a table with some American tourists. We agreed.

And so we had the pleasure of meeting Jack and Jane (not their real names). They were from New Mexico. They owned a small business. That previous year, Jack's tidy company had generated a net profit of over half a million dollars, or at least that's what Jack said as he supped his large glass of extravagant wine. Between courses he also let me know his exact net worth, which happened to be just over four million bucks.

I had trouble eating my soup.

'Yep,' he wore on, 'we've done really well. We work hard. My home is already valued in excess of seven hundred thousand dollars and it's bound to go up. Pass the butter.'

Following this series of revelations, and having known this fellow for exactly fifty-four minutes, Jack proceeded to have a quiet word with our waitress. Unbeknownst to me, and despite my protests when I eventually discovered his intentions, he had arranged to pick up the tab for our dinner. He also left a substantial tip. I suspected that he thought that living as I did in Ireland, I could not possibly afford to buy my wife and I a meal, much less pay for a gratuity. I found his attitude, though certainly well intentioned, absolutely infuriating.

I'm not sure what drives these people to let me know the exact total of their personal fortune. They're not giving any of it to *me*, that's for sure, so why they insist on letting me know of every dollar, Pound Sterling and euro that they've tucked away is beyond me.

The Irish reaction to this declaration of wealth is pretty obvious: they laugh at it. In Ireland, wealth and success — even in the afterglow of a growing economy — is not to be flaunted. Though many young Irish now enjoy the luxuries of driving new BMW's and living in absurdly expensive homes, Irish culture downplays the accumulation and display of wealth. And while it is true that during the 'glory years' of the Tiger economy, Ireland and her people were fascinated by money, and conversations would invariably turn to the value of houses and stock markets and the 'good life', local culture absolutely forbids that a person disclose his or her net worth. That is between God, the bank, your accountant, and the Revenue Commissioners. For that reason, you will never, ever, *ever* hear an Irish person state: 'By the way, Florence, just yesterday, and despite the stock market crash, I'm worth five million big ones.' Unthinkable!

I suspect that the reasons for this are twofold: first, and for hundreds of years, Ireland has been a land of near poverty. People made do with what they had. Such a culture valued kin and friendship much more than it did money in the bank. The reason for this devaluation of money was simple: though some might dream of wealth, the possibility of creating wealth — except for the few landowners, business people, or English Crown-appointed officials who already possessed wealth — was impossible. Knowing that the possibility of creating a financial mountain was beyond them, most Irish developed aspirations that were obtainable: ownership of a small house and a few acres of land, perhaps; food on the table; close friends; clothes that stood up to the Irish winter. Financial wealth, though interesting, could not be obtained and even considering it was akin to fantasy — much like a glittering coin lying on the bottom of the ocean floor.

The second reason for this down-play of wealth was the Catholic Church. The Church promised a life of happiness in the hereafter and cash just didn't enter into that equation. Money, though a necessary evil, was unimportant (except when they took up the Offertory. Then it was a different story.) A life of goodness and faith, an existence that sought to love thy neighbour as thyself, was more important than any pot of gold no matter how large.

In many ways, the creation of wealth was viewed as a sin. And if you were lucky enough to have acquired it, the only way to Heaven was to give it all away. That philosophy is, in many ways, still fostered in the Irish psyche: many wealthy Irish seem positively guilty about the good fortune that they might enjoy. And though they would rather be richer than poorer, they choose not to display that wealth for fear that their neighbours would begrudge them that good fortune. Often, wealth in Ireland is hidden behind closed doors.

Even the poorest of the Irish do what they can to help others. Ireland's population gives more per capita to the world's impoverished and disenfranchised than any other country in the world. For instance, Ireland's reaction to the Indonesian Tsunami was breath-taking in its beneficence. Young, old, rich, poor — it made no difference — the Irish gave and gave and gave. By giving, the Irish not only illustrated the goodness of their hearts, but also, I think, the guilt that they continue to suffer regarding money and the deep belief — often never vocalised but always present — that the doorway to Heaven will be opened through simple generosity.

During Ireland's Tiger Economy years, those values changed a bit, at least among a large minority of people here. Shopping became a way of life, and it seemed that more people spent Sunday at the local mall than attending Mass. The eyes of many Irish were turned by the beckoning glitter of the latest must-have's: that new Gucci bag or the latest from Prada. To be honest, and for the first time in its history, many in this country began to flaunt their stuff, but that didn't go down too well here, at least with some. Oh, there was such a flap as the new values clashed with the old! 'You never saw such behaviour in my mother's time!' many would say. 'These young people, they're getting beyond themselves. There will be heartache surely!' And there was.

With the crash of the global economy in 2010 — along with the Celtic Tiger Dream — many of these would-be global economic gladiators had their dreams torn asunder. More than 10 years later, many are up to their eyes in debt, their credit cards max'd out, the financial value of their homes still underwater (despite the subsequent economic recovery). When many of these young Tigers encountered unemployment, they behaved like Prodigal Sons: they again returned toward the homespun values for which their country is renowned. Conversation today focuses on the simple, urgent topic of survival rather than the colour choice of a new Glittermobile. And while it was sad to see the newly-rich become less rich or even poor, it was also heartening to realise that the Irish are depending on the richer values of family and friends to get through life — just as the Irish have always done in the past.

Therefore, and if you come to Ireland, and especially now, the best advice is this: Don't flaunt your wealth unless you desire a constant stream of suspicion and un-stated ridicule. While you don't want to live like a peasant, shoving your neighbour's face into the bounty that you've managed to accumulate is a sure way to alienate just about everyone around you.

If you get homesick, go home for a visit before you drive everyone crazy.

When I first came to Ireland, I didn't go back to the States for a visit for four entire years. To me, it seemed an eternity. Why, you may ask? Two reasons: first, I couldn't afford the airfare. Second, I thought that I needed to prove to everyone just how tough I was, and that I could live anywhere in the world with no problem.

Well guess what? I got homesick. And because of my overwhelming yearning for my homeland, those four years of self-deprivation nearly drove myself, and everyone around me, crazy.

Homesickness is akin to some sort of deadly poison that waylays the soul and seeks to destroy it. Homesickness can embitter a person. It can make life miserable and not worth living. It causes the sufferer to compare the far away pleasures of home with the ways of their newly embraced foreign lifestyle, and often with horrible results.

My memories of those first few years now seem embarrassing and almost silly. But in talking with other immigrants, I now realise that I was going through a fairly normal cycle of homesickness and feeling sorry for myself.

In short, my behaviour had become crazed.

For instance, I would drive out to Dublin airport and spend a few hours wandering around the airport terminal. There, I would watch passengers bound for the United States, viewing them with a sense of overwhelming envy. Because I couldn't afford a ticket, I would instead pretend that I, too, was about to climb on a flight and in just a few hours I would be able to sink my teeth into a Big Mac (a ridiculous aspiration but in those days a McDonalds in Ireland was only a distant dream), or talk with distant friends, or simply stand with my feet planted on American soil.

On other occasions, I would make my way to Galway and out to the very tip of the Connemara peninsula. There, my gaze would fasten upon the Atlantic and I'd wonder just how far west I could swim before sinking beneath those frothy waves. Though North America was a mere three thousand sea miles distant, hiding beneath the sinking sun, the thought that I could make that swim seemed almost certain. Needless to say, I had sunk into a fugue-like state of depression. Had I tried such a journey I obviously would not have made it far beyond the stony beaches of Galway's coastline.

Or another instance: in those early years, the sound of an American voice could drive me to distraction. Despite the loudness of their voices and the many-coloured clothes that they chose to wear, I was compelled on occasion to make my way toward any American tourist that had the grave misfortune to come within walking distance. My good wife would become annoyed and embarrassed as I interrupted these visitors' conversations with almost any excuse to make their company. I would ask about the state of the American economy, or about the last World Series, or what the price of a hotdog was at the local fast-food joint. My occasional desire to seek people of my own kind, to smell them, to speak with them, to interact with them, helped me to remember that I was still American despite the physical distance from my country. Upon seeing these poor souls, my homesickness would come to the surface like a submerged cork seeking daylight. The sight of Americans, my fellow countrymen and woman, only made my feelings of loneliness much worse.

As you can tell, being an immigrant can be confusing. On one hand, you'll find yourself defending your new homeland (Ireland, in my case) to the hilt against any possible criticism. You will also attempt to minimise any ties that you might have with your old homeland and you'll do everything you can to truly believe that you have settled permanently in your new country.

On the other hand, you'll often find yourself illogically misty-eyed and patriotic about the country of your birth. In my case, and should an unsuspecting Irish person casually criticise the United States, I could go ballistic, defending to the death my country's right to do just about anything. Yet in the same breath, the other half of my brain will again begin to function, and I might start contradicting myself by criticising my country's actions simply because that other part of my psyche truly believes that our politicians just might be wrong.

In other words, the life of an immigrant can become dangerously schizophrenic. Don't be too worried about it if you are pulled apart at times by your emotions and the internal conflict that can arise. In talking with other immigrants, I've discovered that this state of absurd and often bemused confusion is absolutely normal.

But do take this piece of advice: if you get homesick make certain you do something about it. Go home for a visit. Immediately. If you're from the Continent, buy a cheap ticket on Ryanair and taste again the life of Paris or Brussels or wherever you happen to be from. If from the States, cruise back to your hometown. Buy yourself an extra-large pizza with everything on it if that's what you want to do. Take a stroll in the local Wal-Mart. Watch insipid American television.

Plant your feet on your native soil in order to reassure yourself that it hasn't gone anywhere, it's just that you don't happen to be living there anymore.

Then come back to Ireland. Take a big breath of clean air. Listen to the singsong voices of your neighbours. Buy yourself a pint of Guinness in your local. When you do, you'll find that life in Ireland isn't so bad after all.

Learn to drive on the other side of the road.

The Irish drive on the left-hand side of the road. That means that the steering wheel is located on the right-hand side of the car. If you happen to be from the U.K. you will, of course, find this the most natural thing in the world because you already drive cars on that side of the road. However, other people are not so fortunate. If you are from Continental Europe or the United States, do not be fooled into thinking that driving in this foreign manner is going to be simple. It is not and takes some getting used to.

Driving in Ireland is different. For one thing, you'll have to get used to roundabouts. Apparently, roundabouts were devised by an insane traffic engineer who desired to wreak havoc on unsuspecting motorists. Fortunately, most roundabouts are constructed in larger, more populated communities. But unless you plan to continue circling around them for the next hundred years or so, you'll need to learn to drive on them.

My early method was this: come to a stop ten metres or so from the roundabout. Wait for a gap to open in the traffic. Close eyes. Hit accelerator and hope for the best. Over the years I've improved on that method somewhat, though the initial methodology can still work and I have yet to have had a major accident in a roundabout.

In the early days of my driving in Ireland, how many times would I find myself turning down the wrong side of the road, gazing ahead only to find a large juggernaut bearing down on me with possibly terrifying consequences? Or, climbing into the car and looking up, wondering where the steering wheel had vanished to, then coming to the abrupt realisation that I'd sat (yet again) in the passenger seat and on the wrong side of the car?

Or reaching for the stick shift with my right hand and only finding the solid side of a door panel? Or looking for the rear view mirror on my right when it was firmly attached to the window frame on my left?

When you get to Ireland find yourself a School of Motoring. Every small town has one and you can get a list through the Golden Pages (our equivalent to the Yellow Pages) or on the web by Googling 'driving lessons' together with the name of the relevant town or city. Within only a couple of lessons (each costs approximately thirty-five euro — thirty bucks or so), you'll be driving in Ireland as if you'd been born there.

The alternative, of course, is to ask a friend or relative to teach you not only how to motor around a roundabout but also how to avoid turning on to the wrong side of the road. But employing a friend or relative for such a stressful task is only asking for trouble and could possibly lead to murder and dismemberment. A School of Motoring is the much better option.

Be open to the wonders around you.

I vividly remember the first time I flew into Ireland. It was in December of 1980. As you now know, I had met my wife on a bicycling holiday only a few months earlier, and having proposed to her within a few days of our first meeting and then having gone back to the United States to find paid employment, I had finally worked up the courage to board an Aer Lingus flight from JFK with the mission of marrying my newly found Irish beauty.

As we approached Dublin airport, and it being winter, the sun rose late that day. But I remember the magic of that approach. We came into Dublin from the west, flying only a few thousand feet above vivid green fields and between cloud-scud that seemed to have been torn from the pages of a book on Irish Celtic fantasy.

Looking out the window, watching the tiny patchwork fields glow with the blood red of the rising sun, I thought that I'd never seen anything exuding such magic in my entire life.

If you move to Ireland, you'll discover that magic for yourself. Ireland really is a place of magic. That magic may be a little more difficult to find today but it's still here. The country may now be awash with European money, U.S. multi-national companies, millions of cars, telephone systems that work, mobile telephones in every pocket, and five colour televisions in every home, but the ancient magic and folklore that have been at the core of this country for millennia is still here for anyone to find. You'll just have to look a little harder for it, that's all.

The magic of Ireland can be found in both its people and in the country that surrounds you. Try exploring any of the Gaeltacht areas — Gweedore in County Donegal for instance. Walking into a local pub, you'll hear the locals speak in their ancient Irish language and for a moment time will come to a standstill as you drink a pint and take a moment to smell the sweet smoke from the glowing peat fire.

Or drive through any county in the country — County Wicklow for instance. A twelfth century round tower will suddenly appear over the horizon looking abandoned and forlorn and seem anything but beckoning. But do yourself a favour: stop the car and discover its wonders for yourself.

Or do what I finally did in 2010: journey to West Cork and the Beara Peninsula. Here in this isolated, beautiful, and unspoiled corner of Ireland, you'll experience a level of tranquillity hard to find anywhere else. The serenity here in West Cork makes me believe that Angels really do exist, such is the healing nature of this area.

Unlike America, where each historical point of interest seems to come with its own forty-foot billboard, snack shop, tourist guide, and crowds of camera toting visitors, you may initially think that what seems to be an abandoned site only worthy of a wrecking ball wouldn't be worth visiting. If you think that way, you will be wrong.

Such sites of ancient Irish culture are fascinating and you could well have the place completely to yourself. With luck, you'll climb out of the car and that unique and never-to-be-forgotten mixture of recently expunged cow manure, clover and blooming heather will gently assault your senses. The quiet of the place may at first seem unnerving, but listen closely and you'll discover that your nervousness is the direct result of the fact that it *is* so quiet. You may hear the buzzing of bees or the lowing of sheep and cattle from a nearby farm, but that will be about it.

Then look up at the ancient, monumental round tower itself, poised like some stone-aged missile ready for lift-off, the grey of its thousand year old rocks covered with lichen, and you may experience what I have: through the mists you swear that you can hear the calls of local monks yelling in warning as the Vikings approach, swinging their battle-axes with killing on their minds, and watch as the good Brothers flee through the ancient door and up the steep spiral stairs in preparation for a bloody defence. The hairs on the back of my neck usually stand up, and I can swear that the ancient place whispers to me of its many secrets.

Ireland has so many magical places that it is pointless to try naming them all in this one book. As an example of the historic booty that can lie within a stone's throw of almost anyplace you happen to live in this country, let me use Navan and the area near it — a place I lived for over 20 years — as an example.

Within a few minutes' drive of my old house, I can find some of Ireland's most fascinating national treasures: in Kells, a few miles north, rests the massive Cross of Kells. Its long-dead stone carver brought alive a series of biblical passages, all ornately illustrated on its greying, rocky surface. In America, such a treasure would be locked away in a museum. Here, it shines with a steady magnificence from its outdoor location on the main Kells/Navan road, instantly accessible to anyone who chances by.

Or take the Newgrange Mound (or Monument) as another instance. Its immense bulk rises from the surrounding countryside like an alien spaceship. One face of it has been covered completely with white quartz that glitters knowingly in the sunlight. At its entrance, a huge rocky kerbstone, the shape of an immense lozenge, has been carved with ornate swirls, rectangles, and stony cups. Written on its surface may be an explanation of the purpose of the Newgrange Monument itself. However, and at over five thousand years old — older than the pyramids and possibly the oldest human engineered structure on the planet — that explanation has been lost forever. Once a year, and because of the delicate alignment of stones which the Old Ones raised so carefully, the rising sun lights the interior cavern with the glory of Winter Solstice thereby bringing hope that the winter might soon pass. This is a fantastic feat of ancient engineering and those lucky enough to witness it are truly blessed.

Within only a few hundred metres of this wondrous place lay Knowth and Dowth, sister mounds, both created by the same ancient engineers who developed Newgrange. While Dowth has not yet been completely examined by Irish scholars and is therefore closed to public scrutiny, the Knowth Monument has been completely rebuilt. Now open to the public, its multiple mounds and intricate stone carvings offer the visitor another example of the magic that exists in this fabled area of megalithic architecture.

Elsewhere, and only a few miles from my old home, lie: Tara Hill, the ancient seat of the High Kings of Ireland; Slane Hill, upon which Saint Patrick is reputed to have lit the Paschal Fire thereby symbolising the coming of Christianity to Ireland; the King's Belly, a megalithic burial mound and located within the very perimeter of the town of Navan; Trim Castle, originally constructed in the 12th Century and which was — and still is — the largest Norman castle in the country.

The list goes on and on: castles, monuments, burial chambers, faery forts and ring forts, ancient abbeys and monasteries, mysterious standing stones and other magical structures that have been tossed like so much fairy dust only minutes from my front door. In the United States, many of these structures would have long ago been buried beneath cement-grey parking lots. Here, the ancient archaeological artefacts form a living historical fabric that is beyond written description.

Ireland is full of such magic. If you live here, you'll have a chance to discover that magic for yourself. To do so, all you have to do is learn what many of us have never been taught: that reality isn't always what it seems, and that just beneath what our senses tell us lies a different world that perhaps — with a little luck — we may yet tap into.

De-construct your Nationalism before you do anything else.

The point of this chapter is this: while you may well be — and should continue to be — proud of your American, French, British, Norwegian, Canadian, Australian or whatever ancestry might happen to run through your veins, the things that you have learned and that you now value may actually inhibit your ability to settle happily in Ireland.

Ireland is a different country with a different culture and value system. It places less importance on how much money one earns and much more importance on what one knows and how one makes his or her way through life.

Success in Ireland is often measured not by the amount of cash one has in their bank account, but by the number of friends that a person has or the loyalty and courage a person has developed to face the difficulties in life.

For thousands of years, the Irish have faced innumerable challenges and despite everything have managed to overcome them. But the answers to their struggles have never been handed to them on a plate. The Irish have had to develop a sense of patience and humour that borders on the impossible, and a dogged determination to overcome seemingly horrendous odds to achieve what may well have seemed unreachable.

If you immigrate to Ireland, this country offers you all of these values. You may not achieve the sort of financial success that has been set out for you in America or on the Continent; you may have to redefine your own expectations and unlearn what may have taken you years to understand.

But if you can start to develop a different view of yourself, if you can begin to appreciate your own person in a new light, then you stand a much better chance of settling here.

Guideline Ten:
Despite Everything You'll be Criticised So Get Used to It

A friend of mine, another American expatriate, confided to me a number of years ago:

'I don't know about you, but since Trump's election, things have become more difficult. While most Irish realise that I am not personally responsible for American foreign policy, I can't help but feel that people are looking at me differently.

'Being an American living in a foreign land has always had its difficulties, but it's more troublesome now than it has ever been.'

Being a foreigner in a foreign land is difficult at the best of times. While immigrants to Ireland from Continental Europe, Britain, Canada, or other countries might find things a little tough, being American – particularly in the current divisive political climate – can prove daunting. For a moment, I'll focus on the possible heartache that many American citizens face when immigrating to this country – or anywhere else, for that matter.

If you are American, and no matter what political party you belong to or what your stance is regarding recent U.S. policy, make no mistake that folks such as Mr. Trump, the Tea Party, the budget log-jams caused by a fractious Congress, and the general divisiveness in the U.S are making many Irish citizens leery. Even more unfortunately, many Irish now dis-like America with a passion that borders on hatred. This is a huge sea-change in that for years the Irish looked at the United States as a bastion of freedom and goodwill. This new dislike can incorporate not only American foreign and economic policy, but also everything that America stands for.

What's sad is this turning of opinion has happened before. During the Bush administration, many here began to doubt America's intentions and for many years I had to spend time defending the United States. However, when Obama was elected, his policies (and general good nature) once again changed Irish opinion to the positive. When President Obama visited Ireland, he was greeted like a modern-day saviour due to his words of hope, and his continued belief that Ireland, following a hurtful period of recession, would find its feet again. But even during his visit, there were mutterings among my Irish friends that the United States still had much work to do to turn around the damage that had been caused to its reputation due to previous administrations' policies. It dawned on me then that it was going to take many more months — or years —for the Obama administration and their policies to overturn the destructive practices of the previous Bush presidency that resulted in global animosity and distrust of most things American.

When Trump entered office, and following four long years of his presidency, Irish opinion has swung yet again. Unfortunately, there still exist individuals here who cannot, or will not, discriminate between U.S. policies and those Americans who live here, simple folk that we are. For whatever reason American expatriates throughout the world have been caught in the crossfire of foreign hatred and distrust. Rightfully, those feelings should be directed at past (or present) U.S. administrations and not the American people who live in these foreign lands. But occasionally — even in Ireland — those destructive emotions can be vented toward Americans who live abroad.

For instance, in early 2005 and less than one hundred miles north of my then home in Navan, County Meath, two American basketball players were beaten senseless by a group of Irish thugs. The Irish manager of the Irish basketball team for whom the Americans played made two points absolutely clear: first, that the American players had done nothing to incite the incident; second, that those who had beat up the players had done so for one reason only: their victims were American.

With Trump in office and the storms of hatred that swept the United States, and also due to the former president's incessant and careless Tweets, comments, and policies, the Irish once again reconsidered their views of all things American.

American citizens living or visiting abroad became the subject of ridicule and occasional displays of violence. And that is true even in Ireland. While you might have agreed with the policies of the Trump administration (and those American politicians that espouse many of Trumps principles), it may prove positively disastrous to you or your family if you insist on shoving those policies down the throat of the average European should you live or visit here. For instance, many people on this side of the Pond disagreed with the Trump administration's decision to recognise Jerusalem as the capital of Israel. That opinion had been made known in marches throughout Ireland, England and much of the Continent.

Trump's views and policies regarding immigration (and his desire to build a variety of walls) are repugnant to the Irish. America has long been a land of opportunity. Generations of Irish took refuge there in search of survival and new economic opportunity. Due to new policies, that opinion seems no longer valid. Today, the Irish view the America — and the American people — with great scepticism and even ridicule. No longer is America thought of as holding high the values of liberty and equality. No longer is it a country where 'the huddled masses can yearn to breathe free". Trump, and his brand of 'Make America Great' nationalism, changed that.

It's enough to make many American Expat's cry. After all, we have been brought up to view ourselves as citizens of the most caring, most beneficent country on Earth. Most Americans, including many who live abroad, simply can't understand this world viewpoint of our country.

So what do we immigrants do about it?

We wait, that's what. With the election of Joe Biden, the tide of opinion is bound to change again. The Irish look at this new president as one of their own. But even Biden will have a bit of trouble overturning the dismal outlook which most Irish have of the United States. Until such time as Biden can demonstrate a renewed approach, many Expats will have to explain that most Americans still hold as sacred the rich values of welcome and inclusiveness that the United States has long been known for. Of course, if you move here and are a Trump supporter, you have the freedom to express your opinions. You can shout from the rafters that a protectionist America is a good America. However, you may find yourself with few friends. So may I make a suggestion? First, do your best to keep your mouth shut. Second, try to appear open-minded to almost anything your Irish friends may express.

No matter what your feelings regarding current world affairs, Europeans including the Irish have a right to their own opinion. Moreover, that opinion just might be correct. As you know, the Irish have long been supporters of the United States. They recognise that America offered a haven of safety during the times of the Great Hunger. Moreover, they also understand that since then, and right up to the present day, America has been a land of opportunity for millions of Irish who have upped stakes and high-tailed it to the States in search of personal fortune.

But now, that almost instinctual decision to support America is under scrutiny. Due to its long history of occupation, the Irish have always leaned toward the side of the underdog. Yet in the very recent past, America has developed a reputation that is somewhat akin to a bully.

What's sad, of course, is the fact that many American expatriates have to suffer the slings and arrows of our country's policies at all. But as difficult as it is to understand 'foreign' opinion of the United States, and assuming that you stay out of the States long enough, yet another shock awaits you: you will also have trouble understanding and communicating with your fellow Americans.

If you're gone from America long enough you will find it difficult to understand the situation at home, and the values and perceptions that your old friends, neighbours and relatives have. For instance, in my own case I discovered that I had, and continue to have, great trouble relating to the state of affairs in the United States, and the cultural divisions that are now so present in my native country. And while I will always be an American in my heart, I must admit this: I've been gone so long that I can't say I truly understand the people of my country, or what drives them, or what they aspire to.

Following the election and re-election of George W. Bush, the tragedy of 9/11, then the election of Obama as our country's first black American president, the subsequent backlash and election of Donald Trump — all which demonstrate the development of deep fissures in the psyche of the American people, a divisiveness with which I simply cannot relate to because I no longer live there. While America has always been distrustful of many segments of its own population (take race and civil rights issues for instance) I, like many, believe that America is more fractured now than at any other time since the Civil War. Today, Republicans distrust Democrats, the Christian Right distrusts liberals, abortionists distrust anti-abortionists, pro-War supporters distrust anti-War supporters, Tea Party members seem to distrust anyone who is not also a Tea Party member, Trump Supporters distrust anyone who is not a supporter of the former president... the list goes on and on.

At the root of that distrust lies a fundamental re-thinking of the very values that Americans hold to be self-evident, as well as those behaviours that are acceptable within the context of those values. Consequently, great divides now run through the United States. Those divides were made even more apparent during the most recent presidential elections: people argued their positions with anger and fists.

Below that anger, of course, is the fear that was planted in the country's people by the nefarious attack of September 11th. Americans are now afraid. That fear feeds the anger that in turn creates even more distrust as everyone searches for safety. And if you happen to be living abroad things can seem bewilderingly confusing because while you are an American you are not living in America and therefore are not directly involved in these burning discussions. Nor can you take part in, or truly appreciate, the various issues that these discussions centre upon. If you are gone many years, you simply cannot fully grasp what people are talking about or why. All that you know is that people are angry and afraid which, in turn, brings about more confusion on the part of the expatriate.

Today, my problem isn't so much how to get along with those Irish and Europeans who disagree with American policy, but rather how to get along and communicate with other Americans, my countrymen and women, whom I now no longer entirely understand.

Let me give two examples: The first occurred during the Bush presidency. At the time I was fortunate to have kept in touch with a number of American friends, usually by way of the Internet. In fact, some of those friends were responsible for this book in that they form part of the populace that kept asking me about the positives and negatives of living in Ireland.

Right after the re-election of George W, an old acquaintance and I were having a discussion via Email about a topic that I now forget. For some reason or other I made a slight jab at President Bush. The remark went something like 'I think he's a nice guy and would be a great neighbour in that he probably makes a mean barbeque. But as a president? No way!'

This wisecrack to my friend was not made in anger. Nor was it in any way a reaction to something he had said (we never discussed politics prior to this). And that tiny sentence was written in earnest: I believed then, as I believe now, that George W. Bush is a nice enough human being. And I do think that he'd make a great and interesting neighbour. And I also suspect that he makes a mean barbeque (many Texans of my acquaintance really know how to get a steak just right and I'd love to learn their secret). And yes, I never thought that he should be the American president. Despite being a registered Republican, I voted for the other guy.

In times past, such a remark might generate a small amount of intelligent discussion, a trading of points of view, etcetera, etcetera, as both parties attempted to learn and grow from contrary opinion. But this time...oh, my! The reaction was as if a ballistic missile had been fired in my direction.

My friend's subsequent Email was vitriolic, to say the least. He viewed my remark, made so innocently, as a personal attack on his values and his personal opinion of George W, whom he held, and continues to hold, in high esteem. In closing he wrote,

'...you don't like President Bush...that is fine and you are entitled to not like him...but he is not your President since you don't live here...The US is a great country and one of the most generous, always the first to rush in to help. President Bush is still my President and I will treat him with the respect of the office as I have done with the Presidents before him.'

I was flabbergasted. In one short Email he had made it clear that a) my opinion was wrong, b) my opinion was disrespectful of the Office of the President of the United States, and c) my opinion didn't matter anyway because I no longer lived in the United States.

Amazing.

Or as a second more recent, and perhaps even more painful, example: just after the Trump electoral victory in 2016, a very close American friend and I were talking politics. I made no bones about it to my friend. I did not vote for Trump and I couldn't stand the man. However, my friend — a highly educated and articulate woman — did vote for Mr Trump. For years, our relationship moved around politics with little friction. But not this time. This time, despite my efforts to move on to other subjects, she felt that I was not listening and did not understand. She insisted that I listen to her somewhat far-right, rather white nationalist born-again Christian rhetoric. Moreover, following a somewhat one-sided argument in which she determined that I could not comprehend her feelings of fear caused by possible Muslim terrorists, which she saw lurking up almost any old street in any old American city, she told me she was sending me a video CD to prove what she espoused was correct.

"You'll see," she had written at the time. "President Trump understands the threat. He will protect our values and this society from attack. He'll make America Great Again."

When I received the postal package from her, I almost died. Within the thick envelop were three videos, each featuring a far-right Christian minister denouncing the Muslim faith and demonstrating that they worshipped a false God. Frankly, the content was incendiary, when viewed through a prism of local Irish values.

Thank God Irish customs hadn't opened the envelop. If they had I might have been taken for an extremist, placed on some Irish police authority's watch list, and thought of as a potential risk.

I threw the CDs into the trash at my local recycling centre. And I've not talked to my friend since. She stepped across a boundary, one that potentially put me at risk in my adopted country. Not that she'll ever understand the possible consequences of her actions.

And perhaps more importantly, I know I will never understand her actions, either.

To me what is even more shocking is the knowledge that the attitudes held by the people mentioned above are today also held by many of my country-fellows. As far as many U.S. citizens seem to be concerned, expatriates have no inherent right to comment on U.S. policy, values, or behaviour simply because we no longer happen to live within the forty-eight contiguous States, Hawaii, or Alaska. Apparently, the Constitution of the United States makes little difference to these people. After all, I am still an American citizen, I still vote, I still pay U.S. taxes, and I still care deeply about what my country does and how my country fares. As the years go on my emotional ties to the U.S. have actually grown, not diminished.

Yet this makes little difference to those Americans who take a dim view of citizens who live abroad. I guess they figure that rather than love America, I left it. They have of course no understanding of why I moved abroad or what my current thinking is regarding the past president and his policies, or the current president and his view of the world. In that they are unlikely to read this book I doubt that they will ever come to such an understanding.

As importantly, they don't care about my opinion because — at least according to my friend quoted above — my voice does not matter.

It is an unfortunate state of affairs and it is, of course, my own fault. Because despite my own personal decision not to, I have changed since coming to Ireland. I am no longer entirely American. Instead, I have been stretched by European and Irish thoughts and values, and my thinking and beliefs have changed because of that education. Some Americans might say that I've been brainwashed but I don't think so. Instead, I have unwittingly attended the College of New Insights. At this college I have learned that the American Way isn't the only way. Instead, it is just one of many that struggle to ensure that we make it through this life in one piece, and with a modicum of happiness.

If you decide to join the hundreds of thousands, even millions of other people, from America and other countries who have chosen the life of an expatriate, be prepared for a learning process that can only result in personal growth. Your values and opinions will change. What you believe to be right and wrong will be tinged with a global viewpoint and expectations. You will learn to spell differently, talk differently, and interact with others in a manner peculiar to your adopted country. Invariably, but only if you are predisposed, your mind will be opened and a path made clear that will allow you not only to learn more about the attitudes, behaviours, and values of other nations and their peoples, but to appreciate those cultural aspects as well.

But at the same time, a part of you will continue to be rooted to your home nation.

This conflict of values — those that you have grown up with versus those that you have learned in a new land — can lead to some strange happenings: there will be times when you will not only have trouble understanding the citizens of your adopted country, but your friends and family back at home as well. It can all result in some very disquieting experiences.

Being an immigrant in a new country is hard. Being an American immigrant in today's world is even harder. But despite the occasional confusion, frustration, and caustic remarks made to you by either the citizens from your immigrant country or back home, the journey is worth it.

It is worth it because we lucky expatriates have been given the opportunity few other people are given: we can learn and grow by entirely submerging ourselves in a completely different culture. Immigration has always been part of the human experience. Historically, immigrants were most often driven from their home nations by economic disadvantage, prejudice, and similar plights to the human spirit. While these factors can still continue to drive immigration, today's immigrant often has a choice. Often, we move to new countries because we choose to. In doing so, we are presented with a tapestry of local culture from which we can truly benefit.

All we have to do is grasp the opportunity.

Guideline Eleven:
Come to the Ireland We All Love

Chicago, Illinois   July 1, 2001

My dearest Tom,

Congratulations on your nineteenth year of living in Ireland and I'm delighted that you have managed to survive in that land of the ancient Celts. As for me...well, I've discovered that retirement isn't all it's made out to be. Robert has recently been made unemployed by his uncaring multi-national company and can no longer afford to make his mortgage payments. To my displeasure, he and his screaming wife are now living with me in my two-bedroom apartment and I can't possibly get a good night's sleep.

Helen, my wife of thirty-five years, has run off with the used car salesman and the City Council is now tearing up the local park to make way for a new parking structure. My rheumatism is again acting up and I've discovered that my health insurance no longer covers the cost of medication – which will only set me back approximately five hundred dollars a month.

Other than that, things are great. I'm so glad that we've kept in touch all of these years. Do write when you have a chance.

Fondly as always,

Ronald

P.S. Would you mind if I came over for a visit next month? Do let me know if this would be convenient. I've already booked airline tickets but I will cancel them despite the high cost if you don't have room for me...R.

Living in Ireland has been a wonderful adventure, and despite the occasional temptation to bolt and run screaming back to the States I've always made the decision to stay. Time and again both friends and strangers have asked me not only why I moved here and why I choose to remain here but also what they should do when considering a similar journey.

If you have purchased this book you are undoubtedly considering, or dreaming of, a move over. I recognise that many factors may dissuade — or even prevent — you from achieving your dream. As outlined previously, getting permission from the government to remain as a permanent resident (unless you are seeking political asylum, are married to an EU national, or have parents or grandparents who were Irish citizens) really is difficult.

It's also no secret that, depending on your skills and luck, and what with the country's current economic situation, getting a job here can sometimes seem as if it would require an act of God.

And there are any number of other factors that can occasionally drive me, or any expatriate, absolutely around the twist and that might give you pause to move to this country. I've already talked about some of those: the high cost of housing, the high level of taxation, the high price of just about everything.

Then, of course, there is the constant patter of rain. It seems to rain almost all of the time in Ireland. Of course, if it didn't rain the countryside wouldn't be green which would mean that the Irish government would have to change the colours of its national flag and Aer Lingus, the flag-carrying airline, would have to completely repaint its fleet.

But it does rain. It rains constantly, persistently. It mists, drizzles, spatters, and buckets. Sometimes, usually in early May when you're thinking in your wisdom that spring must surely be on its way and that the rain will magically dry up and go away, the heavens open and the entire population begins to realise that the rest of their lives will be spent in dire need of therapy. And sometimes, it rains even longer. As I write this' I note the date on my calendar: 26 February. And I look out the window. For the record, it's an absolutely beautiful day here in Eyeries in County Cork. Of course, it's the first beautiful day that we've had in a month. Since then, it's galed, blown, whimpered, bellowed, and rained in miserable sheets, like a depressant's liquid nightmare. Make no mistake. While it's beautiful today, the rain will be back. Such is Ireland.

The constant rain drives people to distraction. It's also one of the most important reasons why many Irish usually check-out of here at least once a year and head for the Mediterranean or any other sunny climate in search of some much-needed sunlight. Local holiday companies have grown rich because of the rainy plight of Ireland. This year, due to lockdown, things will be different. Because many Irish can't get their quota of sun, I fear we'll all be committed to a looney bin. We can only pray that the sun will shine, and we'll be able to stretch out in our back gardens, isolated but at least able to relax before we're all hauled off to a psychiatric unit.

But despite the bad things I've mentioned — the prices and the rain, the government and the roads — I've stayed. I've stayed and I've prospered.

So why do I? Nothing is really preventing me from going home. To be quite honest there have been many times in the past almost forty years when I've thought of chucking it all in and heading back to the bright lights of Los Angeles, Chicago or New York.

Yet here I am and here I'll stay. And for the following very good reasons:

The Medical System —like everything else, the Irish bitch and moan about it, especially when the government seems hell-bent on turning it into an underfunded monstrosity. I understand that the U.K.'s programme is under similar pressure, but I've also heard that many other European countries have superlative medical systems. While I can't compare the Irish way with other countries on the Continent (simply because I've never lived there), I have had the opportunity of comparing the Irish system with the American Way and I like what I see over here.

First of all, it's pretty inexpensive. Yes, we pay high rates of taxes that are supposed to make it practically free, which it is decidedly not. But a stay in hospital won't turn you into a pauper by destroying whatever nest egg you've put by, as it will in the States if you don't have insurance.

But even though the Irish medical system is supposed to cost users a minimal sum, many Irish carry additional insurance cover in order to top-up standard benefits. In Ireland, medical insurance is offered by a number of companies including: Laya, Aviva, and the VHI. Annual coverage (which can cost anywhere between fifteen-hundred euro and four thousand euro for a family of four) means that people will get immediate help in the event of something major going wrong, such as the need for a bypass operation for instance. You also get to stay in a plush single room rather than sharing the ward with other patients in need of medical help (depending on the type of coverage you pay for, of course). But if you're willing to put up with waiting lists and don't mind sharing common facilities, insurance is unnecessary over here. If you don't have insurance the medical community will eventually get to you, be sure of it, but you'll have to wait in a queue. If your complaint is really serious, they'll do their best to get to you quickly.

However, standard medical costs are relatively small in comparison to the U.S. And while prices have been rising, they won't break the bank. For instance, an emergency visit to the ER ('Casualty' on this side of the Pond) costs one hundred euro. If your GP has referred you for the visit, it's free. If you need to stay overnight, the charge is €75 per day, up to a maximum of €750 in any given calendar year. Charges for other services (for instance, longer-termed stays) are calculated based on the patient's income and ability to pay.

Prices for medical assistance, like everything else, have gone up over the years. In 1982, a trip to my local GP cost a whopping three Irish pounds — about five bucks. Today, the same visit to the doctor's surgery can set back a person suffering from a common cold fifty euro or a little more. That said, and only in the past few months, the government has made things a bit easier for certain sections of the population. Today, kids age 6 and under, and anyone over 70 gets free visits to their GP. Kinda nice, huh?

But despite rising prices the quality of care is still exceptional. Here's an example which still sticks in my heart: a number of years ago, my mother came for another visit. She stepped off the airplane and to her misfortune became seriously ill. Within two days she found herself in hospital. My father — despite his positive change of heart about the country — was decidedly unimpressed. The hospital looked seedy. It needed repainting. The beds looked as if they'd come out of a World War Two Army Surplus Store. He was worried that the quality of care would reflect the decidedly worn environment of the hospital ward.

He needn't have worried. The medical community here, at least for the most part, really gives a damn about their patients. Here, you are not a number but a real live human being. Doctors and nurses work hard to make sure that you stay that way. My mother spent three weeks in our local hospital and came out with a clean bill of health. My father was impressed. So was she, come to think of it. And the bill was modest, and mostly covered by my mother's U.S. insurance.

Another example: my father lives near Tampa, Florida (alone now, in that Mom passed away a few years ago) and unfortunately suffers from a number of medical complaints. Dad told me recently that if he didn't have appropriate medical insurance his meds would cost him over one thousand bucks a month. I couldn't believe it.

Here, on the other hand, we have a drugs scheme. If, say, one of the grandkids gets sick, my daughter goes to her pharmacist ('chemist' in Ireland) and buys the necessary prescriptions. Each month she pays a maximum of one hundred and fourteen euro for drugs. Anything over that is paid for by the government.

If Dad lived here, and though the actual cost of his drugs might be one thousand dollars a month, he would only pay the maximum, or one hundred and fourteen euro a month. Not bad.

Yet another example: recently, my grandson became ill. Their family doctor, afraid that he might get worse by coming out into the cold and damp, made a house call. Yes, a house call. They still have them over here. This is just another example of the care that we are fortunate enough to receive in this part of the world.

It is true that because of the relatively small size of our population the medical community here does not have access to some of the most recent procedures that you may have access to in the States, Britain, or on the Continent. While this country is now relatively wealthy (despite the current COVID situation) it still has a far way to go to fix the problems that have plagued it since the middle of the seventeenth century. But most established procedures — such as heart surgery, transplant surgery, cancer therapy, and similar — are not only available here, but are carried out by well-trained, professional, and caring surgeons and staff. If I ever become critically ill, I will have the confidence of knowing that these people really are concerned about my welfare. And even when I'm old and grey, I will know that in the eyes of the Irish medical community I am not dispensable. They will care for me with the same consideration as anyone half my age, and who might have another lifetime to live.

The School System — if you have younger children, I suspect that you'll fall in love with the school system here. Just like I did. While I have already spoken at length about Ireland's fantastic college and university system, let me spend a little time talking about its primary and secondary education programme.

Initially, you'll be shocked by the lack of school infrastructure. Because of the historic under-funding of the Irish education system, many children are still taught in schools that can seem to date back to the turn of the century. The vast majority of schools don't have those fun emoluments that many Americans or Europeans might be used to: they don't have an indoor pool. They don't have a theatre. They don't have an indoor gym with thousands of bucks worth of weight lifting equipment. Instead, Phys Ed is usually conducted in a multi-purpose room that can often double as the school's cafeteria.

But despite the alien looking infrastructure, the quality of education is outstanding and the kids benefit from it in every way. Here, educators still concentrate on Reading, Writing and 'rithmatic. When graduating from school, Irish kids know how to read, write, add and subtract. They have sound foundations in science and the arts. They are not subjected to new-fangled ways of education nor are treated as guinea pigs and subjected to methods that might improve the learning process and which you will only be in a position to judge when your offspring fail to achieve a satisfactory Leaving Certificate, SAT or A Level score.

The majority of Irish teachers are good. They are patient. They know what they have to do. As importantly, they are still respected by the community. Irish teachers know that they are still involved in a proud profession. Unlike in the U.S., it is still a job of work that many aspire toward.

Irish schools operate differently from those in the States and much of the rest of the world. Kids usually go to school at the age of four, attending a year of Junior Infants followed by a year of Senior Infants. This is sort of equivalent to America's kindergarten.

Following that, they enter Primary School. Kids attend for six years. Then the fun really starts. Upon graduation they enter Secondary School.

Secondary School combines U.S. middle school and High School. Students attend for six years and may have an option of attending a seventh year — or transition year — that occurs following their third year. During transition year many students will work on special projects, set up a small business, or work in the community.

By the way, and for the benefit of American readers, kids in Secondary School don't call themselves Freshmen, Sophomores, Juniors or Seniors as they make their way through the years. Their progress is tracked simply by the year in school: you're a First Year Student, or Second Year, or Third, etc.

Secondary School is a real trip because students come under incredible pressure in that they know from the very beginning that at the end of their schooling they must sit what is known as their Leaving Certificate Exam. The Leaving Cert, which assesses them in all of their subjects and which they sit during one entire week of hell, causes headaches, insomnia, and nervous breakdowns not only for the students but also for their parents.

Let me explain.

Most Europeans or peoples from other global communities will understand this examination procedure. But for Americans, it will be a completely foreign concept — rather like a pressure cooker from which students hope to escape unscathed. In the U.S., as you know, successful college entrance is determined by a number of assessments: your high school grade point average, your SAT and ACT scores, and perhaps an interview or essay that is submitted to the college or university at the time of application. In Ireland, it works much differently.

While kids take exams throughout their secondary school years this sort of continual assessment has nothing to do with whether or not a student makes it into the college of their choice. Neither do Irish kids take an SAT or ACT multiple-choice exam or their equivalent, nor do they submit an essay.

Rather, they sit their Leaving Cert. This series of exams — one exam for each subject that they've studied — is the whole Chihuahua. During this single exam week, students are assessed on their entire six years of Secondary School education. Kids receive points (somewhat the equivalent to the U.S. grade point average) in relation to how well they do on each exam. The better they perform, the more points they receive. The points from all exams are then totalled.

They submit their point totals to Ireland's Central Applications Office, or the CAO, which is a centralised clearinghouse of sorts that has been set up to process college applications. As part of their submission, the students also provide their preferences regarding the college they want to attend and the major they'd prefer. Then the race is on.

Kids who have enough points make it not only into the college of their choice but also into their preferred major. Kids who don't have enough points for their first preferences must make do with something else: either their secondary choice of college or university, their secondary choice of major, or both.

Some unfortunates with low point totals don't make it in at all. These kids can either say to hell with it and get a job, or re-sit the Leaving Cert in hopes of achieving a better point total.

During the Leaving Cert season this country thrums with a feeling of tension that I've never seen anywhere else. Is it any wonder that some parents make sure that they've secreted away a week's supply of Prozac for themselves (not their offspring) prior to the examination?

Perhaps this system is unfair. I'm not sure. I do know that if I had to go through the process, I probably would never have made it into college. Here, kids who deal with pressure and who sit exams well are more likely to get through the exam nightmare in one piece, and achieve a higher points total, than those who don't.

This means that some talented kids who don't perform under pressure are left behind. Irish parents and certain government agencies including the Irish Department of Education are aware of this problem and rumours abound that the college entrance process — including the Leaving Certificate examination requirement — may one day change. But for now, students planning to matriculate into Irish colleges and universities are stuck with it.

As for Ireland's colleges and universities: I can't say enough about them. While colleges and universities in Ireland remain underfunded, these institutions of higher learning continue to produce young scholars who can survive in today's challenging world. Lecturers are first rate. Infrastructure, due to past investments, is solid and provides students with what they need to learn. Ireland has a host of exceptional colleges and universities — from mighty Trinity to National University of Ireland (composed of a number of campuses in Dublin, Galway, and Cork), to UCD and DCU, and smaller private technical colleges and universities. My son Jonathan read for his PhD in Irish at NUI Maynooth. After a few years of frustration, he now lectures in Irish at Dublin City University. His choice of college, his chosen major, and the excellence of the university system here has provided him with a wonderful career.

Despite the system's few shortcomings, I do know one thing. Irish kids are renowned for their intelligence, dedication, and quality of education. They are recognised for the foundation that they have in academic fundamentals. That's one reason why the likes of Microsoft, Intel, EMC, IBM, and a host of other American and European companies have set up shop here. They come, at least in part, for the talent and the quality of Ireland's education system.

Television — yeah, I know, what the hell does television have to do with the decision to come to Ireland? I realise that it shouldn't matter but to me it matters very much indeed. For you see, I have come to hate American television, at least what we see over here. U.S. television production companies and broadcasters must think that the entire population of America is dense. If not, why do they insist on creating inept programming, much of it of the inane reality show variety (ever seen Keeping Up with the Kardashians? I make my point) that could only possibly interest a chimpanzee? It makes no sense.

As mentioned elsewhere in this book I can't say that I like the local broadcaster's efforts that much either. RTE executives surely must have to take courses in such interesting and worthwhile subjects as 'Dumbing Down the Irish Populace' in order to land their highly paid jobs. This might explain the incredibly stupid and ignorant TV programmes that they create.

Of course, they can't create enough of this absolute rubbish to fill all of their broadcasting slots. So what do they do? They import American absolute rubbish. But fortunately, most Irish people have a secret weapon.

We can view British television — and what makes it even more pleasurable is the fact that we can do so almost for free! That's right, folks. In that the BBC, ITV and Channel Four allow their signals to beam well beyond their shores, many of us in Ireland can pick up said signal without having to pay even one penny in additional television licence fees. What a boon!

No matter where in the world you live, you're probably aware of some British programming because a wide variety of global cable stations occasionally buy their outstanding wares. British television is, for the most part, wonderful. Their drama is great. Their documentaries superb and intelligently crafted. Their news programming, unlike much U.S. and Irish television news, tries valiantly to be impartial and usually succeeds.

In that we have purchased SKY satellite programming, the Richards are now able to avail of a whole stream of British treats. My wife watches Coronation Street — the longest running soap in the history of the world — three nights a week and I hate to say it but I've also become caught up in the stories of this series' convoluted characters.

We also love to watch any number of documentaries that are rich in content, information and astounding in their choice. They are created for one real purpose: while they might entertain, they also educate. What a wonderful mission!

We enjoyed a costume drama series entitled Downton Abbey, which is fabulous. And so much more including re-runs of such UK stalwarts as Fawlty Towers, Only Fools and Horses, and The Vicar of Dibley, to name a few. The British have a wealth of history and a rich culture which they as creative fodder their often-irreverent imaginations. Their creativity finds its way into stories that are rich in entertainment values, fact, and fantasy.

If I had to go back to the U.S. I probably wouldn't buy a television at all. Instead, I'd either immerse myself in a series of good books or — if I were lucky — I'd give in and buy that telly but only if I could figure out how to beam in the wonderful television from Britain.

The People — what is it about the Irish people? After all of these years, they can still be an enigma to me and can often drive me around the twist. When asked a favour they rarely say no, nor do they say yes, but rather keep you hanging on the question; they often keep up a ruse of ignorance rather than letting you know up-front that they happen to have a doctorate in philosophy and could talk rings around you.

But the Irish really are the most welcoming people in the world. However, if you come to live here things obviously change a bit. When I initially immigrated to this country, I thought that what you see is what you get: big smiles, hearty welcomes, firm handshakes. Needless to say, I soon discovered that behind the welcoming veneer the Irish are far more complex than first appeared.

History has much to do with this complexity, as it does with most any nation of peoples. The Irish suffered subjugation by their English rulers for hundreds of years. To survive they learned to adapt to constant suffering and the yoke of terror. The Irish learned early on to keep their friends close and their enemies closer. To do so they may chat about the inconsequentials of life but what they are really doing is weighing you up, deciding what you really are and if you are worth their time. If you pass the test, the Irish will adopt you as one of their own.

The Irish people are neat. Behind a smokescreen of provincial blarney, they prove to be warm-hearted and caring. This is borne out by the fact that the peoples of this island contribute more per capita to charities than any other country in the world. They will take time out from their busy schedules for a chat and spend a couple of hours over a cup of tea expounding about your wife's Great Aunt who is suffering from an incurable malady and what a wonderful life she has had, God be good to her. And they will also take time out just to listen to you.

I love the Irish despite their warts.

In my opinion the Irish still have a sense of what is valuable in this world. Yes, like many of us, some can be sadly motivated only by money — and have adopted an underlying sense of greed — as has any other first world culture. Recently, the Irish have lost one of their most reliable anchors as the Catholic Church, struggling with lies, lechery and deceit, has imploded. It's sad to say, but Ireland is fast losing its sense of innocent spirituality that has been part of this culture since time began.

But despite all of this the Irish still seem to embrace one critical value: people are important.

Because of this, the Irish have some interesting characteristics: while family sizes are falling (until recently, the Irish had some of the largest families anywhere) those families continue to be incredibly important to them. This attitude was enshrined in legislation: for instance, only in the past few years has it become possible to obtain a divorce. However, a divorce is only granted following four years of legal separation. Consequently, warring husbands and wives are given every opportunity to kiss and make up.

Children are revered by Irish society. They are not the only peoples who feel and behave this way, of course. Like the Greeks, Portuguese, and other cultures, Ireland's folks place their children at the centre of their nation. They spend millions in caring for their children by supporting great education. They have instituted a Children's Allowance in which each month every family receives a lump sum of cash based on the number of children in a given family, which is to be spent by that family on their children. Poorer families receive government financial help for the purchase of everything from shoes to Confirmation dresses.

This attitude of care extends right down to how we look after each other's progeny. When my kids were small, and if I took one of them in a stroller to the local shopping centre, complete strangers would offer to look after my daughter or son should I have a sudden call to nature. The best thing about it was the fact that I could completely trust these people, knowing that my children would come to absolutely no harm, and might possibly enjoy the few moments of surprising company.

While the Ireland of today has changed somewhat, and though the culture of this country has become wary of the stranger, this child-centric attitude continues to exist. It comes to the fore when things go wrong.

In May 2005, a school bus loaded with over fifty kids that were being transported home from my town of Navan's secondary schools was involved in an accident. Many of the children were injured, six critically. Tragically, five fine young girls — four of them from a school that my daughters attended — lost their lives. The outpouring of grief stretched to the far corners of this country as people realised what had happened. That grief was real.

When the bodies of the young women were laid to rest, Navan literally closed down. Thousands attended the funeral Masses. Messages of condolence came from every city, town, and small village in this country. The Irish people realised that they had lost five individuals who were the future of this country, and who represented the best of Irish society.

It was a tragic event. But once again it illustrated to me just how close to their hearts the Irish hold their children.

The Irish are wonderful. They are surprising, intelligent, knowledgeable, clever, and capable. They make good neighbours, bosses and friends. When they have the time, they'll spend more hours nattering across a fence than almost any group of people I know. If you are in trouble, as I have been in the past, they will do almost anything to help if it's in their power to do so. And if it's not, they'll do what they can to sort it out despite the fact. The warmth of these people, perhaps more than anything else, keeps me here and for one very good reason. They have adopted me as one of their own.

The Countryside — a 'soft' day in Ireland is unlike any other day anywhere else in the world. By a 'soft' day, I mean one full of gentle rain... a mist that tickles your cheeks and gets in through the lining of your coat. Yes, it makes things damp. But it makes it wonderful, too.

Taking a walk through the Irish countryside on such a day is an incredibly fulfilling experience. The world seems to lie under a velvet glove that squishes beneath footfalls of low-lying grass. Sheep bleat as they graze in a nearby meadow. Small purple flowers, defying gravity and covered by tiny sapphires of water droplets, grow from the cracks in worn rock walls that are certain to be more than three hundred years old.

It's magic and difficult to describe unless you've been here.

Like a few years ago, for instance. I'd just finished a two-hour workout at a Yoga class conducted by my guru, another American expatriate. We walked out of the building — in this case a nineteenth century Great House that a local nunnery now owns and within which they occasionally permit the likes of us to congregate — and took a seat on the low stone steps that ran in front of the building.

We were sweating like pigs. My Yoga instructor can sometimes be a monster, and she had taken great joy in seeing her charges suffer through a painful workout that evening. But now the work was finished.

For a long time we just sat, saying nothing. It was after ten in the evening but it being summer the sky still reflected a soft glow from the setting sun. Countless green fields swept like a thick carpet in front of us. The air was full of the fragrance of mid-summer flowers, and we could hear the distant bellow of a bovine critter calling to its mate as it made its way home.

I looked at my friend. At that point she had been living in Ireland for four years. Every now and then she talked to me about going home. Like me, she often wondered what's greener: the sparkling excitement of America, or the green grass that stretched at her feet.

'Are you still thinking of going back to the States?' I asked her.

'Well,' she had said, breathing deeply of the tranquil air. 'Maybe not right now.'

Maybe not forever.

A strange force keeps me captive in this country. It is something that I do not entirely understand, and it is something from which I do not particularly want to escape. In these often fraught and maddening modern times, Ireland can seem a pleasant, mystical anomaly.

In Navan, living as I did for years in the Boyne Valley, the sense of the mystical was close at hand. The countryside was a patchwork of secret places littered with ancient monuments. Around every corner medieval castle keeps, round towers and falling down fortresses confront those with a keen eye. Faery rings, magical circles of trees that are said to be populated by the Auld People — the living ghosts of the Tuath de Danaan, the original peoples of Ireland — abounded. Small round hillocks that are the up-thrusts of megalithic burial mounds, the surviving markers of those who lived here so long before us, grew unmolested in the middle of deserted farmers' fields.

Within the circumference of only a few miles we had some incredible wonders at our fingertips: the five thousand year old burial mound of Newgrange, that fabulous hillock built of ancient stone and quartz, casts its magical spell only ten short miles from my front door. The Hill of Slane, where it is said that Saint Patrick once lit the Pascal Fire resides in the town by that same name and is located just up the road from us.

Five miles or less as the crow flies from my old home rested the Hill of Tara. This ancient seat of the High Kings of Ireland, crammed with overgrown ditches, dykes and foundations dug thousands of years ago, fills one with a sense of awe even though it is now nothing more than a large green field perched on a hill overlooking the valley below. It has been a holy place since time immemorial. Druids are said to have prayed to their gods of nature on this high windswept hill, and walking through the grassy tufts I swear that I can hear the whispering voices of their ancient indulgences at my back.

A few years ago, on June the twenty-first — Summer Solstice — and accompanied by my wife and son, we visited the Hill of Tara and took part in an ancient revelry that goes back thousands of years. Hundreds of people were there, many from as far away as France, Spain and, yes, America to join in the midsummer's night celebrations.

As the sun sank over the horizon a simple brazier was lit. A group of local actors took on the parts of ancient Druids to give thanks for the goodness of this country and the peace of life that can be found here. We looked to the North, East, South and finally to the West where the sun was setting over a far horizon, and we joined in a prayer of thanksgiving.

And as the light of the fire flickered its golden shadows over the people of Ireland, I looked at my family and I too gave thanks for the good fortune that had brought me to this fair country in the first place.

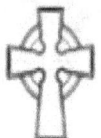

Guideline Twelve:
Holidays. Learning to Love Them Like the Irish

Chicago, Illinois   January 1, 2002

Dear Tom,

Happy New Year and I hope that you had a wonderful and restful holiday period. In that I have been unable to pay for my incredibly expensive medication I have had no choice but to re-enter the educational workforce, and am once again ploughing the furrow in hopes of making a desperate living.

While I must say that I don't particularly enjoy the job anymore, it does have its benefits. For instance, I receive plenty of time off due to the fact that the schools close over the Christmas period. I'm so very lucky, and I know that all Americans are. While we may not get as many days off as you do, we still find time to buy the presents, cook the turkey, make the pies, and even wash out our underwear between trips to and from work.

Robert rang last night. Having finally landed another job (he has at last moved out of the apartment), he called to tell me just how fortunate he has been this year. He managed to get Christmas Day off! What a treat. Of course, he had to go back to work the next day, but he was delighted by his good fortune.

You wrote that you really do enjoy your Irish holidays. Do please explain. I cannot fathom a Christmas spent outside the United States and without the benefit of the various college and professional football games. Happy Holidays,

Ronald

If I ever have to go back to the United States and live there permanently, I will never again be able to become gainfully employed simply because I have been spoiled by an Irish institution that every man, woman and child looks forward to on an annual basis: the Christmas Break.

Christmases, as with every other aspect of this country, have changed significantly over the years. When I first arrived in this country, Christmas was much more of a spiritual and religious holiday than it is today for the simple reason that no one had any money. Consequently, people might give only a single gift to each other but it was the spirit with which it was given that counted, not the monetary value. And in my opinion, that's how it should be.

With the advent of the Celtic Tiger, and the addition of vast wads of disposable income to their lives (or a multitude of over-charged credit cards), at Christmastime the Irish now do what most Americans, British, and other Europeans do: they run down to their local shopping centre, shop until they drop, and spend an incredible fortune that will only be paid down sometime in the following millennia. Unfortunately, and unless you happen to own a department store and thereby benefit from the crazed process of removing hard-earned cash from other people's pockets, spending at Christmas in Ireland has become big business.

Other holidays have their own Irish signature stamped on them: Halloween and Saint Patrick's Day, together with the Summer Holidays, are only some of the reasons why I enjoy living here so much. Let me try to help you experience living through a year of such times just so you know what you're missing, and what you could gain by moving here.

Christmas

What I love about Christmas in Ireland, and what I would miss should I ever go back to America, is rather straight-forward to report: the incredible amount of time we get off here.

Over the Christmas period, and unless you happen to be employed in the retail trade (in which case you'll be working right up until Christmas Eve and possibly can't stand the thought of another Christmas), most of the country's business infrastructure comes to a virtual standstill as it closes down. During that period of Christmas holiday magic — which can last for as long as two and a half weeks, from the middle of December through New Year's and beyond — the Irish go crazy as they begin to prepare for this time of family celebration.

During this period, I particularly enjoy putting my feet into the glowing coal fire and bemoaning the fate of my American friends, many of whom only receive Christmas Day and New Year's Day off as the sum total of their Yuletide holiday period. And while I still miss celebrating Thanksgiving with my American family — and no, the Irish don't celebrate Thanksgiving because that day of gratitude is a decidedly North American affair — we try to make up for it. Every year of our marriage my good wife did her best to put a complete Thanksgiving spread on the table including a turkey and all of the trimmings. So while I don't get to see a live broadcast of the Macy's Thanksgiving Day Parade, at least I'm stuffed to the gills by the end of the day, so I don't particularly mind.

In our house, the Christmas period usually starts in the third week of November when we put together the Christmas Pudding. This amazing concoction, made of breadcrumbs, mixed fruit, a half bottle of Guinness, and a few tumblers of Irish whiskey for added flavour, has been handed down to my wife from her mother Kathleen, who in turn received it from her mother, and so on and so forth and into ancient history.

All of the ingredients are poured into one large bowl and mixed into a batter the consistency of tar. In turn, the batter is split and poured into two smaller bowls of an elegant shape, which are finally turned into a huge pot of boiling water. There, they bubble away for hours and hours, and the house is filled with the smells of spices and fruits and a little homely magic. Everyone holds their collective breath when she finally lifts the finished Puddings from the pot. It's akin to a scene from the Christmas Carol as we wait to see if the Puddings have been properly boiled, or if they will fall asunder in a mass of half-baked breadcrumbs. Thankfully, and for all of our married life, the Puddings have always come out perfectly. They sit in our larder, growing even tastier as the whiskey and Guinness combine to turn the two-pound'ers into alcoholic-tinged Christmas treats, and I must wait until the Christmas Season is really upon us in order to be allowed to imbibe.

As November passes the country shifts up a gear. Christmas decorations and magnificently wrapped presents of shaving lotions, potted plants, and chocolates that might be just the thing for Uncle Michael or Aunt Anna have been sitting in the shops since late October, but now the Irish fly into a mad maelstrom of shopping that can leave me breathless.

They spend and spend and spend, buying everything and anything: chocolate covered nuts that seem to burst from their packaging saying please eat me; huge bushy poinsettias hallowed with red or white leaves that will be placed on windowsills or around fireplaces for that special seasonal touch; twenty speed bikes for junior that he will use to demolish the front garden; brightly coloured, elegantly presented dresses created only for that special holiday party; holiday wreaths composed of fragrant pine or waxy forest leaves of deepest green holly that will be hung on doors or used to adorn the graves of long-lost relatives who reside up at the local Cemetery; books of all types that talk of Irish poets or saints or writers that will sit quietly on some out of the way coffee table until there is nothing left to do but read them; and wax-made angels and small porcelain snowmen that decorate even the smallest corners in festive glory.

As the days pass and the deepest part of the season approaches, it also grows darker. Winter solstice bears down on us and the sun retreats even further, seeming to have abandoned the country in a dismal gloom. Going to work can be a trial: in mid-winter, the sun sets at the miserly hour of four-thirty in the afternoon and keeps its head down until almost 8:00 AM. This means that few of us working stiffs know what our homes look like for a good part of the year. But the Irish make up for this dark imprisonment by lighting welcoming coal and turf fires that keep the cold out and turn many a living room into a boiler house of cheer. Outside, the Irish have imported the custom of their American cousins and many a home is made even more cheerful with multi-coloured fairy lights that turn the towns and villages of Ireland into sparkling magic.

A few days before Christmas, depending upon the year that's in it, the country's employed population says goodbye to their colleagues at work and they all make their way home for the long winter break. Cars are parked resolutely in front of homes and possibly won't be moved for another few weeks. Last minute shopping gets started and the storefronts along the main streets are packed with eager purchasers determined to make this the best Christmas ever. All of these goodly people march home with a spring in their step, loaded down as they are with goodies for what seems to be the entire nation.

Now all of the Christmas trees go up, bought as they have been from the local fruit merchants that also stock them, crammed into the boots of cars as they hurry home to deck their own halls in holiday cheer. With Christmas finally upon us, and the shopping almost done, everyone settles into a joyous quietude filled with expectation.

And finally, it is Christmas Eve. The night is dark and often damp, and the Irish light a candle in their windows, welcoming the Christ Child to the warmth of their homes. Then, turned out in all of their finery, the good people of Ireland make their way to Christmas Eve Mass, and the churches of this country are packed-out with those who choose to give thanks to a God that has brought prosperity to their country, and to whom they can now worship freely. Following Mass, many will go home to put their houses in order. But many revellers choose to find the nearest pub and there celebrate with a quiet pint or a warming hot whiskey made fragrant with cloves and sweeter still with the addition of spoonfulls of castor sugar.

My favourite time is late that night. The roads are almost deserted. We might take a walk through our estate, enjoying the chilly silence, listening to the tolling bells of the distant church echo through the holy night, absorbing the quiet glow of golden candles standing like welcoming sentries in many a window, and sensing the comforting joy of another Irish Christmas.

Then, finally, it's off to home and the quietude of Christmas Eve.

Christmas Day itself is a time spent with family and friends. There's not much else to do anyway because most shops in the country are closed on that day. Gifts are exchanged. The Christmas turkey is prepared and stuffed to the gills with breadcrumb stuffing. The Christmas Ham is taken from its wrapper, washed, and placed into the warm oven or in a waiting pot. Potatoes, carrots and parsnips are peeled and placed in their boiling vessels, there to bang noisily as if wanting to get out.

When everything is ready, these ingredients are massed on to plates like small mountains: first a slice of ham. Then a heaping spoonful of stuffing. The carved turkey laid on top of that. Then a few foothills of mashed potatoes, possibly a couple of roast potatoes, a spoonful of peas, a measure of carrots and parsnips (mashed together and enjoying their new harmony very much), and over it all a gallon of turkey gravy.

Next to our plates rest the Christmas Crackers, those small brightly presented festive tubes that hold miniscule surprises and that help to give even more merriment to the day. Each reveller picks one up, holding an end as their neighbour takes the other. As they pull, the Cracker finally relents to the stress, gives a resounding 'Pop!', and surrenders the undersized treats that have been hidden within. Each Cracker comes with an assortment of small gifts that people haggle over throughout the rest of the dinner: miniature scissors, tiny ornaments, games, and even little books. It's serious business, this cracking of the Christmas Cracker, and the diners will play with their little games as they also pour more gravy onto their mountainous meals.

The Crackers also hold two items that are fundamental to an Irish Christmas: first up is the joke. These absolutely horrid lines are written on a slip of paper possibly no larger than those that are held in any Chinese Fortune Cookie. One after another, each dinner guest must read their joke, the object being to discover who has the worst written, and the revellers practically fall over as they laugh and guffaw at each other.

The final item of each Cracker is the paper hat. Coming in different colours, and of the 'one size fits all' variety, these ridiculous crepe paper items must be worn by all in order to prove just how ridiculous they really are to the world. It works in that everyone wears them —even my mother-in-law when she was still with us — and for a moment at least the child comes out in each of us as we laugh uproariously at each other's stylish new look.

Having gorged ourselves on the piles of turkey and ham, taking the decision to clean up later in the day, and with everyone overstuffed and not able to eat another thing, the Christmas Pudding and Christmas Cake are brought out and the poor population is encouraged to eat just a little more because of the day that's in it. The Christmas Cake, by the way, is a sort of fruity concoction made of raisins, mixed fruit peel, and other savoury delights held together by darkened flour made rich with a mixture of treacle and sugar, and over which a blanket of hard icing has been lovingly trawled.

Having laid a huge section of Christmas Pudding and Christmas Cake side by side on a china plate, many pour a large dollop of fresh cream, hot custard, or — my favourite — a great mound of brandy butter on top of these seasonal creations hoping to hide the high calorie content below.

Glass of brandy in hand, we now pile this mass of sweet on top of a stomach already bulging from the above-mentioned meal. Finally comatose, we sit for the rest of the day in large overstuffed chairs that match the countenance of our constitutions, watching mindless television and pretending that we have not fallen asleep.

But still the holiday is not ended because the next day is Saint Stephen's Day! This day, which is technically the celebration of the first Christian martyr, has little to do with the Saint and much more to do with taking it easy. However, one group of people are still hard at work: the Wren Boys.

This 'Day of the Wren' harkens back to ancient Celtic mythology which suggests that the Robin, who represented the new year and the coming spring, would peck the poor Wren — a bird symbolising the old year and the winter's chill — to death. Since ancient times, the Wren Boys would darken their faces, dress in a variety of black or mysterious clothing, and go from door to door begging for money with which to bury the newly departed Wren. If they should come to your door, they might sing the following:

The wren, the wren, the king of all birds,
On St. Stephen's Day was caught in the furze,
Although he is little, his family is great,
I pray you, good landlady, give us a treat.

My box would speak, if it had but a tongue,
And two or three shillings, would do it not wrong,
Sing holly, sing ivy - sing ivy, sing holly,
A drop just to drink, it would drown melancholy.

And if you draw it of the best,
I hope in heaven your soul will rest;
But if you draw it of the small,
It won't agree with these wren boys at all.

If they should suddenly show up at your house, the best thing to do is reach deep into your pocket and like the song says hand them at least a few bob if you know what's good for you. Otherwise, the poor dead Wren will never get a proper burial, nor will the thirsty lads get a drink. In that the pubs are open on St. Stephen's Day, that's exactly what they have in mind and why they trudge through the winter's cold singing a song that stretches back to times immemorial.

However, Christmas still isn't over. I am delighted to say that the season lasts another few weeks, right up to Little Christmas on the 8th of January, which celebrates the occasion of the Magi bringing gifts of Gold, Frankincense and Mir to the Christ Child. Thankfully, we don't have to exchange gifts on that day, and a good thing it is too, because by that point everyone in Ireland is stony broke.

Christmas in Ireland is a time of magic marked by a pre-Christmas period of frantic shopping, incredible cooking, and enough drinking to sink even the largest of vessels. While it has become commercial here, just as elsewhere in the world, an Irish Christmas is still a time for family and friends; a period of quiet reflection; a breather in the year in which we all thank our lucky stars that we're still alive and kicking.

If you come here you too can take part in an Irish Christmas. It's a holiday that I heartily recommend.

Hallowe'en

Did you know that many Irish, despite these fast-paced modern times, still believe in ghosts and things that go bump in the night? It's true, you know. And at no time is that belief more telling than on Hallowe'en night.

I happen to enjoy this holiday, celebrated as it is in Ireland. There's something wonderfully creepy about the entire affair, a time of dark magic that has not yet been borne off by the commercialism that now surrounds the American celebration. On Hallowe'en night, the dark forebodings of ancient Irish mythology seem to creep out from every darkened corner and hidden floorboard.

The Irish love a good ghost story tinged with horror and suspense, and that's exactly what you get on this night. Years ago, during my wife's childhood, Hallowe'en was a time of dark fun. At that time, pumpkins weren't available in this part of the world. Yet the Irish still had a ghostly way of marking the celebration: they would carve out a turnip, turning it into an image of spectral magic. If you have never seen a turnip — and I hadn't until I came here — you would be shocked at the amount of work it takes to carve a simple lantern from this obstreperous vegetable. Round, but packed as densely as a carrot, my father-in-law would take a knife to it, carving out its innards and creating a spooky face that would later be lit by a candle.

Meanwhile, Ireland's boys would go in search of any burnable rubbish that they could find in order to create the immense Hallowe'en bonfire that would be the highpoint of the celebration. For weeks before Hallowe'en night you could find lads loaded down with old tyres, furniture, wooden pallets, newspapers, and anything else that they could find and that might possibly burn, carrying all of this rubbish into a deserted field, and finally stacking it in a huge mound (at times, more than twenty feet high) that would be lit on that dark night.

In the years before I came here, Hallowe'en night itself was marked with small parties, tricks, ghostly stories and innocent mischief. When it turned dark the kids of the neighbourhood would sneak to each other's house, there to play 'Knick-Knock'. Essentially, they'd bang the hell out of the front door, thereby rousing the occupant within from certain sleep, then run away *pell-mell, finding some dark corner as they watched the homeowner stand at the front door with a worried expression on his or her face.*

Or they would steal front garden gates. At that time, many of the small houses (including my tiny Navan house) had fences of wrought iron that cordoned off each small front garden, one from the other. Each fence also held a wrought iron gate through which one could gain access to their home. Those gates were held down only by gravity and a series of simple hinges.

On Hallowe'en the kids would snatch the gate, laughing like Satan as they ran into the black night. Fortunately, the gates weighed so much that the kids never got very far with them, but it was an innocent way of annoying the neighbours.

Back at my wife's home, her father Luke would hold a small party for the neighbour kids. In front of the glowing fire, he would tell the ancient stories of the Banshee and how its screeching wail would foretell of a coming death to those that heard it. Invariably, the kids would be scared to death. Having finally recovered, they would play games, simple affairs such as an Apple Dunk in which the blindfolded participants were certain to get a drowning as they searched in vain for the apples that floated in the metal basin of water.

Then the lads and lasses would receive treats that might include packets of potato chips and fizzy drinks. And finally, they would cut the Hallowe'en Brack, a dense fruitcake made of flour, nuts and assorted dried and candied fruit. Within the cake, a golden ring lay waiting. He or she who received the ring with their serving of Brack would be sure to marry the next year (unlikely, of course, in that the tiny revellers were all only mere youngsters).

With the cakes and drinks taken, the kids would venture to the bonfire, watching as the older kids (with the help of adults) lit it. The fire would light up the huge pile of tinder-stuff, and within moments the world seemed to come alive in a mountainous conflagration, certain to frighten away even the most remorseless of devils.

Today Hallowe'en is celebrated much as it is in the States, though with certain twists that are truly Irish. The kids dress up as savages and ghouls and walk from door to door in search of sweets. They even screech 'Trick or Treat' when knocking boldly on the door.

But the young ghouls also manage to transport legal (and illegal) fireworks down in to the Republic from their Northern Irish brethren who can purchase these legally. For hours (and even days) beforehand, the Irish countryside comes alive with blossoming fiery displays of rockets and the boom of large explosives.

But despite the modernisation of the holiday, we still have the bonfire and the occasional ghost story. And on a dark Hallowe'en night you can still venture into the Cemetery where you can listen for the call of the Banshee, the ancient ghost of a woman who brushes her hair as she wails her call of doom, and the screech that is certain to mark a quick and uncomfortable passing for those that hear her.

But should you try it, know that you'll be venturing out on your own. Banshees are real. I know. My father-in-law told me so because he heard the wail of the Banshee and two days later a neighbour dropped dead.

Saint Patrick's Day

When coming here I had thought that St Patrick's Day just had to be the day of celebration on the Irish calendar. After all, as the patron saint of Ireland, St Patrick was bound to be a cause for a long and enjoyable bit of craic throughout the country. Having celebrated St Patrick's Day as I had in many American towns and cities in the U.S. (including Chicago, New York, and San Francisco), I had been under the impression that the occasion would be celebrated with much more hoopla in Ireland.

Like many other things about this country, I soon discovered that I was wrong.

While the Irish celebrate St Patrick's Day in a certain Irish style, it is very unlike the celebrations of their American cousins. In fact, the Irish look at the American methods of enjoying that holiday with considerable bemusement. An American St Patrick's Day includes ornate parades and enough green to paint a mile-wide line between New York and the Moon. As you possibly know, everything seems to be green on the U.S. version of the day: green beer, green bagels, and rivers painted a peculiar shade of green. The Irish can only giggle at America's over-wrought efforts.

In Ireland, St Patrick's Day is a much more reserved affair. As a national holiday, everyone has the day off, which is a good thing in that it allows many more people to run to the local pub. But the Irish would never put a green tinge in their beer: that would be a sin and a waste of a pleasurable pint. Nor do they paint their rivers green, nor fill their bellies with green bagels; they do not hang signs that say 'Kiss me, I'm Irish!', nor adorn their homes with green outdoor lights.

Instead, the Irish celebrate in a much more homely fashion. First, they troop to the stores, there purchasing live green shamrock which they plant firmly in the nearest buttonhole. Many put bacon and cabbage on the boil, the cooking process of which fills their homes with the scent of salt and vinegar.

In that Saint Patrick's Day occurs during the season of Lent, and because many Irish give up the drink for forty days during that period, the Day is also a time of leniency because many will cast off their abstinence and head to the local establishment for a few well-deserved pints of black if only for the day. 'Drowning the Shamrock' on St Patrick's Day is a national institution, and one that can be enjoyed by anyone old enough — or brazen enough — to sidle up to their local bar.

If you live in a larger village or town, the next stop is the local parade. On this day hundreds of such parades take place all over the country. In most places, the St Patrick's Day parade committee will consider just about anything to add to the parade and hence make it more colourful. Therefore, you might spend an hour in the damp cold of March 17th watching as what seems to be the entire county marches down the main road. When I lived in Navan, there was the Ceili band from Athboy, the Pipers from Kells, the accordion players from Kentstown, almost all of them dressed in green, orange and white. Local clubs, holding their broad and colourful banners high, stepped proudly down the street as neighbours called out in welcome or with catcalls, depending on their predisposition.

Clowns might come next, throwing sweets to the children that nestled protectively between their parents. Farm tractors followed, each towing a small float created by local schools or businesses, their owners perched precariously on their uneven surfaces, freezing in the damp.

This mad spectacle will wind its way around the town, finally ending up in the village square. There, a forty-foot flatbed trailer will have been decked out in the green and gold of Ireland. On it, a Ceili band — an assortment of pipers and fiddlers — will play madly as dancers slap the floor in imitation of the much larger Riverdance.

The pubs, now well opened, will be serving pints and small ones of Irish whiskey to beat the band. Locals will wander out clutching their large glasses, bravely pushing away the cold by wearing thick anoraks and topcoats.

When the parade is finished, we'll all troop home, there to enjoy the meal of bacon, cabbage and spuds. If we can fit it in there might be a small slice of apple tart and cream together with a cup of tea. After that perhaps we'll all march back down to the pub to finish off the day in a particularly Irish manner: drinking a pint while listening to a small group of fiddlers play rebel songs, their voices reaching to the sky.

Saint Patrick's Day is the national holiday. Yet it also represents something else: the coming of Christianity to this country. And though we Irish can seem to forget it, we recognise that Patrick in many ways defines this small island. It was he, after all, who helped to bring the light of hope into Ireland. And despite our somewhat drunken revelry, that coming of the light is still remembered.

On the Hill of Slane, only a few miles distant from my old home, a group of people will light the Pascal fire, a small bonfire within which burns the Irish hope for a future of goodness. Hundreds of years ago a similar fire was lit, purportedly by Patrick himself. On his Day we replicate that simple gesture, acknowledging the freedom that this country now enjoys after so many years of servitude.

And the Summer Holidays

If you decide to live in this country, one of the first things you'll discover is the fact that the Irish — as well as most Europeans — have something in vast quantities that Americans and many other nationalities can only envy. And that something is holiday time.

In Ireland, employers are legally obligated to give their employees almost a month of paid annual holiday leave. If you work hard to properly string these days of freedom together, you will not only be able to take a considerable amount of time off over the Christmas period, but will also be able to manage two whole weeks off over the summer. And the joy of it all!

As already mentioned, the Irish winters are often an impossibly horrid period of dark nights when we all believe that the sun has deserted us forever. However, as the winter turns to spring and then to summer, the sun reverses itself. Sun up is so early that it surprises even the earliest of early birds. Twilight can last almost to midnight. It's wonderful! During the summer, the Irish make certain that they enjoy themselves by taking advantage of the incredibly long days and that two weeks of liberty. In that the country is located so far to the north (look on a map — Irish latitudes are as far north as Canada's Hudson Bay), summers can be rather chilly compared to similar periods in, say, Chicago, Berlin, Florida, London, or New York. A good day, with the clouds driven away by a summer sun, can get up to the mid-70's (low 20's Centigrade). While we can have even warmer days, with highs of eighty degrees Fahrenheit and more (high-20's C), those periods are positively unusual and the Irish almost die in the poxy heat.

But when the sun is out, and though it might be cooler, the days feel warmer than what might be reflected on any thermometer, undoubtedly due to the high latitudes that we enjoy. Again, there is something magical about a proper Irish summer. Not that we have them every year, mind you. Many is the summer that we've all stood looking up at a dark blanket of cloud, temperatures in the low 50's (10 degrees C), the streets awash with a cold pouring rain, and wonder what the hell happened. Occasionally, summer will entirely forget to come to Ireland and we'll all go nuts thinking that now we'll have to wait for a whole year to see the sun, while also realzing that our Vitamin C intake will have to be increased in order to avoid scurvy.

But despite the occasional disastrous years, we have our wonderful summers, too. And during those periods you won't have to go anywhere else in the world to enjoy yourself.

Being social animals, the Irish love to get together in vast flocks that don't have to work very hard to enjoy each other's company. The beaches are awash in people. Kids throw themselves into the cold Irish Sea on the east coast, or the even colder Atlantic on the west coast, hoping to create an Irish version of Bay Watch. While they do this, their parents plant large screens of fabric on the beach in hopes of keeping away the chilly Irish breeze. Behind these thin bulwarks, they search desperately for a tan with which to impress partners and friends, invariably burning their unprotected skin to cinders in the process.

If not the beach, the Irish will venture to any number of festivals and gatherings held throughout the country. Fleah's, an Irish celebration of dance and music, and Country Fairs will be held in many towns and villages countrywide. At these affairs the populace gathers for singsong, many pints, and great craic as they enjoy the music and dance of their ancestors. Ploughing competitions, celebrating the nation's agrarian roots, will be mounted on fields throughout the country. There you can watch tractor go head-to-head with tractor, or see ancient steam threshers at work, or learn how farmers used the wide blade of a scythe in the old days with which they broke their backs in cutting the acres of hay from their stony fields.

If you'd rather avoid the crowds then visit the old castle that will invariably reside just down the road and spend some time sitting in the warming grass, perhaps breaking out a fulfilling lunch of sandwiches and flasks of tea. Or if you'd rather get some exercise, then put on your hiking boots and take off for long walks upon Ireland's miles of hiking trails. It being the summer, you're bound to run into hundreds of foreign tourists who are also enjoying the natural beauty of Ireland and you'll have the guilty pleasure of knowing that they would envy your position if they knew that you had thrown caution to the winds and had emigrated to this country, and are now free to take the pleasure of the Irish countryside whenever you choose to do so.

But the Irish aren't content to spend their summers only in their home country. In the hunt for guaranteed sunshine, they search the world for new corners to enjoy. And why wouldn't they when the rest of Europe beckons, and with foreign holiday prices and airfares so low? With the coming of new competition in the airline and travel industries, the Irish have hundreds of summer destinations to choose from.

For years, Spain was by far the favourite. Back when I came here, and with the national economy in the gutter, an Irish person who was fortunate enough to visit Torremolinos for a week was considered to have found heaven. But now such a place is considered something of a dive. Instead, the Irish pack their bags and head to the four corners of the globe: in Europe, favourites include Portugal, Greece, France, Turkey and the Cannery Islands. Moving farther a-field, Thailand and Vietnam are now visited more frequently by the Irish. Going in the other direction, Florida and much of the Americas — including Cuba — are now firm favourites.

But wherever they go, the Irish bring with them their joy of life and uniquely-Irish sense of conviviality. They'll be the first up to the bar, the first on the dance floors, the first to be cajoled into taking part in a ridiculous stunt by a floorshow host, the first to start a conversation, and the first to break out in belly laughs full of living. For you see, the Irish enjoy themselves so much because they really do their best not to take life too seriously. And when on holidays, the Irish can't seem to take life seriously at all.

The Irish enjoy their summer holidays just as much as they enjoy Christmas, Hallowe'en, St Patrick's Day, and all of the other days in between. They do their best to embrace these precious days of freedom, experiencing each new person, each new place, each new activity, to its very fullest. The rest of the world might be puzzled at the antics of the Irish but the Irish don't seem to mind a bit. I've come to understand the hard-earned secret in Irish smiles: they've learned how to enjoy the greatest gift of all.

Life itself.

Guideline Thirteen: Understanding of Mania

Toward an Ireland's Sporting

Upon being asked why his team was so successful in the 1990 World Cup, an unidentified Irish Football fan replied:

'Like it's pretty straightforward, like. The team was great, the manager was great, and as for the fans? Fecking brilliant!'

I must admit that I am not the greatest sports fan in the world. This predisposition probably goes back to those heady days of my childhood: at a mere ten years of age, and believing as every other kid on my block did that I was certain to be the next Mickey Mantle (a Superman of a professional baseball player in case you didn't know), I tried out for the local Little League Baseball Team. With a pop fly hit in my direction, and knowing that my actions were being scrutinised by a cadre of adult coaches and sneering, weasel-like school chums, I backed up ... up ... up ... reaching for the ball, never taking my eyes from it...and promptly fell on my ass. With the laughter of coaches and other ten-year-olds ringing in my ears, I fled the field, deciding then and there that sports of any description just weren't my thing.

But despite my lack of interest in the sporting world, no book on Ireland can be complete without a chapter devoted specifically to sports. For you see the Irish are mad about sports. And they have so many to choose from! Gaelic sports, football (read: soccer), horseracing, rugby, polo, golf, billiards and snooker — the list seems endless.

If you decide to become one with the Irish, and no matter what your own predisposition regarding sports, you will undoubtedly be sucked into this exciting madness just like I was.

When I first moved to Ireland I admitted to a complete ignorance of the local games. I had a hard enough time understanding the basics of American sports. Baseball, American football, basketball and ice hockey were the sum total of my sporting universe, and I had enough trouble struggling with those. Consequently, and when my wife and I would wander into the local pub for a well-deserved drink, I had a difficult time talking with the local natives and in particular the males of that species in that all they seemed to do was converse about the matches, players, and scores of the teams that had beaten each other senseless only the day before. For the longest time I would take my drink alone, thinking that I would never fit in simply because I had no interest in what my Irish cousins were so very focused on.

All of that changed in 1990.

If you are an American reading this, you possibly understand that soccer is the world's most popular sport. Known as 'football' in this part of the world — and the rest of the world as a matter of fact, bar America which insists on calling the game 'soccer' — and not to be confused with the American variety, billions of people passionately follow the 'beautiful game', as it has become known across the globe. Nowhere is this truer than in Ireland.

Football in Ireland is played at a variety of amateur, semi-professional, and professional levels. But while the Irish might follow some of their local teams, their real passion is focused upon English teams. I still can't figure this out. Though the Irish are supposed to espouse a negative view of the English due to history, and though they may seem to desire to punch the English senseless whenever the Irish National Football Team happens to share a football pitch with an English National Football Team, never ask an Irishman or woman to betray their loyalty to English soccer. Many follow Manchester United, Liverpool, Arsenal and a host of other English football clubs as if their lives depended on it.

The International Football season changes all that, of course. In Europe and the rest of the world — even in the United States — each nation fields its own national soccer team. Every four years those teams pit their skills and national honour against each other as they vie for the World Cup, one of sporting's most prestigious championships. If you are European or from most other countries in the world, you will instantly understand the passion and general craziness that surrounds this series of matches. If, on the other hand, you are from North America, and though football is gaining traction due to successful U.S. soccer teams, you possibly won't understand why what seems to be the entire world becomes so obsessed during the World Cup season. If you are one of those unfortunates, and should you decide to reside in Ireland or most anywhere else in the world, you'd best become educated.

For many years, the Irish didn't have very much to get excited about when it came to the World Cup Championship. The Irish national football team, those erstwhile Irish players assembled from other national squads to play for the World Cup, had never achieved very much. Then in 1988 and 1989 Irish soccer fans noticed a difference. A new manager had taken over. An English fellow as it turned out; a tall man who wore a soft cap and carried a loud voice, and who knew exactly how he wanted his team to play. And the Irish team started to win. Suddenly, the locals had something to natter about.

Having no interest in sports, I didn't notice much, of course. But in 1990, as the World Cup approached and with my parents once again in town on a visit, my goodly wife suggested that we all troop down to the local pub to watch what at that point were the beginnings of the 1990 World Cup play-offs. As it turned out, the Irish team was in the thick of it.

'You mean you want to spend an entire evening watching soccer?' I had croaked. 'It sounds so boring! What about my father? He'll fall asleep!'

'It's called football over here,' she had replied, not taking no for an answer. 'Stop snivelling. You'll all love it.' And so I packed up my parents, put on a bright green woolly hat that my wife insisted I wear, and headed down to our local drinking establishment, believing we were facing in to an evening of certain boredom.

The pub was packed. And I don't mean just crowded. I mean *packed*. When the four of us squeezed into the standing room only crowd, you couldn't have put a toothpick between us. 'What the hell is going on?' my father wanted to know. 'Shut up, lad,' the fellow next to us stated reverently. 'Charlton is taking the field.'

We looked up at the giant television screen that had been bolted to the wall for this special occasion, watching as the Irish manager took the field, followed by his team of seasoned players. In the pub, the sea of Irishmen and women peered anxiously toward the television's flickering screen as if watching the Second Coming. 'Who's playing?' I asked my wife.

'Where have you been?' the guy next to me stated. 'It's Ireland versus England. If we beat them — if we even get level with them — we're off to Italy and the finals!'

The game — called a match over here — started. I knew that I was going to be bored to death. What I hadn't counted on was the emotion that the Irish fans would display. As the game moved along, and when England scored one over on the Irish, the entire pub descended into a pit of despair. I turned to my father, noting the glazed look on his face, thinking that maybe it was time to go home.

'We're not going anywhere,' my wife hissed.

And so we waited. The eyes of the Irish fans were all locked on the television. The ball moved downfield. The packed pub sensed an opportunity. On the TV screen the Irish forward swung back a large boot, kicked with all of his might, and the ball rocketed into the English net.

The pub exploded in delight. Honestly, you would have thought the roof of that small building would have come off. The Irish fans roared their pleasure like a pride of victorious lions. The decibels that they generated would seem to have broken glass. They jumped up and down. They pounded each other's backs. They poured beer over one another. Obviously, a sporting miracle had taken place.

This same scene of revelry was replicated in small towns, larger villages, and entire cities over the width and breadth of Ireland as the entire country came unglued. Even today, over thirty years later, the Irish talk about that match and that single goal with hushed voices approaching reverence.

I had never heard or seen anything like the uproar that took place that night, not at any game that I had ever attended, anywhere. I was hooked. Ireland was a participant in the 1990 World Cup, and finally — after eight years of living in that wonderful country — I finally began to understand just how important sports were to that populace.

The Irish people take their sports very seriously. Many Irish people follow their chosen brand of sport like a religion. When a national team plays, the country's fans bleed green and orange. Legions of Irish men and women will travel the globe to support their teams.

During that World Cup for instance, many Irish took out second mortgages or otherwise incurred substantial debt in order to parade around the world in support of the national football team. Those Irish who couldn't afford to travel took special delight in closing down the country as they headed toward their local pub in order to watch the various matches as Ireland clawed through the competition. During those games, the roads were deserted. The country had come to a standstill as Irish fans everywhere watched their team play against stiff competition.

The Irish have been a sporting nation since time immemorial. Their official national sports — Gaelic football and Gaelic hurling — illustrate the competitive, yet crazed, nature of the Irish.

To this American, Gaelic football seems rather like a combination of soccer, rugby, and American football. Fifteen insanely strong, athletic players on each team (or 'side' as a team is called in this part of the world) attempt to get their hands, feet, or body around a round ball. The objective of the game is to either score by kicking the ball through an upright at the end of the field (or 'pitch' as the playing field is known over here) for a single point, or by putting the ball into a net that rests underneath the upright for three points.

Like soccer, the game is non-stop. Players must 'dribble' the ball, meaning that they can only hold it for three steps. Otherwise, they must kick it, bat it, or throw it to another team member. Each county in Ireland has their own Gaelic football team. The players are 'non-professional', meaning that they don't receive any pay. Yet their commitment and professionalism is unquestioned as they attempt to bring honour to their county by winning the All-Ireland Championship.

My old Irish hometown of Navan resides in County Meath. The county, for all intents and purposes, is Gaelic football mad. Come the GAA season, the county's folk troop down to the local County Football Pitch to watch the Meath Team as it attempts to beat other county teams senseless, and thereby win the match. Over the years, the Meath players have done a fairly good job at this. Not only have the managed to destroy their opponents upon numerous occasions, but in the time I lived there, have also managed to win the All-Ireland Championship any number of times. Upon those occasions the town of Navan has gone crazy as the victorious Meath players march through its small streets and the roar of drunken revelry is raised in joyous approval.

This celebration of victory must certainly harken back to times thousands of years ago when the Kings of Tara, based only a few miles from modern Navan, would march home from their wars to the acclaim of their fellow Irishmen and women. I suspect that Gaelic Football is simply a reflection of those days long ago, and gives the Irish something to cheer about without the need to resort to conflict of the bloody kind.

But if Gaelic Football is crazed, its sister sport — Gaelic Hurling — is insane. In my humble opinion, this is a madman's game. Like Gaelic Football it is a game played between fifteen players on each side. Again, the objective is to get a ball either over an upright for one point, or into a net for three points. But there the similarity ends.

Hurling is one of the fastest, wildest, and possibly most dangerous of games, in the world. It originated in Ireland before the days of Christianity. The earliest written reference to Hurling is contained in the Brehon Laws of the fifth century A.D. While I've never read the Brehon Laws, I'm certain that it must contain a list of casualties that were suffered by local players as they attempted to hack through the opposition. For you see in this game of wondrous skill, each player is armed with an incredibly strong ash stick, seemingly as deadly as a steel girder, known as a hurly. Approximately three feet long, and with a flat surface carved at one end, players use this stick to move a small, hard ball called a zlither downfield in hopes of scoring a goal. These fellows run pell-mell down the pitch, keeping an eye out for the uprights at the end of the field, all the while balancing the small ball at the end of the hurly. In a flat run, and approaching the goal, hurling players will then toss the ball straight up while pulling their sticks back, finally smashing the zlither toward the far goalposts in a mighty blow.

Should an opposing team member's head, arm, or back happen to get in the way of that strong ash stick, so much the better. Heads, arms, legs, and assorted body parts might litter the field after a match but that's just part of the adventure. Unlike American football where players wear padding that protects them much like armoured knights of days gone by, hurling players wear very little to offer them protection from the shattering might of a hurly stick.

But the Irish penchant for sport does not stop at soccer or Gaelic games. The Irish also field winning professional rugby teams. Only a few years ago, the Irish Rugby Team won International Rugby's Triple Crown. Since then, they have become feared by their international opponents. The Irish have also participated successfully Six Nations Cup (where they are feared). In a very different sport the Irish have honoured this country in the Olympics, winning Gold, Silver, and Bronze medals in horse jumping, swimming, and track.

Many Irish love to follow horse racing, doing so as if their lives depended on it. Betting shops — or Turf Accountants, as they are called over here — are often crowded as the Irish put their hard-earned money down on the warm nose of their choice, watching the flickering television as they determine whether they have won or lost a fortune.

Ireland is sports mad. When their teams are playing, the entire country might come to a stop as the locals determine whether or not their favourite teams are winning or losing. If they are winning, you can be certain that much of the country will be crowded into the local pubs in order to watch the excitement. If they are losing, you can be sure that many Irish will be gathered in the pub anyway, if only to commiserate over a tall, cold pint.

While you can survive in this country even if you do not particularly enjoy soccer, rugby or hurling, it does help if you know enough to be able to hold up your end of a sporting conversation down at the local. Otherwise, you may end up sitting in a dark corner, forlorn and forgotten. But if you can learn enough about sports to roar madly at the local teams like the Irish do, you'll find life here much more enjoyable. Do that and Irish will surely embrace you as one of their own.

Guideline Living & Dying  *Fourteen: the Irish Way*

Overheard at a local country wake as the recently departed was being viewed:

'Ah, now doesn't he look like himself? And he really did know how to live didn't he? Now let's get out of here and grab a pint before he wakes up and spoils the day on us.'

When I first came to this country, I decided to take a tour of our small town and spent a day walking through its narrow streets and byways. The roadways were deserted because of the light rain that fell and having taken a look at the small variety of newsagents, chemists, picture houses, green grocers, coal merchants, and drapers in which I could spend my non-existent cash, I suddenly felt a certain parching of the throat and knew that it was time to get out of the rain and grab a pint.

In that Navan had over thirty pubs to choose from back then, I knew that a pint would soon be resting at my elbow. Looking across the small main street I spied Fitzsimmon's Pub, a well-known local watering hole, and made a mad dash across the potholed surface of the road, entering the establishment where I hoped to find warmth and company.

The pub was packed but the good-natured locals made room for me as I sidled up to the bar. 'Pint of Guinness,' I called, shaking the rain from my jacket.

'Soft day,' the barkeep observed as he poured.

'Is it?' I stated shortly, feeling the cold fingers of rain run down my neck. I watched as he filled the pint, then put it aside to rest.

As I waited, my eyes adjusted to the dark warmth of the bar. And as they did I noticed a curious thing. The bar was roughly split into three sections. In the middle section, the owner kept his supplies of beverage, enough to sink a ship: taps that poured what seemed to be endless quantities of Guinness, Smithwick's

Ale, and Harp Lager rose from behind the counter like a small forest of stainless steel; large bottles of spirits were bolted to the wall, resting vertically, draining into the small optics that held exact measures of fiery whiskies, ports, gins, and vodkas. Resting on shelves behind the counter were other bottles containing dark porter and mixers. But it was the other two sections that made me realise that I was living in a different world.

To the right of the dark mahogany wood of the bar was an area devoted entirely to foodstuffs: tins of baked beans, spaghetti hoops, soups, pots of mustard and the like rested on narrow shelves that completely covered one wall, rising, it seemed, into the dark recesses of the high ceiling. A whole cooked ham and a block of cheese sat regally behind a glass case. Loaves of sliced bread filled a wide shelf. One of them had been opened, sitting on a block of wood, breadcrumbs and bits of ham and cheese covering the counter. Obviously, the barkeep's customers had recently taken their lunch here.

But it was the third section of the bar that really grabbed my attention, though what I saw seemed so entirely out of context with the rest of the establishment that I had trouble believing what my eyes were certainly communicating to my rain-soaked brain.

Memorial wreaths of every description covered one wall. Plastic flowers of reds, pastels, whites, and mauves, wrapped in tight ovals, hung like grim sentinels above me. Wine coloured ribbons overprinted with white epithets bearing remarks such as "In Deepest Sympathy", were tied reverently to the wreaths, seeming to whisper their grim intentions.

Just below the display of wreaths I noticed a small but carefully painted sign:

Padraig Fitzsimmons, Undertaker

Funerals and Memorials Available

I picked up my pint and took a deep drink.

'Ya' all right?' the barkeep asked, having noticed my disbelieving look.

I pointed to the contents on his wall with a somewhat unsteady hand. The barkeep smiled broadly, reached over and patted me on the shoulder. 'Ah, it's the Irish way,' he stated. 'Don't you know, you can drink, eat and die in this place.'

While such an all-in-one facility might well be available in the United States, I have never seen one. For all I know, Wal-Mart might be thinking of such a strategy in order to further increase its market share, though I doubt it.

But no matter what is happening in the U.S., and upon further reflection, the Irish ability to develop an establishment that allows a person such an all-encompassing facility all under the one roof seems entirely appropriate and is indicative of the Irish attitude to life. For you see, the Irish know not only how to live but also have developed an uncanny ability to accept the inevitability of death. And they celebrate the lives of those who have died in a way that at first seemed entirely foreign to me but which now seems entirely appropriate and sensible.

Death, of course, is inevitable and unless an archaeologist manages to locate the Fountain of Youth or a geneticist finally discovers a method to manipulate our genes, a visit by the Grim Reaper will always be humanity's final outcome. In the U.S., however, the inevitability of this certain outcome is not taken lightly. Americans will do almost anything to postpone this final curtain: they will try to halt the aging process with help from the latest dietary fad; they'll spend vast fortunes on unguents and lotions that promise to delay the day of aging; they'll struggle with exercise regimes that could kill even the strongest of them. No matter what they do, of course, death is always around the final corner, waiting to take its due. But until that grim day, many Americans seem to do what they can to push the grisly thoughts of the inevitable from their minds.

The Irish, on the other hand, seem to recognise that Death is a part of living. While it is not exactly embraced (who in their right minds wants to die?), it is recognised as being an unavoidable part of the circle of life. This practical attitude results in some unique and very human customs.

Saying Goodbye

I've never been to a first-class wake, even after all my years of living here. Wakes, as they used to be performed, seem to have gone out of fashion in Ireland though I've heard of them still happening particularly in the West of the country. Apparently, a true wake is something to behold.

On the day of death, the surviving family members will drape all of the mirrors of the house in simple cloth and open the doors and windows of the home in order to provide the soul of the dead with an easy departure. With his or her soul now on the way to Heaven, family members will also quickly gather the material possessions of the departed, distributing them to relatives, friends, or charities. In this way, the soul has nothing to beckon them back from their Heavenly journey.

Now the wake begins in earnest. As I understand it, a wake not only allows friends and relatives a chance to say goodbye to the departed and pay their respects to the surviving family, but also provides a great excuse for a few days of uproarious living.

The dearly departed, dressed in their best and laid out in the simple mahogany casket, will have been delivered to the family home the day following their death. Usually laid out in the living room and surrounded by all that they knew and loved, the entire village might turn out to pay their last respects.

Mourners will form a huge line, passing through the family home, saying goodbye to the dearly departed, shaking hands with the survivors, and saying a small prayer for everyone involved. Back in the old days, a group of hired Wailers — women who have been asked to cry and wail for the sake of the dear one's soul — would stand outside the house, creating a terrible cacophony that might rival that of the Banshee.

As part of the wake, the local publican might have delivered a huge supply of porter and whiskey, and the locals will stand in the garden drinking themselves toward oblivion as they recount tremendous stories of the person who has passed away. Sometimes, and depending on the status of the departed, a successful wake could last for days.

In most of today's Ireland, wakes are a thing of the past. That said, the Irish still manage to honour their dead in a manner that also allows them to embrace the glory of living. Possibly the most celebratory funeral I was fortunate enough to attend was that of Jenny (which is not her real name), a close friend of mine. She died young, at the age of only fifty-two. Her funeral was held in her mother's home, a simple structure located only a few doors down from my wife's parent's house.

Jenny died of cancer. For a few weeks prior to the end, she was confined to hospital. But in the last few days she was permitted to go home. Because we all knew that she had only days left, we spent a great deal of time visiting with her. Jenny wasn't too worried about what the future would hold. Instead, she revelled in the company of her family and friends. Each of us, in our individual ways, said goodbye. And finally, succumbing to the inevitable, she left us.

Jenny's death occurred during the Christmas season. She was lovingly dressed in a new tracksuit that her husband gave to her and placed in a beautiful mahogany casket which rested in her parent's living room. Because the house was small, all of her friends gathered in the freezing December weather at the front of her home. We formed a small queue and by turns entered the house to bid our final goodbyes.

Many of us took Jenny's hand to say farewell. We each sprinkled holy water on her head. Then we stepped back out into the night. I will never forget it: the frosty cold of the Christmas evening and the clear bells of the local church as they tolled a clarion of Silent Night. When all of us had paid our last respects, the casket was closed and brought from the house. We then formed a funeral cortege, walking behind the hearse that held Jenny's remains to St Mary's Church, located just down the road.

There, the local priest helped us to say our goodbye's within the dimly lit yet Christmas bright confines of the Church. And when he had finished, we again formed a queue, each of us shaking the hands of Jenny's relatives, letting them know of our love for this woman and the fact that she had helped us experience life a little more fully.

The next day Jenny was buried in a simple ceremony. Again, those that loved her walked behind the hearse as it made its way up to the cemetery. At the graveside, we all said one last farewell. Finally, Jenny was laid to rest.

Later that day, some of us gathered in a local hotel, there to have a drink and a sandwich, laughing at the memory of this remarkable woman, recounting the many joys that she had brought to us all. It was a gathering that not only cherished and celebrated Jenny's life, but that also celebrated our own. When we had finished, we walked out of the hotel determined to make the most of the days that we each had left on this planet.

Dying is inevitable. But somehow the Irish have learned to make it a part of living. To that end, they also have figured out a way to make it not quite as frightening.

A Walk with Past Friends

On any given Sunday afternoon, when we had nothing else to do, my goodly wife might look across the living room at me, toward the lump snoring behind the Sunday papers, and asked: 'Want to go up to the cemetery?' And rather than say, 'What, are you out of your mind?' I'd reply instead, 'Sure, why not?'

We'd throw a rake into the back of the car, perhaps bring the dog, and motor off the mile or two to the local repository for the dead of Navan.

In many places throughout Ireland cemeteries are treated somewhat like public parks. On a sunny day you'll find these places crowded as people tend to the graves of their loved ones, enjoy a chin-wag or two with living friends or neighbours, take a walk to see who has recently met their Maker, or simply enjoy the day.

When I first arrived in Ireland, I thought this to be a rather macabre custom. After all, I had never before taken a trip to a cemetery with the intention of simply visiting the place unless it was of some historical importance. Visiting the graveyard in Ireland is different. It offers a chance to take some much-needed time out. At the same time, it allows all of us to confront and accept the inevitable.

For instance, when Kathleen, my mother-in-law, was still alive we would regularly drive up to the cemetery with her in order to visit the grave of her late husband and weed the plot and visit with whomever happened to be around. In that Luke, my late father-in-law, happened to be interred in the family grave and in that wives are invariably buried beside their husbands, Kathleen recognised that someday she too would be residing next to him. Yet her reaction to the inevitable was not a cause for tears but rather for jokes:

Me: 'Are you sad when you visit, Nana (we always called Kathleen "Nana")?'

Her: 'Not at all. One day you can plant me right here. I'll be pushing up the daisies. And if it's full, just put me in the back garden. I'll do just fine there.'

I'd smile uncertainly, then she'd laugh gaily and we'd all get back to pulling weeds from the small gravesite.

Kathleen passed away a couple of years ago at the relatively young age of seventy-five. We buried her next to her husband, and we do our best to visit them both a couple of times a year. I know now that visits of this type help all of us not only to accept what has happened to our loved ones, but to also realise that this final inevitability will also happen to ourselves.

And in doing so, many also gain a certain acceptance that perhaps death — as a part of living — isn't so bad after all. Not if you can rest in a pretty park, with a huge variety of marble and stone monuments surrounding you, listening to your friends and neighbours as they walk over to say hello and pull a weed or two.

Guideline Fifteen: When You Come Here You Might Never Leave

Navan, County Meath   September 11, 2001

Dear Mom and Dad,

Are you both okay? I couldn't believe what I saw. We rang Junior. He had been driving along the 57th Street Bridge when it happened and saw one of the towers collapse. He thought it was Armageddon. Thank God he came out of it all right.

I can't believe it nor can anyone else. I just wish I was home right now. Today, more than any other day, I know that while I've made my home here, I am still an American. And rightly proud I am of it.

The Irish have been wonderful. You wouldn't believe the outpouring of sympathy. While I would rather be with you, at least I know just how much these people care for us. Everyone seems to be praying. Their prayers have helped me enormously to cope with the unthinkable.

I'll write again later and phone you this evening if I can get through.

I love you,

Tom

The trouble with Ireland is simple. If you come here, you might never, ever find the strength to leave no matter if you suffer from grave misfortune or experience an incredible stroke of good luck. You might moan about the place. You might find yourself to be intolerably homesick. You might even find perfectly logical reasons to journey back to your homeland: the distance from relatives, the prospects of an incredible job and career move, or the simple emotions of wanting to go home.

Move here and the odds are that you'll never go back. But though you may stay, you will undoubtedly be torn apart by uncertainty, wondering if you've made the right decision. Often, you may be wracked by a sense of loss and despair that perhaps your decision has been the wrong one and that you should move back home. But then you'll put off the decision and stay another day in Ireland, and then another. But even as the days pass, you'll still hear a confused voice in your inner-ear once again saying: 'Am I really doing the right thing by staying in a country so distant from my own?'

I offer this warning because it's something to think about before you choose the path of immigration, and the emotional plight of an immigrant is an issue that I find is rarely discussed. Immigrating is hard work. It can be an emotional roller coaster out of which few emerge unscathed. But something magical happens when a person moves here. Despite all of the difficulties of immigrating to this country that I have previously mentioned, Ireland seems to root itself into the very fabric of your being. And once the roots have become established, it's very difficult to shake yourself loose.

Let me tell you two stories: one a riddle, the other a story from my own experience that might explain this point.

The riddle goes like this: a friend of mine, an Australian immigrant, recently asked me to name the second most miserable person in the world. I guessed and guessed and couldn't come up with an answer. It turns out that the second most miserable person in the world is an expatriate.

Then he asked me to name the most miserable person in the world. Again, I couldn't come up with the answer. It turns out that the most miserable person in the world is an expatriate who has returned home.

Departing on the adventure of immigration is not to be taken lightly. For years I second-guessed my decision to stay in Ireland, thinking that I would be much happier and much more successful if I had moved back to the States. When in the dark throes of homesickness, I would look to the West and think that the grass beyond the horizon had to be much greener than the Irish variety that I found growing beneath my naked feet. At times I believed that I was going to go crazy with the thoughts of my homeland.

And on occasion, when I'd return home on a holiday, I'd seriously think that perhaps I should really consider a move back to the U.S.

But there's a problem. I've changed. I am no longer just an American. Because of the length of my stay here I am also Irish and hence also a European. And I find that I've come to think with a somewhat European view of things. This means that I am no longer entirely comfortable with the U.S. And I realise that if I went home I would in all probability find it as difficult to fit in there as I did when first making the move to Ireland. In short: the United States is now a foreign country to me.

It's a sad state of affairs because I've always loved my homeland. But I realise now that perhaps I can never go home.

Ireland has captured my heart. I've already written about many of the aspects of Irish life that have caused this. But if you come here, you'll understand that which I often have so much difficulty in putting into words. For this reason, perhaps this next story will illustrate that which I can't adequately describe. The start of this story occurred on what is a dark day in the world's history, and certainly what must rank as one of the darkest in American history. It starts on September 11, 2001.

That day I had a meeting in Dublin with a business client. I was sitting in a boardroom when one of the client's secretaries ran in. She announced to all of us that an attack had occurred in New York.

Knowing that I was American my clients — who have now become close friends — were more than a little concerned for me and mine. Rather than just expressing sympathy and continuing with the meeting, they reached out with their minds and hearts and supported me because they knew instinctively how upset I had become.

They walked me out of the conference room to a television that was tuned to CNN. I arrived just in time to see the collapse of the second World Trade Centre tower.

Like many Americans throughout the world, I too collapsed. The client's marketing manager held me in his arms as I cried and cried. And you know what? He never made me feel in the least embarrassed. Instead, he let me know that it was perfectly okay for me to be a human being as, on that terrible day, I cried for my fellow citizens.

When I finally got home on that dreadful evening, I found my house to be awash with neighbours who had come to express their concern. Their eyes were also filled with tears. They were stunned by the uncontrollable events that had engulfed us.

They offered me, a person who in their eyes represented the people of the United States, their sympathy, their support and their prayers.

Two days later, the Taoiseach — the Prime Minister of the Irish government — decided that the events that had taken place in the United States required an appropriate response. For hundreds of years America has held a special place in the hearts of the Irish. For that reason, the Taoiseach determined that the best way that the nation could possibly express its sympathy was to close the country down in a Day of Mourning, a day that would demonstrate to the world the extent of Irish grief and solidarity.

And that's precisely what he did. To my knowledge, Ireland is the only country in the world that marked this desperately sad occasion with a National Day of Mourning.

That night, what seemed to be every person in the country flocked to their local church. My wife and I went to St Mary's Church in Navan with our children. I've never seen so many people there, not even at Christmas. The Altar of the church was set alight with the sparking, hopeful flames of hundreds of small candles. And in front of that bright river of glittering hope came the outpourings of sympathy from the heart of a nation, and from the hundreds of local people who expressed their own emotions of condolence so freely.

After Mass many people whom I had never had the opportunity of meeting came up to me. They had been told that I was an American who had chosen to make Ireland home both for himself and his family. Many took my elbow as they whispered words of sympathy. Others touched me gently on the chest or arm in a simple gesture of kindness and comfort, and told me how very sorry they were. I had never been as proud to be American as I was on that day. Since then, it is true to say that I am also incredibly proud to be Irish.

Perhaps that is one of the reasons why I will probably never leave this country. If you come here, you will begin the journey toward an understanding of what it means to be Irish. Ireland is much more than its beautiful landscape. It is much more than its rich history or its magical ancient structures or even its people. Somehow, it is a combination of everything that has been woven together to form a rich tapestry for living; an attitude and joy for life that I have been unable to find elsewhere.

Should you come here on a similar journey, you will not only be captivated by the experience, but you will also know what it means to be truly blessed.

Guideline Sixteen: That's What!  Now What? Plan, That's What!

Planning vt 1 : to arrange the parts of : DESIGN 2 : to devise or project the realisation or achievement of 3 : to have in mind : INTEND

Webster's Seventh New Collegiate Dictionary

So, you've read the books, whipped through the tourist guides, talked it over, thought about it, spent a year of sleepless nights, and now you're determined to uproot your existence and move to Ireland. For whatever reason, perhaps because you've watched The Quiet Man one too many times, you've decided that your life would become much more fulfilled if you chucked everything in, sold the house, packed up your boxes, and became one with the Irish and all that their country has to offer.

What do I advise? Hold everything, that's what.

For God's sake, take it from me: don't do what I did. Prior to moving here, I had visited this country for all of two weeks. I didn't know my arse from my elbow as they say over here, and didn't have any idea of what I was getting in to when I finally arrived.

I didn't understand that I was about to move to a completely different culture. And it is, you know. Perhaps because the Irish speak English with such a wonderful lilt, many people — particularly Americans — automatically believe that living here will be akin to residing in Peoria only without the benefit of a local Wal-Mart.

Ireland is different. Take my word for it. Some people love the place. Other people simply hate it. For instance, I know of one couple from Canada who moved over because the husband had been born here. His family had immigrated to Canada when he was a mere lad and he had never returned — until his ill-begotten journey.

Working from his home near Toronto, he had landed a job with an Irish company over the Internet. Having painted a world of Irish charm to his Canadian wife, he then proceeded to sell up everything. He loaded wife and children on a plane and flew over.

A couple of weeks later a twenty-foot container holding what remained of their worldly possessions — including the family car — arrived. The family bought a house near us. They put their kids in school. They tried to settle.

As it turned out, prior to their move over, his wife had never had the benefit of even a short visit here. Leaving Canada, she had no idea at all that she was moving to a country whose reality was very different from the green-tinged musings of her homesick husband.

Less than two years after their arrival, the wife and kids packed their bags and made their way back to Canada. The bemused husband was left behind to sell his recently purchased Irish dream home. Having finally sold, he left without so much as a whimper.

I've never seen them since. I worry that they are now divorced and that he is living near a squalid pond populated by bellowing moose as punishment for his insane judgement.

If you're considering a move to Ireland, for God's sake be careful. Think about it. Do some research. Then take some time out and visit the place. Make it a thorough visit.

Rent a car and drive through the countryside. Along the way, take the opportunity to stay at some of the best bed and breakfasts anywhere. You'll find them delightful, relatively inexpensive, and you'll have the pleasure of knowing that your Irish host will be taking incredible delight in parting you from your hard-earned money with the very best of intentions. Invariably, they'll give you and your family a cup of Irish tea to make the process that much less painful.

Then climb back into your rental car. Go see the rest of the country. Take a drive through big cities, small cities, larger towns, and wee villages. Get some idea of what it is that you're looking for.

Visit a few pubs and see how well you can handle your Guinness. If you're standing when everyone else has fallen, you'll know that you're more than able for this country.

Find out if you can tolerate the constant rain. See if you go ballistic as the occasional pothole knocks the fillings from your teeth. Discover the outrage of high Irish taxes and prices for yourself, and see if you can not only sympathise with your Irish compatriots about the extortionate cost of living here, but also grin and bear it as everyone else does.

If you can do these things you might just make it here.

Then, do the other stuff. Stay away from the tourist trail and instead take a walk on a fine soft Irish day. Breathe in the peat-filled air. Climb a couple of mountains. Get drunk and roar at the sheep just like some of the locals do.

Sit facing the ocean and watch as the sun sinks over the far horizon and visualise that you now live here permanently, that the next stop over that misty sea is Boston Harbour or Liverpool or Paris or wherever you're from and ask yourself: how do you feel about it? Would you be so homesick that you would brave anything to make the swim to the far shore and seeming civilisation? Or would you know that your home town still exists as always, only without the benefit of your presence, and that you will be incredibly happy in this small yet beautiful country?

If your answer is the latter, then you just might do it. You could uproot yourself from your present existence and settle into a culture that sparkles like a glowing, living tapestry of life.

You could survive in Ireland just as I have.

Guideline Seventeen: Learn to Talk Like the Irish, A Dictionary of Irish Slang and Phrases

Overheard, as an English couple received a warm welcome from a local Irish tour guide:

Irishman: 'And a Cead Mile Failte to you. Yer sure to enjoy the stay, and you'll take pleasure in the back of beyonds of our country for certain or I'm a gobshite to be sure. When you go to the West, do try the poteen if you can get it down you and make certain that you have the bubble and squeak for tea.

'But stay away from Lorcan on yer travels for he's a cowboy and he'll banjax you entirely. He's only a Gossan so you shouldn't take any notice of him because he has much to learn. Now be off with you, for me throat is parched and I'm blathering on like an eejit.'

English husband to his wife: 'Audrey, what did he say?'

Both Irish and English are the official languages of this country, which means that while not all Irish understand Gaeilge (even though that is their beautiful native tongue, many Irish don't speak the traditional language at all) all of them do speak English just like you possibly do. But just because they speak English doesn't mean that you'll understand them. To survive here and really integrate into this society, you'll need to absorb the colourful English language of the Irish. Trust me, it isn't so hard and within a few months you'll be chatting, fecking and blinding just like they do.

The only problem with learning Irish slang and phrases is that they become second nature. And when you decide to go back on holidays to America or Canada, Germany, Australia — or wherever you're from — your relatives and friends will look at you as if you've gone nuts because your tongue can't help but utter those new pieces of Irish vernacular you've picked up. However, it is a small price to pay knowing as you do that you live in a country far, far away and have learned to talk the talk within a culture that is decidedly different from your own.

If you're an American writer or have some sort of job that insists that you use the written version of the English language, all I can say is Good Luck to you. The Irish, as do the English, spell many words a little differently. You know most of them already, of course. 'Color' is 'colour'. 'Realize' and most words ending in '...ize' is 'realise'. 'Favorite' is spelled 'favourite'. But after a few months of going crazy as you attempt to remember which country you're writing for, you'll soon get the hang of it. If all else fails, and you write using a Bill Gates 'Word' product, there's always Spell Check to fall back on. Just make certain that you're using the U.K. default settings.

This small dictionary will hopefully help you to navigate through some of the Irishisms that pepper the conversation of the locals. If you study it well, it might help you to avoid the many difficult situations I managed to get myself into when I first moved here. Though I heard what they said, and while I thought I understood, I discovered that I didn't understand at all!

For instance, check out the Irish meaning of the word, 'Rubber', below. When I took my first job as a weighbridge salesman, I had the pleasure of working with a charming and absolutely gorgeous young woman. One early morning, and without the appropriate amount of caffeine in my blood to ensure a working brain, this woman Cheryl casually asked me to lend her my Rubber.

I could swear I had heart palpitations. I began sweating. I was certain that a heart attack would follow. As my guilt-wracked *mind wondered what my young wife would think of this unprovoked advance, I attempted to think of how I might answer the sweet woman who gazed at me with a face that grew more perplexed as the moment following her simple request wore on.*

With my body frozen into a ridiculous posture, and with Cheryl probably believing that I was having some sort of psychotic episode, the poor woman finally reached across me, pulled open my desk drawer, and grabbed an eraser.

My suddenly sheepish look was filled with the knowledge that what I had thought to be an early morning flirtation had only been a request for a small office supply item. 'Rubber' is an 'eraser', now isn't it? From that day on I realised just how little I knew about the local language and vowed to myself that I would listen carefully to understand the real context of a discussion or question before I put my own brain and mouth in gear.

I hope that the following helps you to avoid a similarly embarrassing situation.

A

Acting the maggot – behaving foolishly, incompetently, or like a complete eejit. Often accompanied by a few pints of porter.

Afters – dessert, not to be confused with anything else that might come 'after' a meal such as a cup of coffee or tea. An 'after' is the sweet course following the main meal.

Arse – a person's backside, as in 'His head is up his arse.' Can also be used as a verb, e.g. 'All you did was arse around all day!'

B

Back of Beyonds – a reference to almost anything outside of Dublin or a large city or town; a country location that's not quite with it as in 'You wouldn't get me to live there. It's the back of beyonds for sure.'

Bacon – a particular cut of ham. Usually boiled to cook.

Banjaxed – broken beyond any hope of repair, as 'The car is banjaxed for sure!'

Beyond the Pale – the Pale refers to Viking times, and the area immediately surrounding Dublin and the local environs. 'Beyond the Pale' refers to anywhere outside of Dublin and is used in the modern vernacular to mean an area anywhere other than Dublin. The Dubs take particular delight in letting the rest of us know that we live 'beyond the pale'.

Biscuit – is a cookie. If you ask for a cookie all you'll get are blank stares.

Bird – a woman, usually a good-looking one.

Blackguard – enemy, evil, mischievous, and generally behaving badly. "Don't you be acting the blackguard or I'll send the dogs after ya."

Blather – as in talking nonsense, e.g. 'All she did was blather on and on.'

Blow In – a recent (like in the past 20 years) arrival in a community, e.g. 'That Richards only arrived here in '82. Don't be talking to him because he's only a blow in and will probably leave in the morning!'

Bog – while ostensibly a watery part of the Irish geography, can also refer to the toilet, as in 'Where's the bog? I'm dying to take a piss.'

Bollocking – a noun that indicates a verbal tirade as in, 'I'm going to give that fellow a bollocking when I catch him!'

Bolloxed – a noun indicating that a person is either very tired, very drunk, or both as in 'I'm bolloxed tired.'

Bonnet – an automobile's hood.

Boot – an automobile's trunk.

Bowsie – a noun or adjective used to describe an oafish or overtly dirty person: 'He's a real bowsie, that one!'

Bril – shorthand for brilliant.

Brilliant – meaning a wonderful experience, e.g. 'The play was just brilliant!'

Bubble and Squeak – an Irish dish of leftover mashed potatoes, cabbage, and a little seasoning all mixed together and fried on a pan. Wonderful!

C

Casualty – emergency room.

Cat – a negative term for something bad, as in 'This film was cat and I'd never recommend it.'

Chance Your Arm – to take a chance, often used in a negative manner, as in 'I'll chance my arm and have another drink. The Garda will never catch me out.'

Chemist – pharmacist.

Chin-wag – a discussion or chat, as in 'I met Breda at the shopping centre and we had a lovely chin-wag.'

Chipper – a fast food restaurant that serves Chips, among other greasy titbits.

Chips – French Fries. Ask for chips expecting Potato Chips and you'll be in for a surprise.

Cock – the male reproductive organ, not to be confused with a male chicken.

Cooker – the Irish term for a stove, e.g. 'Put the pot on the cooker.'

Cop – to discover or understand as in, 'I couldn't balance the bank book but then I copped the error.'

Cowboy – a dishonest businessperson, as in 'Don't trust him. He's only a cowboy!'

Craic – not to be confused with a mind-altering drug, 'Craic' means Great Fun, as in 'Let's go to the pub and have some mighty craic!'

Crisps – potato chips.

Cuppa – a cup of tea as in, 'Go on, have a cuppa. I know you want one!'

Cute – usually used in a negative context to describe a person who is being inappropriately clever as in, 'That cute hoor will never succeed. Wait 'til he falls on his arse.'

D

Deadly – a term meaning 'cool', as in 'That new coat you're wearing is deadly!'

Dense – usually a pejorative word, meaning stupid as in *'I don't know why I talk to the lad because he's so dense!'*

Dickeyed Up – dressed up to the nines, e.g. *'You've dickeyed yourself up for the occasion, I see.'*

Divil (as in Devil) – usually a humorous observation of a person with a rude, troublesome, or cantankerous disposition as, *'Yer Uncle Harold, now he's a real divil.'*

Doing a Line – exclusively courting or dating a person, as in *'She's doing a line with Jason so keep your distance.'*

Donkey's Years – a great deal of time as in *'I haven't seen you in Donkey's Years.'*

Drawers – undergarments, usually of the female variety.

Drink Link – a standard *'hole in the wall'*, or ATM. The handiest place to get cash for a much-needed pint.

Dry Shite – an exceptionally unfunny and boring person, as in *'He's such a dry shite I don't know how his wife stands him.'*

Dummy – a baby's pacifier.

E

Eat the Head Off – verbal abuse, as in *'Stop eating the head off me and calm down!'*

Eejit – a true idiot, as in *'You eejit, you! Get the feck out of my gob.'*

F

Fag – a cigarette, not to be confused with a person of a homosexual persuasion, as in 'Give us a packet of twenty fags.' Irish people abroad must be circumspect if standing in a New York tobacconist and ordering a pack, realising that they must do their level best to avoid using this word without attracting trouble.

Fair Play – a phrase that has absolutely nothing to do with a theatrical play, it roughly translates into 'Good for you!' as in 'You've passed your math test? Fair play to you then!'

Fanny – ummm…this does not refer to a person's posterior, but rather to that part of the female genitalia located directly opposite. Use this word only with extreme caution (by the way, this also means that the term 'Fanny Pack' is not used at all in Ireland).

Feck – the socially-acceptable version of the F-word and used whenever possible, as in: 'He's a cute fecker', or 'Would you ever feck-off!' Feck rapidly descends into the four letter common word when in heated discussions. Get used to it.

Fine Bit of Stuff – a good-looking woman, as in 'Now there's a fine bit of stuff! Wonder if she'd give us a go?'

Fiver – a five-euro note, as in 'Stop being cheap and give us a fiver.'

Flummoxed – inordinately puzzled, as in 'You've confused the shite out of me and now I'm completely flummoxed.'

Fry – an Irish breakfast (or occasionally an evening meal) often consisting of rashers, sausages, black and white pudding, fried tomatoes, fried mushrooms, toast and tea.

G

Garda Siochana – the Police. *In my opinion, the Irish have one of the best police forces around. They are usually courteous and effective. You address them as 'Garda', as in 'Garda, I've lost my wallet. Can you help me?' If you encounter any problems they are always a good point of first contact.*

Garden – yard. *The Irish spend their summers in their back gardens here, not their back yards.*

Gas Ticket – *roughly translates as a person who is out of his or her mind but who also has a lot of fun, as in 'She's a gas ticket when she has a pint on her.'*

Gear – *clothing, usually the better stuff, as 'I see you have your party gear on.'*

Gersha – *Irish language slang for Young Girl, as in 'Ah, you're only a gersha and don't know a feckin' thing.'*

Gob – *a face or mouth, as in 'He has dirt all over his gob.'*

Gobshite – *a person who is worse than most idiots, as in 'You know, Pat? You're a real gobshite!'*

Gosson – *Irish language slang for a Young Boy, as in 'Yer only a mere Gosson and don't know a thing yet!'*

Gurrier – *an evil person who is always bent on wrecking everything around them: 'That young gurrier will land in prison yet.'*

H

Half-One – *a glass of whiskey often purchased together with a half-pint (otherwise known as a Glass) of stout.*

Hard Neck – a person who will try anything yet not suffer from any consequences, e.g. *'Janet will be okay. She has a hard neck and nothing will bother her.'*

Header (or Head Case) – a crazy or mad individual as in: *'Mad, isn't he? A real header (head case).'*

Holiday – vacation.

Hooley – a party or other wild get-together, e.g. *'We got drunk as hell. It was an incredible hooley!'*

Hoor – as in *'He's a cute hoor'*. Usually a pejorative expression meaning that a person will do almost anything to get what they want, usually through deceptive or manipulative means.

Hot Press – built within a house, the closet for airing clothes that often contains the hot water heater.

J

Joy, The – or Mountjoy, is Ireland's premier prison. If someone tells you that they have recently come out of The Joy, then you'd best beware.

Jumper – a common sweater.

K

Knacker – also known as a Traveller or Gypsy, this is a derogative word describing someone who belongs to the Travelling Community.

Knickers – a woman's underpants.

Knob – male genitalia.

L

Langorous – absolutely shit-faced drunk, as in *'He's languorous, so stay away from him because he's going to puke!'*

Lift – an elevator.

M

Maggot – a selfish, abusive, troublesome, or unclean/uncaring person, often used as *'Stop acting the maggot!'*

Messages – usually used as a noun and roughly the equivalent of *'errands'*, as in *'I'm going into town to pick up the messages.'* This word has nothing to do with communication at all, but often alludes to the purchase of groceries or other day-to-day items.

Mickey – male genitalia, as in *'He's got the weirdest looking mickey that I've ever seen!'*

Mitch – to play truant from school, as in *'He mitched school today and he's likely to get suspended.'*

Mobile Phone – cell phone.

Muck – dirt, soil or mud.

Muck-in – to get involved, e.g. *'Come on, muck-in and help us get this thing finished so we can go to tea!'*

Muppet – a derogatory though often humorous observation of a crazed or not-quite-together individual. Also translate as *'eejit'*, e.g. *'What a muppet!'*

N

Nappies – diapers.

Narky – bad-tempered, e.g. *'Do you have a headache or what? Then stop being so narky would you?'*

Nine-Nine-Nine (999) – the Police/Fire/Ambulance emergency number. *If you're American, dial 999 (not 911)*

Nixer – a small job usually done in someone's spare times and completely *'off the books,'* e.g. *'If you want to make a few bob I've a nixer to be done if you don't mind building some bookcases in your spare time.'*

Not the Full Shilling – a disparaging remark that means a person is incompetent or mentally deranged as in *'He's definitely not the full shilling and shouldn't be allowed anywhere near anyone.'*

O

Off License – a Liquor Store.

P

Pants – lady's underwear. Not to be confused with trousers. Tell a woman that you like her pants and you might get a slap in the gob.

Path – a sidewalk. People walk on paths over here, not sidewalks.

Perishing – exceptionally cold, as in *'It's perishing outside!'*

Pissdabells – dandelions. At least that's what my wife calls them.

Poteen – illegal Irish spirit, equivalent to moonshine but distilled from potatoes.

Pub Crawl – a time-honoured profession in which the drinker travels from one pub to another, finally descending to hands and knees because of the amount of drink taken.

Pudding – desserts as in, *'After dinner we have a selection of fine puddings for your culinary delight!'*, unless the word is associated with Breakfast or an Irish Fry in which case it will refer to a meat sausage, known as black or white pudding.

Pull – getting lucky with the opposite sex as in *'Do you think we'll pull one tonight?'* meaning *'Do you think I'll have some luck picking up a woman?'*

Poof – a person of the homosexual persuasion.

Q

Queer – a wonder, mystery, or used as an accolade, e.g. *'It's a queer night and I'm glad that I'm home.'* Not to be confused with homosexual.

Queue – a line. That is, people form a queue over here, not a line. A line is used to define a straight edge, e.g. to draw a line.

Quid – money, usually referring to whole but unspecified amounts as in, *'Dad, can I borrow a couple of quid so that I can go out with the lads tonight?'* A *'quid'* in the old days could also mean one Irish pound. Today, it can mean a euro.

R

Rashers – the Irish equivalent of strips of bacon.

Ride – having sex as in, *'Come on, honey. What about a ride tonight?'*

Rubber – the equivalent of *'eraser'*. A rubber is not a prophylactic device but rather an instrument used to remove unwanted pencil marks.

Rubber Johnny – this is the prophylactic devise: a condom.

Runners – training or track shoes.

S

Sambo – sandwich, as in 'Do you want a sambo for lunch?'

Scoops – a few pints of Guinness as in 'Let's go down to the pub for a Couple of Scoops."

Scuttered – drunk beyond belief; 'He's been drinking all night and is absolutely scuttered!'

Session – yet another drinking term foreshadowing a great night of drinking full of craíc, to wit: "Ah sure but wasn't it a great session we had last night!"

Shag – errrr, the Irish version of sexual intercourse.

Shattered – exhausted as in 'It's been a horrible day and I'm just shattered!'

Shite – the socially acceptable word for 'shit,' as in 'What a load of shite!'

Slainte – Irish for 'Cheers!' and said in a similar situation. To use this word correctly, raise your glass, say 'Slainte!' and drink!

Small One – usually refers to a single glass of Irish whiskey.

Snog – to kiss or make out, e.g. 'Mum, stop embarrassing me! All we were doing was snogging...!'"

Spuds – potatoes.

Starter – appetiser.

Stir the Shit – to tease or attempt to cause trouble, usually in an innocent way: *'Would ya stop telling everyone about how drunk I got at the party last night? All ya try to do is stir the shit.'*

Strange – shy, as in *'The baby is acting strange with you.'*

Surgery – a General Practitioner's doctor's office.

Sweets – translates as *'candy'*. Candy is a word not used at all over here.

T

Taking the Piss – joking, as in, *'Don't get mad. I'm only taking the piss with you.'*

Teatime – often refers to dinner or the evening meal. It is never used as the English use the word (e.g. a mid-morning or mid-afternoon tea).

Thick – usually meaning that a person is obstreperous, angry, or intentionally stupid, as in *'He's as thick as a plank and won't listen to anyone.'*

Tinker – a derogatory word for a person of the Travelling Community but based on fact in that many Travellers were tinsmiths in days gone by.

Toilet – exactly what it means: e.g. a Men's or Women's bathroom. The Irish do not use the term Restroom. If you ask for a Restroom they'll probably think that you're looking for a place to lie down for a week or two.

Trap – mouth, as in *'Close that trap, would ya, and give me some peace!'*

Travelling Community – are a native Irish minority group, set apart from the mainstream of Ireland's more settled community, and known for their nomadic way of life, and unique language and culture.

Trousers – used as a replacement for Pants, as in 'Put a belt on those trousers before they fall down around your ankles!'

Turf Accountant – a Betting Shop. A great place to put a few quid down on the horse of your choice.

W

WC (Water Closet) – the Irish do not use this term for the toilet or loo; my understanding is that it is a term applied only in the U.K. and other British lands.

Wellies – outdoor boots.

Y

Yoke – one of the most versatile words in the Irish vernacular, a 'yoke' can be used in place of the American 'thingamabob', e.g. 'Hand me that yoke over there!' A great word if you're suffering from a hangover and have trouble remembering anything including your own first name.

Yonks – 'like forever' as in "I haven't seen him in yonks."

Afterword

"The doors we open and close each day decide the lives we live."

Flora Whittemore

Life changes. I suspect I've learned that more than most people. It is how we learn to deal and cope with change that gives our lives substance, depth, meaning and, if we're lucky, a little joy.

In 2010 my life turned upside down. Following a marital separation and a fire in which I was almost burned to toast, I realized that I needed to find a place to heal in order to also find peace of self. For a brief moment I considered going back to the United States. But I realised that I had changed too much. I realised too that such a move would be a bridge too far: my children live in Ireland as do my grandchildren. Once again, I decided to stay.

In November of that year, I moved yet again. This time to the small, beautiful and nay I say it, "quaint" village of Eyeries in County Cork. This small coastal village of only sixty souls or so, located in West Cork (not too far from where the fellow on that black Raleigh bicycle gave me those confusing directions so many years ago) has been my salvation. I look out the back door of the cottage that I've purchased, and onto a large body of water:

Coulagh Bay glistens beneath a warming sun in the summer, and in winter tosses with the white furious manes of storm-force gales. In the distance, Scariff Island rises like a majestic whale, the glimmering wave-tossed Atlantic Ocean beyond. And beyond that, North America and my ancestral home.

I have been fortunate. I have survived in this country, and have prospered at least somewhat due to the opening arms of the Irish that have become my friends and neighbours. Here, in Eyeries, I shall learn again how to survive, this time in a place as unspoiled as a fragrant wild rose.

Perhaps, in time, I will write another book about surviving in this beautiful part of southwest Ireland. But that's for another day. In the meantime, I shall enjoy living in this simple place that seems to have been created for just that...just living.

At the same time, I'll finally learn how to understand the wildly difficult accent of those from West Cork. To be sure, to be sure, as they say here, and you can count on that. And you can also count on my continuing survival. After all, I've learned how to survive from the best. From the Irish, themselves.

Slán abhaile.

References

A Note for 2021: the pandemic has wreaked havoc on so many aspects of Irish, and global, life. Many of the items I refer to below have been subject to cancellation or deferral, at least as of this writing. However, I'm assuming that most will be reinstated as the impact from the virus wanes.

How to Get Here

Ireland is now served by a wonderful choice of airlines and ferries. In the old days, we had to get here via charter jet or the ubiquitous and expensive Aer Lingus daily flight from New York City. Now, things are better and prices have come down too. By the way, prices have also fallen for trips to and from the rest of Europe, making it wonderfully inexpensive to fly in from or return to the Continent.

This country has also seen a steady increase in Tourism. Each year seems to outdo the previous. For that reason, more airlines than ever are choosing to serve the country. However, there's a downside because the list of airlines serving Ireland is in constant flux. For that reason, please use the following list as an indicator only. For current information on how to get to and from Ireland via the skies, make good use of Google or other search engines.

Airlines:

*Aer Aran (*www.aerarann.ie*) – with flights serving the U.K. This airline also serves Ireland's Aran Islands, located on the west coast of this country.*

*Air Canada (*www.aircanada.com*) – with flights to Montreal and beyond.*

*Air France (*www.airfrance.ie*) – flights to and from Paris and onward through France, the rest of Europe and the world.*

*Aer Lingus (*www.aerlingus.com*) – to/from the United States, with arrivals in Dublin and Shannon and departures from New York, Boston, Chicago, Washington DC, and Los Angeles; to/from Europe, check out their website for an extensive list of European destinations.*

*American Airlines (*www.aa.com*) – serving much of the United States.*

*British Airways (*www.britishairways.com*) – for inexpensive service to and from the U.K. and beyond.*

*City Jet (*www.cityjet.com/*) – serving London City Airport and Spain.*

*Czech Airlines (*www.czechairlines.com/en/worldwide/ww_home.htm*) – direct flights to and from Prague.*

*Delta Air Lines (*www.deltaairlines.com*) – with service to Atlanta, Georgia and onward.*

*Etihad (*www.etihad.com*) – go global with this wonderful airline.*

*Finnair (*www.finnair.com*) – for direct flights to Finland.*

*Iberia (*www.iberia.com*) – direct flights to Spain.*

*Lufthansa (*www.lufthansa.com*) – direct to Germany and the continent.*

Ryanair (www.ryanair.com) – great prices to destinations all over Europe.

SAS Scandinavian Airlines (www.scandinavian.net/) – direct to Copenhagen and beyond.

Singapore Airlines (www.singaporeair.com) – with flights to and from the US... and the rest of the world.

Swissair (www.swiss.com) – with flights direct to/from Zurich.

United Airlines (www.united.com) – with services from Dublin to many parts of the world.

For more listings of airlines serving Ireland go to www.dublin-airport.com. This website will only provide you with airlines serving Dublin Airport, Ireland's main aerial terminus. However, do remember that Ireland is also served by other International Airports including Shannon Airport, Cork Airport, Galway Airport and Kerry Airport.

Ferries:

Irish Ferries (www.irishferries.ie) – sailings from Dublin Port and Rosslare Harbour, and transporting you to/from either Liverpool or Holyhead. Connect by bus or train to London or vice-versa.

Stena Ferries (www.ferryport.com) – as above plus sailings from Northern Ireland to the northern parts of Britain.

Staying Here

B&B's (www.irish-bnb.com)

As part of my day job I've had the pleasure of working with any number of Irish B&B's located throughout the country. The constant stream of compliments from their foreign guests is always wonderful, though unsurprising. Invariably, tourists never forget the warmth of the Irish welcome. Prices have gone up a little, but the price is worth it if only for the incredible breakfast.

Hotels:

Ireland has plenty. Some of the major hotel chains include:

Great Southern Hotels (www.gsh.ie)

Ryan Hotel Group (www.ryan-hotels.com)

Jury's Hotel Group (www.jurys.com)

Adare Manor (www.adaremanor.ie)

Renvyle House Hotel (www.renvyle.com)

A particular favourite of mine is The Park Hotel Kenmare (when I can afford it). Yes, it is expensive. But what a treat! See: https://www.parkkenmare.com/

Ireland also has its fair share of 'international' groups including Holiday Inns, Best Western, and similar.

Irish Citizenship

For more information on Irish Citizenship, go to:

www.justice.ie *(the official website for the Irish Department of Justice, Equality and Law Reform).*

www.oasis.gov.ie *(search for 'Irish Citizenship').*

Irish Taxes

Search the following, depending on your requirements.

Motor Tax – www.eforecourt.com/php/cartax.php

Income Tax and VAT – www.revenue.ie then click on their FAQ's button, and choose your poison for more information.

Buying a House

Just like the US, Ireland has any number of Internet sites available that are devoted to this subject. Simply go to your favourite search engine and search 'Ireland Property'. That said, here are a couple that I recommend:

www.sherryfitz.ie

www.gunne.ie

www.myhome.ie

www.daft.ie

Getting that Job

If you can, try to get access to a couple of the local newspapers. They're filled with jobs especially during the weekends:

National Newspapers:

The Irish Examiner

The Irish Independent

The Irish Times

The Sunday Business Post

The Sunday Times (Irish Edition)

Internet Job Sites:

www.jobs.ie

www.irishjobs.ie

www.irishtimesjobs.com

www.recruitireland.com

www.monster.ie

Starting a Business

A variety of Irish funding and support agencies are available to help would-be entrepreneurs. You might check out the following websites:

IDA (Industrial Development Authority) – www.idaireland.com

Enterprise Ireland – www.enterprise-ireland.com

Small Firms Association – www.sfa.ie

Other Useful Sites

Simply search 'Ireland' on your favourite search engine and see what comes up. Some of mine include:

www.ireland.travel.ie *For more information on B&B's and general travel.*

www.beamish.ie *Take a virtual pub crawl from this old-world producer of stout.*

www.guiness.com *Learn more about the history of the grand-daddy of all stouts.*

www.irishcountrykitchen.ie   *Real Irish recipes, and boy are they good!*

www.2fm.ie   *News, sports, and what's happening from this leading Irish radio broadcaster.*

https://www.rte.ie/player/   *Catch the latest on local TV*

And if all else fails why not just climb on an airplane and find out for yourself?

Acknowledgements

In this section the author is supposed to thank all those people who helped to produce their book, no matter how large or small that contribution might be. In that I'd like to continue living here, I'd best get to it before being summarily kicked out of the country.

So to Michael Scott, friend and fellow writer, who spent any number of cruel hours reading and rereading the original manuscript, suggesting changes that were (often) completely ignored. To Liam O'Neill, fellow expatriate, my best friend who was always there for me. I miss your steady support and guidance.

To Paul Tierney, brilliant graphic designer, who struggled valiantly with the cover of this book.

To Bernadette, who also read the rough draft despite deep misgivings, to ensure that I wouldn't tell too many lies. To Colette Ducie and Sarah Parke, office colleagues and bestest friends, who put up with my idiotic blathering as I slaved over these few words.

To the people of Navan, my friends and neighbours, who opened their hearts and minds to this poor Yank - no more so than on September 11th 2001 - as I fought to find my way. And finally to my old boss at Avis Rent-a-Car who fired me back in 1982 despite the fact that I had a newly arrived daughter and a humongous house payment. If you hadn't done so I never would have made it to Ireland. You are forgiven.

Slán libh agus sin á.

(Photo by Cathy Richards)

Tom Richards is a best-selling children's novelist and a produced screenwriter. Today he lives in Eyeries Southwest County Cork, Ireland, a small village located on the unspoiled Beara Peninsula. Someday he might decide to live somewhere else. But not today, thank you very much.

A Survivor's Guide to Living in IRELAND

2021 the Final Edition

"Come for a week – stay for a lifetime, that's the lure of Ireland."

Is Ireland the land of your dreams? Have you ever thought of staying for a prolonged visit, establishing residency, or creating an Irish business? Have you ever wondered what it would be like to live in Ireland?

In 1982, American Tom Richards, fresh out of UCLA, took a four-week holiday in Ireland. He's still here.

Witty and insightful, Tom tells how he overcame the culture shock of living in the Ol' Sod, learning to twist his middle-class American thinking into a more European point of view while managing to pay his bills at the same time. Along the way, he's learned some practical lessons that he now shares: From how to understand the Irish to how to drink a perfect pint; from finding a job to how to get a work permit; from purchasing your first Irish dream home to learning to take soaking walks on a soft Irish day.

He reveals that to survive in Ireland all you have to do is discover the magic of this wonderful country for yourself.

LEARN HOW TO
Talk like the Irish
Drink like the Irish
Eat like the Irish
Live like the Irish

"Absolutely essential reading for anyone thinking of moving to or visiting Ireland."

"Funny, thoughtful, useful."

"Bill Bryson has some serious competition."

ISBN 0-9550212-0-0

Front Cover image: Paul Tierney
Cover Design by: Avalon Point & Design

Many thanks to Gerry & Barbara for the use of their bar.

Printed in Ireland
Non-Fiction / Travel

www.ingramcontent.com/pod-product-compliance
Lightning Source LLC
Chambersburg PA
CBHW072043110526
44590CB00018B/3022